ETHNOCENTRISM AND INTERGROUP ATTITUDES

ETHNOCENTRISM AND INTERGROUP ATTITUDES

East African Evidence

MARILYNN B. BREWER
University of California (Santa Barbara)

DONALD T. CAMPBELL
Northwestern University

SAGE PUBLICATIONS

Halsted Press Division
JOHN WILEY & SONS
New York—London—Sydney—Toronto

To Jean . . .

M.B.B.

Distributed by Halsted Press, a Division of
John Wiley & Sons, Inc., New York

Printed in the United States of America

Library of Congress Cataloging in Publication Data

Brewer, Marilynn B.   1942-
  Ethnocentrism and intergroup attitudes,

    1. Ethnocentricism. 2. Prejudices and antipathies.
  3. Ethnology—Africa, East. I. Campbell, Donald
  Thomas, 1916-   joint author. II. Title.
  GN495.8.B73   301.2'1   75-26930
  ISBN 0-470-10330-2

FIRST PRINTING

CONTENTS

Chapter 1

OVERVIEW

Intergroup attitudes—ethnocentrism, social distance, prejudice, nationalism, tribalism—are among the oldest and most persistent topics in the social sciences. If social scientists are to be lucky enough to build a truly cumulative theory of social beings, this would seem one problem area in which it might first emerge. In his *Folkways* of 1906, and in his posthumous *The Science of Society* (Sumner et al., 1927), Sumner was able to consolidate a substantial literature on group self-images and attitudes toward neighboring groups under the terms *ethnocentrism, ingroup,* and *outgroup.* A sociologist, he primarily used materials from anthropologists, explorers, and the like, often of a very anecdotal nature. He also gave us some theory—predictions about social-organizational universals and about the relationships among variables—some of which we will be testing in this volume. Most explicit in Sumner's statements are the hypotheses that high self-regard, preservation of ingroup idiosyncracies, hostility and contempt toward outgroups, and ingroup solidarity occur together, are a part of the same functional syndrome, potentially confirmable by correlational studies using a population of groups. He also proposed the causal hypothesis that intergroup warfare and perceived threat of attack cause increases in all these attitudes. So concise and rich is his founding statement that it is worth citing in full:

> *The concept of "primitive society"; we-group and others-group.* The conception of "primitive society" which we ought to form is that of small groups scattered over a territory. The size of the groups is determined by the conditions of the struggle for existence. The internal organization of each group corresponds to its size. A group of groups may have some relation to each other (kin, neighborhood, alliance, connubium and commercium) which draws them together and differentiates them from others. Thus a differentiation arises between ourselves, the we-group, or in-group and everybody else, or the others-groups,

out-groups. The insiders in a we-group are in a relation of peace, order, law, government, and industry, to each other. Their relation to all outsiders, or others-groups, is one of war and plunder, except so far as agreements have modified it. If a group is exogamic, the women in it were born abroad somewhere. Other foreigners who might be found in it are adopted persons, guest friends, and slaves.

Sentiments in the in-group and towards the out-group. The relation of comradeship and peace in the we-group and that of hostility and war towards others-groups are correlative to each other. The exigencies of war with outsiders are what make peace inside, lest internal discord should weaken the we-group for war. These exigencies also make government and law in the in-group, in order to prevent quarrels and enforce discipline. Thus war and peace have reacted on each other and developed each other, one within the group, the other in the intergroup relation. The closer the neighbors, and the stronger they are, the intenser is the warfare, and then the intenser is the internal organization and discipline of each. Sentiments are produced to correspond. Loyalty to the group, sacrifice for it, hatred and contempt for outsiders, brotherhood within, warlikeness without—all grow together, common products of the same situation. It is sanctified by connection with religion. Men of an others-group are outsiders with whose ancestors the ancestors of the we-group waged war. The ghosts of the latter will see with pleasure their descendants keep up the fight, and will help them. Virtue consists in killing, plundering, and enslaving outsiders.

Ethnocentrism is the technical name for this view of things in which one's own group is the center of everything, and all others are scaled and rated with reference to it. Folkways correspond to it to cover both the inner and the outer relation. Each group nourishes its own pride and vanity, boasts itself superior, exalts its own divinities, and looks with contempt on outsiders. Each group thinks its own folkways the only right ones, and if it observes that other groups have other folk-ways, these excite its scorn. Opprobrious epithets are derived from these differences. "Pig-eater," "cow-eater," "uncircumcised," "jab-berers," are epithets of contempt and abomination. The Tupis called the Portuguese by a derisive epithet descriptive of birds which have feathers around their feet, on account of trousers. For our present purpose the most important fact is that ethnocentrism leads a people to exaggerate and intensify everything in their own folkways which is peculiar and which differentiates them from others. It therefore strengthens the folkways [Sumner, 1906: 12-13].

In these few paragraphs, Sumner has postulated a functional and mutually reinforcing interaction among attitudinal, ideological, and behavioral mecha-nisms that promote ingroup integration and outgroup hostility. In his view, these attributes of ethnocentrism are invariably intertwined as a universal concomitant of the formation of social groups. The concept of *social distance* was soon added as an integral part of this syndrome (Bogardus, 1925, 1928), if not already explicit in Sumner. Studies of nationalism by political scientists independently discovered most of the same syndrome (reviewed by Rosenblatt, 1964). (Sumner explicitly included patriotism and chauvinism in his syndrome [1906: 15].)

THE PRESENT STUDY: THEORETICAL RATIONALE

Sumner's conceptualization of ethnocentrism is a rich source of hypotheses regarding intergroup orientations which can be empirically probed. Yet, in spite of some fine examples (e.g., Buchanan and Cantril, 1953; Klineberg and Zavalloni, 1969; Lambert and Klineberg, 1967; Mitchell, 1956), studies of intergroup attitudes collecting reciprocal data in more than two groups are very rare. Still rarer is the effort to quantitatively relate such data, with an N of groups, to theories of intergroup relations. Such a study we undertake here, in limited degree and with fallible tools.

The theories being tested by our data are most conveniently presented and evaluated set by set in connection with the analyses presented in Chapters 3 through 8. However, some preliminary discussion of theory belongs here. The present authors are heirs to, and participants in, the compilation of a systematic propositional inventory (LeVine and Campbell, 1972) in which some eight theories, or classes of theory, from the social sciences have been milked for empirically testable propositions regarding the features and correlates of ethnocentrism. The process of derivation resulted in between 148 and 331 propositions, depending upon the level of refinement chosen. Of these, some 50 or more would potentially have been testable by data on reciprocal attitudes such as we have collected here. (Hypotheses relating ethnocentrism to child-rearing practices have been excluded because of the absence of the latter data in this inquiry. Hypotheses dealing with societal complexity have been ruled out by the fact that, of the thirty groups studied, twenty-nine were "stateless" prior to European colonial control. Related hypotheses dealing with group size and degree of group modernization are, however, examined.)

For Sumner and Bogardus, for the political scientists studying nationalism, and for the anthropologists, the unit of description was the social group. In the 1920s and 1930s, psychologists started studying individual differences in race and nationality prejudice within a single culture (e.g., U.S. college students), using Bogardus's questionnaire for this new purpose, as well as attitude scales in the Harper, Thurstone, and Likert traditions. In *The*

Authoritarian Personality (Adorno et al., 1950), if not earlier, the term "ethnocentrism" itself became used for the individual tendency to endorse hostile statements about a variety of outgroups. These two levels of analysis— group versus individual—should be clearly distinguished, even though they have many independencies. The present book is focused on groups. Its laws, correlations, and tests of significance are based on Ns consisting of ten to thirty groups. Of course, to achieve each group's score on its attitudes toward each of its neighboring groups, individuals were interviewed, making possible subsidiary studies of individual differences and their correlates.

The basic data for the study were collected by public opinion poll procedures in 1965 in thirty ethnic areas of Kenya, Uganda, and northern Tanzania. Members of each of these thirty ingroups were interviewed regarding their attitudes and images about fourteen ethnic groups—thirteen outgroups and themselves. Chapter 2 gives details on the sample, interview content, and general methodology of the survey.[1]

The selection of East Africa as the site for the survey was largely a matter of convenience and opportunity. It provided a desirable location because of the presence of a large number of fairly well-delineated social groups with a history of cultural identity and intergroup relations extending prior to European influence. However, the purpose of the survey was not the study of ethnic relations in East Africa per se, and thus the major analyses of the data have been devoted to identifying regularities in patterns of intergroup attitudes that supersede conditions specific to the East African locale. In order to reinforce this emphasis on generalized relationships, most of the results are reported without reference to specific group identities, except where such identification proved necessary to make a particular theoretical point.

The content of the survey interview schedule and the directions taken in analyzing the results were dictated by the assumptions underlying Sumner's (1906) conceptualization of the ethnocentrism syndrome. Implicit in this conceptualization is a cognitive representation of intergroup relations that is essentially unidimensional, similar in many respects to the model underlying hierarchical cluster analytic techniques (see Figure 3.1 in this volume). In such a model, each social group is represented as a solid, bounded unit separated to a greater or lesser extent from other such units along a single continuum, and sometimes subsumed within a higher-order grouping. Variations in degree of ethnocentrism in this model can be examined from only two perspectives: (1) variations in the "boundedness" of social groups reflected in measures of ingroup cohesion, bias, and exclusiveness, and (2) variations in the psychological or social distance separating the ingroup from various types of outgroups. Essentially the same factors were presumed to influence both.

What we found, as we proceeded with analyses within the above frame-work, was a need to progressively revise the underlying structure until we wound up with a model much more akin to that of multidimensional scaling. In our revised conceptualization, the undifferentiated social unit is replaced by a multifaceted system, each facet representing different dimensions of interpersonal responding, and the distance between two groups represented in terms of extent of overlap between the systems. The need for such a reconceptualization, and its implications for our understanding of intergroup relations, emerged only gradually as we worked our way through analyses of the survey data. The following chapters provide an essentially historical account of our progressive revision of the ethnocentrism model based on results of those analyses.

CONTENT OF THE VOLUME

The presentation of results in the following chapters is organized to correspond to major subsections of the survey interview schedule. Following a chapter describing the background of the survey and the context in which it was conducted, Chapter 3 discusses the development of an index of inter-group attraction. The index—based on responses to survey questions regarding liking for, social distance toward, and familiarity with each outgroup—is essentially a quantification of the relative distance at which each ingroup holds various outgroups. Correlates of this distance measure are then system-atically examined in Chapter 4.

Following these analyses of attitudinal data, Chapters 5-7 report on various explorations of the content of intergroup perceptions—the trait characteristics ascribed to ingroups and outgroups by our survey respondents. Chapter 5 begins with a theoretical discussion of the complementary relation-ship between loyalty toward the ingroup and hostile disregard toward out-groups as a rationale for the development of an index of ethnocentrism based on positive bias in the attribution of evaluation-laden traits to the ingroup. Chapters 6 and 7 describe the search for systematic variations in the attribu-tion of outgroup characteristics—first in evaluative content and then in terms of descriptive content. Our attempts at this stage of analysis to "map" the content of outgroup stereotypes onto the social space derived from the intergroup attraction index revealed some inconsistencies. The factors that most influence the nature of specific outgroup perceptions appear to be different from those that determine generalized affective relations between groups.

The two chapters in the final section provide a discussion of findings at a higher level of abstraction than the essentially descriptive presentation of preceding chapters. Chapter 8 discusses the discontinuities between affective and evaluative dimensions of intergroup attitudes in light of changing political and social conditions in East Africa at the time of the survey. The purpose is to account for our failure to find the expected convergence of facets of ethnocentrism and to speculate about what social-environmental conditions would promote such convergence. Finally, the concluding chapter provides a concise summary of major findings in broader theoretical perspective, with implications for our conceptualization of ethnocentrism.

Most of the data analyses reported in this volume were guided by a hypothesis-testing orientation, although a number of emergent relationships were also explored that had not been dictated by a priori theorizing. Interpretation of results has been tempered by an awareness of the limitations inherent in correlational data, but confidence in reported relationships is buttressed by use of multiple indicators and replication across different populations of survey respondents. Where possible, findings have also been cross-validated with data from other regional surveys and with materials from ethnographic fieldwork. However, the unique features of this survey lie in the elicitation of *mutual* perceptions, attitudes, and social relations among groups within a regional cluster, and these have yet to be replicated in any wide variety of settings.

N O T E

1. The survey was undertaken as one facet of the Cooperative Cross-Cultural Study of Ethnocentrism project (CCSE), funded by the Carnegie Corporation of New York. Reports on other aspects of the project can be found in Brewer (1968a, 1968b), Campbell (1967), Campbell and LeVine (1970), LeVine (1966), LeVine and Campbell (1972), and in the *Ethnocentrism Interviews* series of the Human Relations Area Files, New Haven, Connecticut, 1972.

Chapter 2

THE SURVEY AND THE SITES

The data on which this volume is based were collected by public opinion poll methods from 1,500 respondents distributed among thirty ethnic groups in East Africa in 1965. Respondents provided information on their contacts with and perceptions of fourteen ethnic groups, including their own. Analyses of these data were guided by a search for regularities in intergroup liking, social distance, and stereotype content, as reported in the following chapters. The present chapter provides background material on the methodology of the survey, the sample selection, the groups studied, and the rationale for the modes of analysis employed.

It is important to note at the outset that, as methodologists, we have some ambivalence about the survey. On the one hand, we are convinced that it constitutes a precious body of data, the best of its kind, and probably irreplaceable under present conditions. The data collection activities of the Cross-Cultural Study of Ethnocentrism involved anthropologists spending from two to six months obtaining interviews from a single ethnic group. Resulting from these efforts are extensive bodies of qualitative data on some twenty-three societies the world around,[1] which are rich in detailed information but difficult to analyze quantitatively. Because time and cost limited extensive data collection to one, at most two, societies in any one area, these ethnographic data contain little information on reciprocal relations among groups within a geographic region. In comparison, the East Africa regional survey provides readily quantifiable data on interrelated groups at considerably less cost of time and money, and we feel fortunate that we made the spur-of-the-moment decisions to take advantage of the transient opportunities that made it possible.

On the other hand, the conditions of data collection were far from ideal, and the survey methodology was, at best, equivalent to the "quota-control" sampling procedures of U.S. polls of the early 1930s. In order to provide perspective on the conduct of such opinion polling in the Africa of 1965, it seems desirable to present some background on the survey operation and the polling agency involved.

THE SURVEY OPERATION

Marco Surveys operated out of Nairobi during the 1960s under the direction of its founder and owner, Gordon Wilson, who had previously worked as a government anthropologist among the Luo of Kenya. The agency did a mixture of opinion survey work, including market research for various commercial importers and opinion research for U.S. overseas agencies such as A.I.D. On its own, it did some public service or journalistic opinion research that was published and sold in the form of mimeographed research reports. A dozen or so of these were available by 1964, including one elaborate study of interethnic perceptions in Kenya (Wilson, 1961) which we subjected to various secondary analyses (Campbell and LeVine, 1968; LeVine and Campbell, 1972: 178-181). In addition, we had access to an unpublished study of interethnic attitudes, covering all of East Africa, done for Fred Burke in 1963. This experience recommended the services of Marco Surveys to us as relevant to our study of ethnocentric attitudes.

Marco Surveys made no pretense of getting representative opinions as defined on a total population base. Instead, it concentrated on people in towns or cities, neglecting the entirely rural areas. Within the sites studied, respondents were sampled primarily from among the literate and relatively sophisticated. While quota controls were used to get some female and some nonliterate respondents, these quotas were set in the spirit of exploring a range of responses rather than in any effort to parallel population distributions. Thus, similar to other Marco Surveys samples, the overall sample of the present study is composed of sixty-six percent literate respondents, seventy percent males, and sixty-eight percent within the twenty- to thirty-five-year-old age range, in marked disparity to what an accurate East African census would have shown.

Social scientists are so thoroughly trained in the advantages of representative sampling that some case must be made for the value of a survey conducted under these conditions. To begin with, it may be noted that for most of the rural, nonliterate population, no "public opinion" on nonlocal issues exists. However arbitrary Marco Surveys' selection of respondents, it was more representative of existing public opinion in East Africa than a population-based representative sampling would have been. In many ways, this parallels our dependence, in other aspects of our research, on anthropologists' informants, persons selected as specially capable of reporting on opinions and customs rather than as randomly chosen representatives of the local culture.

One disadvantage of the quota-control approach used by Marco Surveys is that a great deal of the sample selection was left to the discretion of the local interviewer, with quota assignments the only curb on his idiosyncratic choices. A large part of the advantage of probability sampling techniques in modern survey research lies in the rigid rituals of respondent selection which provide replicability, rather than representativeness per se. Lacking these, the sample selection is of uncertain comparability across times and places. This weakness is made worse by the fact that only one interviewer was used within any given ethnic group. Thus, some of the group-to-group differences found in the present study must surely be due to interviewer idiosyncracies in sample selection and interview administration. In the analyses to be reported, we continually raise the issue of the contribution of interviewer bias or other methodological weaknesses to the results obtained. For these reasons, major emphasis is devoted to findings reflecting *relationships* replicated across respondent groups, relying minimally on differences among groups as a source of variance.

The plan of operation for the East African survey provided that interviews be conducted individually, among respondents who were members of the local ethnic group in residence, and in the local language (although some, at the respondent's preference, were conducted in English or Swahili). Each interviewer was to have a copy of the interview questions written out in the local language in a translation (from an English version that had been revised on the basis of pilot interviews conducted in three regions) that was checked through back-translation procedures (Werner and Campbell, 1970). The mimeographed interview-record form was in English and all responses were recorded in English. In order to meet these procedural requirements, the selection of ethnic groups to be included in the study was constrained by the availability of a dependable and experienced Marco Survey interviewer who was a native speaker of the local language. These interviewers had secondary school education or better and were often local school teachers.

If we had it to do again, we would make two changes in the fieldwork procedures. First, we would have arranged for direct, continual consultation with the interviewer during the data collection.[2] Second, we would have tried to get two interviewers, rather than one, to collect data in each area, each being given the same sampling instructions. This might have eliminated a few areas from the survey because of lack of staff, or required the breaking in of a few inexperienced interviewers, but it would have greatly increased our confidence in the validity of responses aggregated at the group level. As it now stands, ethnic differences in response are inextricably confounded with interviewer idiosyncracies. Problems generated by such confounding are illustrated by the social distance ratings discussed in Chapter 3, for which unusually high average scores (i.e., lacking in social distance) were obtained for respondents among the Gusii and Kipsigis of Kenya. Inspection of the original interview forms revealed that the interviews in these two groups had been conducted by the same interviewer (with extensive previous experience and language competence in both groups). In this case, it seems likely that the level, if not the pattern, of responses was influenced by the biases or expectations of the particular interviewer.

THE INTERVIEW CONTENT

The focus of the survey interview was upon interethnic contacts and attitudes. The content was adapted from the field manual prepared for the central ethnographic aspect of our study of ethnocentrism and intergroup relations. The final version of this field manual and a discussion of the theoretical issues leading to the selection of its contents are presented in LeVine and Campbell (1972). The manual was designed to provide a standardized format for collecting information on intergroup contact and attitudes, as well as material on social structure, child training practices, and other aspects of intragroup culture that various theories hypothesize to be related to intergroup relations. It was prepared for use with elderly informants being asked to report on their culture as it existed before Europeans established colonial rule. Thus, much of its content was unsuitable or unfeasible for inclusion in the present survey of contemporary intergroup attitudes. The items selected for the survey interview covered four content areas quite similar to the standard U.S. or European surveys of intergroup attitudes except for some variations in response format.

The final version of the survey interview included several questions on the respondents' personal contacts with each of the thirteen groups (other than their own ethnic group) selected for consideration. It also included four social distance questions asked about each of the other groups, and more general questions regarding liking and perceived similarity. Finally there were two lengthy sections dealing with group stereotypes. Rather than attempting to obtain ratings for individual ethnic groups on each of the forty-eight specific traits of interest (which would have entailed 672 items), stereotype information was elicited through two orthogonal sets of free response questions. First, each group was named and the respondent was asked to provide two salient characteristics; second, each trait of interest was named, and the respondent asked to specify the group that it characterized most. The interview items in detail were as follows.

Section I contained five questions related to intergroup social distance and familiarity:

(1) Would you willingly agree to work with a _____ ?
     (Asked for each of the thirteen outgroups.)
(2) Would you willingly agree to have a _____ as a neighbor in your house?
(3) Would you willingly agree to share a meal with a _____ ?
(4) Would you willingly agree to become related to a _____ by marriage?
(5) Do you know any _____ ? Do you speak their language? Have you ever lived with them? Where? For how long?

Section II consisted of open-ended responses elicited for each of the thirteen outgroups:

(6) The most important good thing about _____ is . . .
(7) The most important bad thing about _____ is . . .

In Section III, specific intergroup perceptions were elicited by asking: "Of all the peoples we have talked about (fourteen groups, including the ingroup), which one of these people is the most . . ."

(8)   peaceful among themselves, honest and generous?
(9)   peaceful with other groups?
(10) quarrelsome among themselves?
(11) quarrelsome, unfriendly with, or suspicious of other groups?
(12) obedient to rulers?
(13) independent, disobedient, and unruly?
(14) dishonest and treacherous among their own people?
(15) honest and trustworthy in dealings with foreigners and strangers?
(16) dishonest and treacherous in dealings with foreigners and strangers?
(17) hardworking (men)?
(18) hardworking (women)?
(19) lazy (men)?
(20) lazy (women)?
(21) brave?
(22) gentle, mild, cowardly?
(23) appear to be friendly, but backbite and are two-faced, hypocritical?

(24) dirty?
(25) clean?
(26) intelligent, clever, wise?
(27) lacking in wisdom?
(28) weak physically?
(29) strong physically?
(30) handsome, good-looking (men)?
(31) unattractive, ugly (men)?
(32) beautiful (women)?
(33) interested in using witchcraft and poison?
(34) powerful in its magic to help themselves?
(35) friendly?
(36) strict concerning sexual matters?
(37) men are like women, effeminate?
(38) sexually loose, immoral?
(39) cruel?
(40) uncivilized, backward?
(41) hot-tempered?
(42) pushy, keen to advance themselves?
(43) uninterested in personal advancement?
(44) progressive?
(45) conservative?
(46) light in skin color?
(47) dark in skin color?
(48) wealthy, rich?
(49) poor, impoverished?
(50) thrifty, like to save money?
(51) lacking in thrift, like to spend money?
(52) lacking in generosity?
(53) religious?
(54) proud, despise other people?
(55) lacking in pride?

"Of the peoples other than your own (thirteen outgroups), which one of them . . ."

(56) do you like the most?
(57) do you dislike the most?
(58) is the most similar to your own people?
(59) is the least similar to your own people?

The form of the questions was determined with consideration for the level of sophistication of potential respondents and for ease of translation across languages. The response restriction introduced by the use of single-response item formats, rather than rating scales, was deemed necessary even though it placed some limitations on potential levels of analysis. For many dimensions, the only quantitative measure that could be derived had to be based on proportions of responses from the total for each respondent group, thus restricting these data to the intergroup level of analysis. The problems associated with developing appropriate indices for such analyses are discussed as encountered in the following chapters.

THE PEOPLES STUDIED

A sample of fifty persons was interviewed in each of thirty ethnic groups in East Africa. In Kenya, the ten groups sampled were the Kikuyu, Embu, Meru, Kamba, Luhya, Gusii, Kipsigis, Nandi, Masai, and Luo. Respondents were asked to answer the interview questions with respect to each of these ten groups and also the Ganda and Teso of Uganda and the Sukuma and Chagga of Tanzania.

In Uganda, the ten groups included in the survey were the Ganda, Gisu, Toro, Nyoro, Soga, Ankole, Teso, Acholi, Lango, and Karamojong. Ugandan respondents were also asked about the Kikuyu, Nandi, Luo, and Luhya of Kenya. For Northern Tanzania, the ten groups sampled were the Chagga, Pare, Sambaa, Meru, Arusha, Sukuma, Nyamwezi, Luo, Masai, and Gogo. In addition to responses regarding these ten groups, Tanzanian informants were asked about the Kikuyu, Kamba, and Nandi of Kenya and the Ganda of Uganda.

These groups were selected as the major peoples with compact territorial identity. For most of them, some anthropological literature was available and is referenced in Appendix A, which contains brief background information for each of the thirty groups, including data relevant to the economic development of the group and its relations with neighboring groups. For more general context information, the following overview of the region in which the survey was conducted is provided.[3]

The thirty ethnic groups of the sample lie in a broad, continuous band that extends from Western Uganda, around the west, north, and east shores of Lake Victoria, diagonally through southwest Kenya, and across the northern part of Tanzania, almost to the Indian Ocean (see sketch map of the region in Figure 2.1). The lands of the northernmost group in the survey, the Karamojong, extend about 275 miles north of the equator, and those of the southernmost group, the Gogo, extend about 500 miles south of the equator. Within this region there are dramatic and economically significant differences in topography and climate. The most important differences concern rainfall; the amount of rainfall increases quite regularly with increasing altitude,

Figure 2.1 Sketch Map of Survey Region

variations in which include the volcanic cones of Mt. Kilimanjaro (19,340′), Mt. Kenya (17,040′), and Mt. Elgon (14,178′), and the rift valleys, with sheer drops of up to 4,000′ in Kenya. Since the volcanic loams of this region are extremely fertile as well as abundantly watered, the groups that inhabit the mountain slopes tend to be quite prosperous.

Most of Uganda is a plateau between 3,000 and 4,000′ above sea level. It is bordered on the west by the Ruwenzori and the western rift valley, in which lies the chain of lakes that includes Lakes Albert and Edward. Most of the plateau receives more than forty inches of rainfall per year; only scattered areas in Uganda are too dry for agriculture. Consequently, the nationwide population density is greater than for Kenya or Tanzania. Both Kenya and Tanzania exhibit more geologic and ecological variation than Uganda; more than half of each is presently not arable due to aridity or the tsetse fly. Population is concentrated in the higher land masses, where rainfall is heavier, and the low nationwide population densities conceal local concentrations of up to 1,000 per square mile, as in parts of the (formerly) North Nyanza and the Kiambu Districts of Kenya.

It is a reliable rule of thumb for the thirty groups in this sample that areas with a mean annual rainfall of forty inches or more can supply subsistence for a substantial population and produce cash crops. Areas with a mean annual rainfall under twenty-five inches, however, cannot support agriculture, and the people who live in these areas must rely on livestock for subsistence and lead a pastoral life that includes some nomadism. In marginal areas with mean annual rainfall between twenty-five and forty inches, other variables, such as rainfall distribution and soil type, have some effect. Populated areas with rainfall in this range, such as large portions of Sukumaland and of the Kamba districts, have been the scene of recurrent famine, yet they continue to support population densities of 25-100 per square mile.

There are three distinct linguistic groups in the survey region—the "Bantu," the "Nilo-Hamitic," and the "Nilotic," as they are often referred to in the literature. In the modern linguistic classification of Greenberg (1963), the Bantu languages are in the Bantoid branch, Benue-Congo subfamily, Niger-Congo family (1963: 8-9); the Nilo-Hamitic languages are in two sub-branches (one including Masai and Nandi-Kipsigis, the other, Karamojong and Teso) of the Nilotic branch, Eastern-Sudanic subfamily, Chari-Nile family (1963: 86); and the Nilotic languages (including Luo, Acholi, and Lango) are in the Western sub-branch of the same Nilotic branch that includes the Nilo-Hamitic languages (1963: 85). (The languages within each of the three groupings are related, but not necessarily mutually intelligible.) These linguistic divisions were thought at one time to correspond to physical and cultural differences, the Bantu being dark-skinned cultivators with negroid features and the Nilo-Hamites instrusive pastoralists with sharper features and taller and thinner bodies. However, if clear-cut distinctions ever did exist, they have been obscured by many generations of intermixture and cultural exchange.

The traditional beliefs of East Africa included ancestor spirits, nature spirits, witchcraft and sorcery, and a remote high god, but the relative importance of these elements and their patterning in cultural symbol systems varied from one ethnic group to another. As Richards (1969) has noted, indigenous variations of this kind did not become a focus of ethnic antagonism and are not prominent in the perceptions of a group by its neighbors. The only exception seems to be reputation for practice of magic and sorcery, for which certain groups are noted in parts of the region.

The area was explored by Europeans only about a century ago, after which trade between the coast and some hinterland peoples was intensified. In the last decades of the nineteenth century and the first part of this century,

European (after World War I, exclusively British) colonial administration was established in the three territories of Uganda, Kenya, and Tanganyika. In many localities of the interior, the period between first European contact and independence was no more than sixty years long. It was a period of rapid political, economic, and social change, however, in which ethnicity and ethnic relations—like so many other aspects of life—were transformed. The Europeans found a multitude of ethnic distinctions based on language, culture, and political boundaries. As Richards (1969: 7) states:

> In its ethnic composition, East Africa is characterized by its large number of small tribes: 120 in Tanzania, 31 in Uganda, and 27 in Kenya. Many of these tribes number only 150,000 to 200,000, and the only groups which reach anything like the size of the Ashanti, the Ibo, or the Yoruba are the Kikuyu speakers or the Ganda, reckoned at about two million people each.

Even before colonial administration, the participation in trade of certain groups, and not others, laid the basis for future ethnic distinctions in some areas. Austen (1969: 136) has this to say about the Nyamwezi and Sukuma of Tanzania, two of the groups included in our survey:

> Political, linguistic, social, cultural and ecological evidence all suggest that the very distinction between Nyamwezi and the Sukuma as separate peoples dates only from the commercial impact of the nineteenth century. Both share similar traditions of Ntemiship [chieftaincy] ; their languages are today still mutually intelligible (Sukuma means "north" in the common tongue); and many aspects of their social structure, customs, beliefs and methods of subsistence in their home environments remain similar.

In other cases, boundaries were set and fixed by Europeans:

> Tribal organizations were created during the colonial period when the desire for orderly administration led administrators to amalgamate formerly independent communities into larger units under officially appointed leaders. Wherever possible, European officials drew political boundaries to coincide with language or cultural boundaries, since they assumed this would provide a natural cohesion and stability to the administrative unit. The importance given to "language" and "nationality" as political factors in nineteenth- and twentieth-century Europe no doubt encouraged such endeavors [Colson, 1969: 29].

The result is that contemporary ethnic or "tribal" boundaries bear some relation to pre-European divisions but are by no means identical with them; and the relatively autonomous and (in some cases) loosely connected groups of the past were quite different entities from the competitive, often communalist, ethnic components of modern Kenya, Uganda, and Tanzania.

The Luhya of Kenya provide a particularly marked example of such a recently formed ethnic unit composed of subgroups of highly diverse historical roots, incorporating not only Bantu groupings (with which they are now largely identified) but some with ties to the Masai and Nandi and others related to the Soga and Nyoro of Uganda. Detailed case studies of the evolution of ethnic identity in several East African groups, and the part that colonial administration played in creating ethnic groupings and attitudes, are provided in Cohen and Middleton (1970).

One of the most prominent influences of the colonial period on present-day ethnic attitudes relates to economic and educational development. The decisions that Europeans made concerning the location of towns and plantations, the railways and roads connecting them, and the schools that provided them with literate African employees, favored nearby ethnic groups over those farther away. Groups like the Kikuyu and Ganda, located in and around the major cities of Nairobi and Kampala, respectively, got an early start in schooling and European employment which gave them greater access to the prosperity created by the commercial development of East Africa, in comparison with groups less favorably located. Many of the early differences among regions in economic and educational development were maintained throughout and after the colonial period, as Soja (1968) has systematically documented for Kenya. This differential access to the benefits of "modernization" laid the basis for competitive attitudes between ethnic groups and regional blocs which found political expression at the time of independence in both Uganda and Kenya, and which are being tapped in the present study.

Of the thirty ethnic groups in the sample, four—the Ganda, Nyoro, Toro, and Sambaa—had developed centralized kingdom states before European contact. Six—the Soga, Ankole, Acholi, Sukuma, Nyamwezi, and Chagga—were conglomerates of chiefdoms or petty kingdoms. The remainder were acephalous societies in which political power was in the hands of (a) clan or lineage elders, (b) the senior sets in an age set system, or (c) the elders of a hierarchical series of territorial units such as homesteads, villages, parishes, or some combination of these. Among the pastoral Nilo-Hamites, political power was allocated through an age set system; in other groups, kinship and territorial units, sometimes combined with age sets, were more important.

Political power in the immediate postindependence period in East Africa centered around political parties which bore some, although imperfect, relation to ethnic affiliations. The year 1965 in Kenya was a period of transition in party politics. From 1960-1964, the national political scene had been polarized between two major parties: KANU (Kenya African National Union) and KADU (Kenya African Democratic Union). KANU, the nationalist party, which stood for strong centralized government, represented a Kikuyu-Luo alliance also supported by the Kamba, Gusii, and most other Bantu (although a majority of Kamba deserted the party temporarily in 1962 when Paul Ngei broke away and formed the African Peoples Party; in 1963, Ngei rejoined KANU which then regained Kamba support).

The opposition party, KADU, supported regionalist policies and attracted votes from Masai, Kipsigis, Nandi, and Coastal Bantu groups, as well as about half of the Abaluhya (the only Bantu group in this study without a majority identified with KANU). In November 1964, about one year prior to this survey, the KADU party was officially dissolved and its membership absorbed by KANU. That this new union was not a stable alliance is indicated by the fact that, shortly after our survey (in April 1966), KANU was divided, partly along Kikuyu-Luo lines, culminating in Oginga Odinga's resignation as vice president of Kenya and the formation of the Kenya Peoples Union (KPU).

In Uganda, postindependence rivalry formed along a north-south division, pitting the more-developed peoples of the south, particularly the Ganda, against the less-developed northern peoples such as the Teso, Lango, Acholi, and Karamojong. In Kenya, the politics of independence also for a time pitted the larger and better-developed groups, notably the Kikuyu and Luo, against the smaller and less-developed ones (including the Kipsigis and Masai). In both countries, however, there was also considerable competition among the better-developed groups for political dominance during the same period. Tanzania, on the other hand, with its large number of small ethnic groups and relative lack of economic and educational development, reached political independence with a low level of ethnic competition. Thus, in many ways, the Tanzania interviews provide the best sampling of groups that have not been polarized by major economic and political factors associated with development in the other two countries.

GENERAL METHODOLOGICAL NOTES

Each of the following chapters deals with specific methodological and analytical issues that are best discussed in context. In this section, we wish to comment on two methodological considerations that transcend a number of decisions regarding data analysis and presentation.

Ethnic Group Anonymity

After much internal debate, we have decided to present most of our findings in such a manner as to keep specific ethnic groups from being identified with particular reputations, stereotype attributions, or other response patterns. Given the major focus of analysis, this presents no serious problem; the findings are in a statistical form in which groups are naturally as anonymous as are individuals in a typical correlation coefficient. For anthropologists and political scientists interested in particular groups, however, this decision represents a double loss: both a loss of descriptive information and a loss of some of the contextual cues that would permit a cross-validation of our survey against their own knowledge of intergroup relations in the region.

These costs seem to us justified by a number of considerations. It is by now well recognized that respondents cooperating in a social science study should be protected from the potential damage to their reputations which might result from release of the information they have provided. Increasingly, it is coming to be recognized that groups have a similar legitimate claim to safeguards against release of information which could be identified with them. The data generated by our study—in particular, the documentation of negative attitudes and unfavorable stereotypes—could potentially be found offensive to many of the groups involved. While only attitudes which were already publicly available have been assembled by this study, their effects could be magnified by documenting them in a scientifically authoritative manner and making convenient summaries readily available in a form inviting invidious comparison.

These problems are exacerbated by the particular setting in which our study was conducted. As developing nations come to monitor more carefully the studies they permit within their borders, there is increasing sensitivity to the implications of studies dealing with intergroup hostility. The potential for immediate damage from stirring up internal animosities may well outweigh any long-term benefits associated with contributing to social science theory. Even such thoroughly European nations as Belgium and Yugoslavia have found it politically expedient to discourage or suppress studies of intergroup attitudes among polarized segments of their nations. The fact that a replication of the present study would be likely to meet similar resistance, of course, contributes to its value and to our willingness to invest special efforts in refining the often inadequate data. In particular, we feel an added urgency to our concern for determining to what extent the European pattern of ethnocentrism and nationalism would hold for those raised under different conditions of social authority and family structure. But we feel it would be an abuse of our privilege to publish the data now in a form that would lead our hosts to regret having permitted their accumulation.

The group anonymity provided in the following chapters is not perfect, and with discretion we breach it ourselves where the scientific issues seem important and general enough, and potential damage seems unlikely. A few well-informed readers may be able to identify some of the groups from knowledge of popular stereotypes. We do not encourage this game and believe that such guesses will often be wrong; due either to the thinness of our data or the lack of popular consensus on stereotypes, we doubt that anyone will be able to identify the attributions of a particular group with much certainty.

Types of Correlational Analyses

Most of the analyses we will be presenting are, broadly speaking, "correlational," though many of them take somewhat unusual forms. While the details of these are best presented in context, an overall typology of correlational analyses may provide a useful perspective. Four types will be distinguished: (1) correlation over persons, (2) correlation over groups, (3) correlation over dyads, and (4) correlation over referenced groups.

Figure 2.2 shows a scatter diagram expressing a generally linear relationship between attributes A and B for fifteen observational units. Each point represents one such unit plotted at the intersection of its values on A and B. The scatter shows a generally positive though imperfect relationship such that the higher the value on A, the higher the corresponding value on B. When computed, the product-moment correlation coefficient representing this relationship is +.91. The N of fifteen units that the correlation is computed over provides the degrees of freedom for tests of statistical significance. The four types of correlation to be discussed differ as to the nature of this observational unit.

In the *correlation over persons,* the observed values are characteristics or attributes of individual people. For this case, Figure 2.2 might represent the relationship between number of years of schooling (A) and acceptance of other ethnic groups (B) computed over fifteen respondents. Correlations of this kind are the most common in social science research, especially that done by psychologists. We employ them in secondary analyses in Chapters 5 and 6, and in Chapter 3 we report reliability coefficients and Guttman reproducibility coefficients corresponding to this level of analysis. For the most part, however, this type of analysis is not central to the questions we ask, nor are the individual data always detailed enough to support this level of analysis.

Somewhat more characteristic of this study is the *correlation over groups,* in which each of the fifteen points in Figure 2.2 would represent an ethnic group, and A and B would refer to attributes of those groups. Sometimes these will be attributes derived from aggregated individual data (for example, mean educational level and mean score on acceptance of other groups computed for fifteen groups of respondents). More often, the attributes are such as to be appropriate only to groups or measurable only at that level. The quantitative cross-cultural correlations of Murdock (1949) and Whiting and Child (1953) are of this type. We use them primarily for the analyses of intergroup differences in self-ratings as reported in Chapter 6.

Correlations over dyads are conceptually appropriate where the focus of analysis is on group interactions or intergroup relations. One group-to-group (pairwise) relationship can be designated a dyad, and Figure 2.2 could represent the correlation of two relational attributes across fifteen such

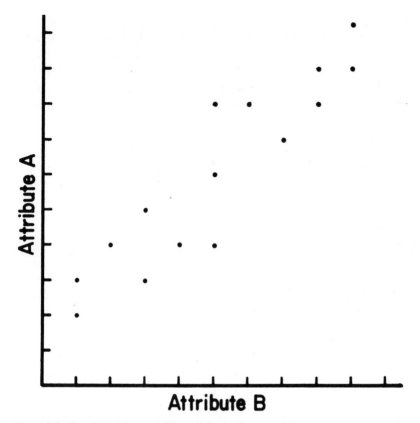

Figure 2.2 Correlation Between Two Attributes Computed Over
A Population of 15 Observational Units
(r = .91)

dyads. For example, it might represent the correlation between similarity (A) and proximity (B) of groups considered two at a time. The ten ethnic groups within each of the nations in our survey generate 10 x 9/2 = 45 nonredundant dyads. Correlations across these 45 pairs have been utilized in analyses of reciprocity in Chapters 3 and 4.

In contrast to correlations across individuals or across groups, the correlation across dyads presents special statistical problems in that the observations are not all independent of one another; that is, each of the groups appears in more than one of the dyads so that an eccentric observation on one group will generate several eccentric dyadic values. (To make this problem more concrete, consider an illustration from our setting. The Kenya Masai, because of their distributed locations, would be scored high in proximity to a number of other groups in the Kenya sample. At the same time, as the only nonagricultural pastoralists in the sample, the Masai would tend to be scored low in cultural similarity in each dyad in which they appeared. What is in some sense a single coincidence of traits, then, becomes represented in numerous dyads and could significantly affect the size and direction of the assessed relationship between similarity and proximity.) In order to avoid this problem of statistical nonindependence, studies would have to be conducted in which groups were paired such that any particular group was represented in only one pair.

For many of the relationships that could have been assessed in the present study by correlating dyadic measures taken on all possible pairs of groups, we have instead used *correlations over referenced groups.* The inspiration for this orientation comes from studies of social perception or cognitive mapping. In our setting, a particular ethnic group is treated as a reference point, and correlations are computed between various aspects of its relations with multiple outgroups. Typical questions posed in this type of analysis are (1) within Group X's imagery, what is the relationship between A, the degree of social distance at which each of nine outgroups is held, and B, the net favorableness of traits ascribed to those groups, or (2) for Group X, what is the relationship between measures of A, proximity to each of nine outgroups, and B, perceived similarity to those groups. Each such correlation, computed over an N of nine outgroups, represents a "mini-study" that can be replicated thirty times (once for every ingroup) and then averaged across replications. This approach overlaps the dyadic analysis in that it amounts to computing the dyadic correlation separately for the dyads in which each given group is involved. While this does not completely resolve the statistical nonindependence problem, the contribution of any one group to the relationship as measured in each replication of a referenced-group correlation is restricted relative to its contribution to the same relationship assessed by the pooled dyadic approach.

In summary, the analyses presented in this volume represent two basic strategies of cross-cultural comparison. In one paradigm, each culture represents an opportunity for replication of some pattern of covariation, much analogous to the role of the individual subjects in repeated-measures research designs. Within this model, cross-cultural repetition provides checks on the reliability of relationships between variables, to assure that any systematic covariation obtained in one culture is not a spurious finding due to small Ns or confounds peculiar to that particular group. For this purpose, it is not essential that groups be comparable in terms of measurement levels on the relevant variables, but only that some measure of each variable be available that differentiates among cases within each group, in the same way for all groups.

In the second paradigm of cross-cultural comparison, it is necessary to obtain measures that differentiate *among* groups on some common dimension because the groups themselves become the variable of interest (or the representation of some hypothesized variable) and intergroup differences in response make up the relevant data. For this purpose, the equivalence of dimensions must be enhanced by measurement procedures that permit equivalent scaling. For such response dimensions in the present study, we have relied on the use of what Przeworski and Teune (1967) refer to as "identical indicators," translation-equivalent items that "behave" the same way (i.e., covary with other indicators) among respondents pooled across all groups. The procedures involved are best illustrated by the derivation of trait-rating dimensions through factor analysis of pooled responses as reported in Chapter 6.

Throughout the following chapters we have highlighted for interpretation only those findings that meet relatively stringent criteria of consistency or replicability. Despite the problems of data inadequacy discussed in this chapter, the survey has produced a remarkable number of lawful relationships that have justified a theory-testing orientation.

NOTES

1. Edited versions of these interview protocols are available through the *Ethnocentrism Interviews* series published by the Human Relations Area Files in 1972.

2. This requirement stems not from any faults we are aware of in the East African data but from an unfortunate experience with a parallel sixteen-group study conducted in Nigeria, contracted through Marco Surveys and handled by their short-lived Nigerian affiliate. Our suspicion was aroused by some unusual response patterns from one of the groups surveyed and, through a friend who had been in the area at the time, we learned that the data for that group were collected in a classroom setting from secondary school pupils who were instructed to fill in their fathers' names as respondents. In addition, it was possible to have a colleague's research assistant in Ibadan look up the names and addresses of the fifty respondents in that sample. This assistant could not locate or confirm the existence of a single one of the interviewees and became convinced all were fictitious. As a result, we had to judge all of the Nigerian data not credible enough to be worth analyzing. A careful check of the original interview report forms from the East African survey produced no evidence suggesting that the field work had not been conducted as planned. We were also somewhat reassured by the fact that our contact network for learning of fraud was better for East Africa than for Nigeria, and that we received no disquieting reports.

The survey in East Africa was conducted during September and October 1965. In 1970, Marco Surveys ceased operation and Gordon Wilson left Kenya for unknown places, under circumstances that cast doubt on the financial integrity of his operation. Although this has not affected our own confidence in the authenticity of the data obtained from the East Africa survey, it is something we feel the reader should be aware of in evaluating the results reported in this volume.

3. Recognition is due to Joan Prims, who compiled most of the materials on which this overview and the data in Appendix A are based.

PART I

INTERGROUP ATTITUDES

Chapter 3

ASSESSING INTERGROUP ATTRACTION

The theoretical perspective behind this study of ethnocentrism (LeVine and Campbell, 1972) treats ethnocentrism as a multidimensional concept with aspects referring to individual cognition and emotion, cultural ideology and shared stereotypes, and collective action—all theoretically interrelated but logically separable. The major facets of the ethnocentric syndrome— ingroup solidarity and outgroup hostility—are both subject to multiple levels of analysis (e.g., individual affect for ingroup and outgroups, occurrence of overt interpersonal aggression, practice of institutional warfare, etc.), with no guarantee that relationships obtained at one level will be replicated at other levels. Thus, the scope of the present survey research, limited to the attitudinal-cognitive-perceptual level of response, cannot permit an exhaustive probing of variations in ethnocentric behavior. However, to the extent that multiple aspects of attitudinal phenomena follow the same patterns of variation, generalization to other aspects of the syndrome can be expected, or, conversely, to the extent that attitudinal symptoms do *not* systematically converge, the theoretical validity of a unified syndrome of ethnocentrism can be questioned.

Intergroup relations on the attitudinal level can be assessed along at least two response dimensions—the direction and intensity of intergroup attraction (affect) and the content of intergroup perceptions (cognitions). Not all of the theories reviewed by LeVine and Campbell deal directly with either of these two dimensions, but it is probably reasonable to assume that most predictions regarding variations in intergroup conflict can be extended to the expression of attitudinal hostility as well. The content of perceptions, on the other hand, is of more restricted theoretical relevance, and the present study of its relationship to intergroup attraction is largely exploratory.

DERIVATION OF THE INDEX OF ATTRACTION

Given the normal problems of measurement error, compounded by potential translation errors in cross-cultural settings, we could not rely on any single response elicitation for an adequate assessment of dispositional concepts such as intergroup attraction. Thus, the development of an index of attraction for the present study was preceded by an exploration of several available indicators for the purpose of assessing shared variation and cross-societal comparability.

Measure of Intergroup Liking

The items in the survey questionnaire most directly related to intergroup attraction were nos. 56 and 57, those which requested respondents to name the one outgroup "most liked" and the one "most disliked" by their own group. However, since each question required respondents to name only one outgroup, using them to derive an index of liking between each ingroup and respective outgroups posed some problems. The primary difficulty was that of response biases regarding highly visible outgroups, those with a high probability of being named in response to any question by the informants from some ingroups. Among the fifty respondents of one group, for example, such a visible ethnic group as the Kikuyu of Kenya may receive thirty mentions in response to the "most liked" item and twenty mentions in response to the "most disliked" item. If an index of liking were computed as simply the net difference between "most liked" and "most disliked" votes, the Kikuyu would receive the same liking rating as another, less visible outgroup with ten "most liked" mentions and no "most disliked" mentions. On the other hand, if some ratio between the number of mentions in response to the two items were used as the index of liking, one or two votes received by some low-visibility outgroup would be drastically overweighted. This problem of differential response probability was compounded by the inclusion of some highly visible outgroups that were consistently negatively evaluated across all ingroups. Large net negative liking scores assigned to such groups would seriously affect any correlations computed between intergroup liking and other measures of intergroup perception, in the direction of overweighting characteristics peculiar to these specific groups.

A solution to these problems was arrived at by computing, for each ingroup-outgroup dyad, a measure of liking based on deviation scores. A deviation score was obtained by subtracting from the actual number of mentions of a particular outgroup by ingroup respondents, an "expected" number (E) based on the tendency to name that outgroup, across all ingroups, and the tendency of the particular ingroup respondents to respond to the item. In order to compute these E scores, the responses to the "most liked" and "most disliked" questions among respondents in each country were arranged into 10 x 10 matrices. The cells in these matrices contained the number of mentions, for each respondent group in that country, of each of the outgroups surveyed in the same country. The three matrices for each of the two items then provided the raw liking-disliking responses from which deviation scores were computed.

For each cell in each matrix, an expected score was calculated by multiplying the overall tendency to name the target outgroup (column total) by the overall response tendency of the respondent ingroup (row total) and dividing by the total number of responses in the matrix: $E = (R \times C)/T$. The difference between obtained and expected number of mentions in each cell provided a deviation measure comparable to Guilford's technique for computing "halo" error scores (Guilford, 1954: 284), and corresponding to an index of relative liking or disliking for each outgroup by each ingroup. Finally, the net liking score for each ingroup-outgroup dyad was obtained by subtracting the deviation score for that outgroup in the "most disliked" matrix from its deviation score in the "most liked" matrix. Thus, an index of intergroup liking was computed that measured each ingroup's tendency to like or dislike each outgroup beyond the degree expected from response biases alone.

To illustrate the computational procedure, an example can be drawn from the Kenya matrix, representing the response of Group A (Row 1) toward Group C (Column 3). In response to the question regarding "most liked" outgroup, the row marginal for Group A was 28 (i.e., a total of 28 of the 50 respondents from this group named an outgroup from the Kenya sample in answer to this question). The column marginal (the frequency with which Group C was chosen in response to this item across all Kenya respondents) was 23, and the total number of responses in the matrix was 380. Thus, the "expected value" for A's choice of C was $(28)(23)/380 = 1.7$. The actual frequency of C responses from Group A respondents was 6, a deviation of +4.3 from expected. In response to the "most disliked" item, Group A gave a total of 32 choices (row marginal), and C received a total of 19 mentions (column marginal) of the total 397 responses. Thus, the expected value for A-C choices was $(32)(19)/397 = 1.5$, a deviation of -1.5 from the obtained frequency of 0. Thus, the net liking score for Group C from Group A is $+4.3 - (-1.5) = +5.8$, as reported in Appendix Table D.3.1.[1]

The results of the remaining computations of intergroup liking scores for mutual ratings of the ten ethnic groups in each of the three countries are reported in Table D.3.1 in the Appendix. (The diagonal in these matrices is empty since respondents were not permitted to name their own ingroup in these items.)

A measure of reciprocity of liking was obtained by computing the correlation between liking given and liking received for the forty-five nonredundant dyads in each matrix. (The resulting correlation is reported with each matrix.) The overall reciprocity correlation, averaged across the three countries (i.e., combining the results from the three matrices in Appendix D.3.1) is .30. This value, representing the degree to which liking ratings are mutually recipro-cated across groups is significantly greater than .00 (p < .05), but not impressively high (and note that the correlation for the Kenya matrix alone is not reliably different from .00). One reason for this may be that liking, being a relatively abstract relationship, is inaccurately perceived by both evaluators and recipients. To assess the effect of perceptual inaccuracy on reciprocity of liking scores, the ethnic groups in each matrix were ordered according to geographical distance and cultural similarity, so that groups next to each other, whose mutual ratings appear along the diagonal of each matrix, should be closer on these dimensions than any groups elsewhere in the matrix. Presumably, mutual visibility between these groups should be high and, therefore, the correlation between the nine pairs of scores along the diagonal of each matrix should provide a measure of reciprocity of liking under conditions where opportunity for accuracy of perception is maximized. The computed diagonal correlations (Kenya: r = .18; Uganda: r = .67; Tanzania: r = .91) were consistently higher than the reciprocity correlations for the corresponding matrices as a whole, providing support for the hypothesized influence of perceptual accuracy.[2]

Other Measures of Intergroup Attraction

Apart from responses to the questionnaire items involving most liked and most disliked outgroups, the survey provided additional measures of inter-group attraction that did not share the same response bias factors as the liking index. One such measure was derived from responses to the social distance questions included in the first section of the interview (nos. 1-4) (see also, Brewer, 1968a, 1968b). Respondents in each survey sample were asked whether they would willingly engage in four types of behavior, representing different levels of intimacy of social interaction with members of each outgroup. Presumably, degree of permitted intimacy in social relations reflects favorability of attitudes between those groups, and combined responses to the four social distance questions should provide a scale of intergroup attraction. For this purpose, responses to the items by each ingroup relative to each outgroup were scored 2 for a "yes" response, 1 for "don't know," and 0 for a "no" response. Then the four item scores were summed to obtain a total social distance score for each respondent toward each outgroup, ranging from 0 to 8 (with 8 representing least social distance, highest attraction).

To test whether this measure was acceptably comparable across ethnic groups in meeting the assumptions of unidimensionality and scalability of items, the set of social distance responses was subjected to scale analysis and internal consistency analysis within each group of respondents. The results of these analyses for each of the thirty respondent samples in the survey are reported in Table 3.1. The Guttman analysis and Kuder-Richardson reliability were computed for dichotomized scores (responses 0 and 1 recorded as 0, and response 2 as 1) and were based on an N of 650 for each tribe (ratings by fifty respondents of thirteen outgroups each). The split-half respondent reliabilities were computed by randomly dividing the fifty respondents from each sample in half and correlating their mean ratings across thirteen outgroups.

The values in Table 3.1 reveal that the reproducibility coefficients (Rep) were uniformly high, indicating that the scalability of the items was good. However, of more interest is the order of scaled items obtained for each of the respondent groups (based on item marginals, or proportion of "yes" responses, reported in parentheses in column 2 of the table), since these provide a test of the implicit assumption that there is some commonality in the rank ordering of social distance steps across groups. The items as listed in the interview schedule were intended to be ordered from least intimate (no. 1) to most intimate (no. 4), but this rank ordering was obtained for only six of the thirty groups in this study. For nineteen of the thirty, the obtained order was 3-1-2-4. (Considering all possible item orders as having an equal chance of occurring, the binomial probability of this one order occurring so frequently by chance is less than .00000001.) To test whether the obtained deviations from this modal item order would be expected by chance, a multivariate analysis of variance was performed on the item response patterns for the thirty groups, dividing the respondents of each group randomly in half to get an estimate of within-group variation. No significant difference was found. Thus, there is strong indication that among the groups surveyed there was a regular ordering of social distance steps as follows (from least to most intimate):

(1) willingness to share a meal with outgrouper
(2) willingness to work with outgrouper
(3) willingness to have outgrouper as a neighbor
(4) willingness to become related to outgrouper by marriage.

That sharing a meal is considered less intimate than working together or living in the same neighborhood is not surprising among ethnic groups in which hospitality, including treating visiting strangers to meals, was traditionally an important factor in group prestige. In this case, shared traditions regarding social contact contributed to the comparability of scale steps among groups from this one cultural area.

The lack of significant differences among respondent groups can also be

TABLE 3.1
SOCIAL DISTANCE SCALE ANALYSIS RESULTS

Ethnic Group	Item Order and Marginals				Rep	K-R20	Corrected K-R	Respondent Reliability
Kikuyu	3 (.56)	1 (.54)	2 (.43)	4 (.23)	.94	.76	.84	.95
Embu	3 (.38)	1 (.36)	2 (.35)	4 (.29)	.95	.86	.88	.98
Meru (K)	3 (.94)	1 (.72)	2 (.53)	4 (.41)	.98	.71	.89	.97
Kamba	1 (.74)	2 (.57)	3 (.56)	4 (.35)	.98	.86	.96	.96
Masai (K)	1 (.23)	2 (.22)	4 (.20)	3 (.16)	.98	.93	.96	.99
Gusii	3 (.93)	1 (.91)	2 (.84)	4 (.74)	.98	.76	.87	.97
Kipsigis	1 (1.00)	3 (.96)	4 (.76)	2 (.68)	.96	.00	.00	.97
Nandi	1 (.21)	2 (.18)	3 (.17)	4 (.16)	.92	.53	.55	.99
Luo (K)	3 (.74)	1 (.50)	2 (.46)	4 (.33)	.93	.64	.72	.88
Luhya	3 (.50)	1 (.32)	2 (.25)	4 (.16)	.92	.61	.70	.93
Ganda	1 (.63)	2 (.53)	3 (.49)	4 (.34)	.96	.86	.94	.96
Teso	3 (.78)	1 (.71)	2 (.62)	4 (.49)	.94	.73	.81	.98
Banyoro	3 (.77)	1 (.57)	2 (.56)	4 (.51)	.91	.72	.77	.99
Batoro	3 (.54)	1 (.50)	2 (.45)	4 (.42)	.94	.86	.89	.98
Ankole	1 (.62)	2 (.58)	3 (.52)	4 (.35)	.95	.83	.90	.99

TABLE 3.1
SOCIAL DISTANCE SCALE ANALYSIS RESULTS
(continued)

Ethnic Group	Item Order and Marginals				Rep	K-R20	Corrected K-R	Respondent Reliability
Basoga	3 (.41)	1 (.39)	2 (.38)	4 (.30)	.97	.90	.93	.97
Bagisu	3 (.69)	1 (.60)	4 (.54)	2 (.40)	.93	.73	.80	.93
Acholi	3 (.79)	1 (.78)	2 (.61)	4 (.34)	.96	.74	.87	.80
Lango	1 (.68)	2 (.64)	3 (.53)	4 (.47)	.94	.80	.86	.97
Karamojong	3 (.38)	1 (.35)	2 (.26)	4 (.17)	.97	.85	.92	.97
Sukuma	3 (.71)	1 (.40)	2 (.29)	4 (.13)	.98	.74	.91	.97
Nyamwezi	3 (.51)	1 (.37)	2 (.31)	4 (.18)	.97	.82	.92	.97
Gogo	3 (.49)	1 (.40)	2 (.37)	4 (.27)	.95	.81	.87	.98
Chagga	3 (.50)	1 (.48)	2 (.43)	4 (.18)	.95	.79	.87	.94
Masai (T)	4 (.13)	1 (.12)	3 (.12)	2 (.10)	.99	.95	.97	.96
Arusha	3 (.89)	1 (.88)	2 (.85)	4 (.69)	.97	.79	.88	.94
Meru (T)	1 (.87)	2 (.86)	3 (.85)	4 (.59)	.98	.82	.93	.88
Pare	3 (.51)	1 (.50)	2 (.49)	4 (.37)	.99	.94	.98	.92
Luo (T)	3 (.61)	1 (.46)	2 (.40)	4 (.15)	.92	.56	.65	.96
Sambaa	1 (.58)	4 (.50)	3 (.35)	2 (.34)	.94	.80	.87	.99

attributed, in part, to the fact that differentiation among items (in terms of proportions of yes responses) was generally quite small. Examination of individual response patterns revealed that this was not due to variation in respondents' interpretations of the four items but rather to a tendency to give all-or-nothing ratings to outgroups. Thus, although all the obtained Rep values were greater than expected by chance (based on item marginals), their size was largely due to high proportions of "all yes" or "all no" response patterns. Some respondent groups, particularly the Kenya and Tanzania Masai, were characterized by very large proportions of "all no" response patterns, as indicated by very low and undifferentiated item marginals. Other groups like the Gusii, Kipsigis,[3] and Arusha made high proportions of "all yes" responses, while the rest of the groups were more differentiating among outgroups.

The internal reliability of the social distance scale, as measured by the Kuder-Richardson Formula 20 (KR20) was consistently high across most of the thirty samples, especially for a scale of only four items. Applying the Horst correction for uneven item marginals (corrected K-R) produced even higher reliabilities. (Lack of variation among the responses of the Kipsigis respondents accounts for the occurrence of the one .00 correlation—see note 2.) Across groups, the split-half reliability of respondents was .99 (N = 30), and it was also consistently high within groups. However, at least part of this internal consistency of respondents may be accounted for by the fact that only one interviewer handled all the interviews within each group.

Some indication of the reliability of the social distance measure across time is available from a comparison of some of the data obtained in the present survey with that obtained in a more abbreviated survey conducted in Kenya in 1969 (Edari, 1971). Using only the data from those groups included in both surveys, on a comparable four-item social distance scale, mean social distance scores for the two years were as follows:

1965

	A	B	C	D
A		4.00	4.32	4.62
B	2.86		5.94	6.86
C	6.12	4.44		4.68
D	3.22	3.50	2.50	

1969

	A	B	C	D
A		3.46	6.32	4.60
B	3.67		5.98	7.31
C	6.15	3.83		4.49
D	2.33	4.49	3.67	

Although the two sets of data reveal some differences in level of responding (reflecting both differences in respondent sampling between the two studies and changing political alignments across the time period represented), the patterns of response are remarkably consistent, reflected in a correlation of .82 between the two matrices.

Given that respondent groups in the present study differed significantly in their average response level on the social distance scale, an index of social distance that was more comparable across groups was obtained by reporting the rating for each outgroup as a *difference score*, relative to the mean rating given by the fifty ingroup respondents across all outgroups. (These ratings for the ten groups in each country are reported in the 10 x 10 matrices in Table D.3.2 in Appendix D, along with the reciprocity correlations for each.) The average reciprocity across the three countries is .56 which is significantly greater than .00 (p < .01) and considerably larger than that for liking ratings. This probably reflects the fact that social distance is more closely linked to observable behavior than is liking and is therefore likely to be perceived with greater consensus both within and between groups.

Closely related to social distance, as a measure of accepted intimacy in intergroup relations, is the actual degree of contact, or familiarity, between members of different groups. Familiarity is expected to be bidirectionally related to intergroup attraction, being both a source and a consequence of interpersonal liking. Information regarding the acquaintance of each respondent with outgroups was available from items in the first section of the interview (question no. 5). Responses to this item, regarding living among outgroup members and speaking their language, were coded to compute a measure of acquaintance for each respondent relative to each outgroup ranging from 0 (never lived among them; does not speak their language) to 5 (lived among them three years or more; speaks their language). An index of the familiarity of each ingroup with each outgroup was obtained from the mean acquaintance scores of the fifty ingroup respondents relative to that outgroup. (The 10 x 10 matrices of mean familiarity scores for the three countries are reported in Table D.3.3 of Appendix D, along with the reciprocity correlations for each.) The reciprocity values are again consistently positive, averaging .52 (p < .01) across the three countries. Since the acquaintance measure is based on actual experience of respondents, the size of the reciprocity correlation in this case is probably less a reflection of accuracy of perception than of the representativeness of the sample of ingroup respondents of the experience of that group with intergroup contact.

Derivation of the Combined Index

The indices of liking, social distance, and familiarity were all presumed to reflect favorability of intergroup attitudes, although with differing sources of error or inaccuracy. To test the validity of this assumption, the intercorrelations among the matrices of liking, social distance, and familiarity scores were computed for each country. For each pair of matrices, the average correlation was computed, based on within-group correlations across the ten respondent groups, with the following results:

(1) Liking and social distance: Kenya: $r = .64$; Uganda: $r = .65$; Tanzania: $r = .58$.

(2) Liking and familiarity: Kenya: $r = .40$; Uganda: $r = .64$; Tanzania: $r = .56$.

(3) Social distance and familiarity: Kenya: $r = .74$; Uganda: $r = .74$; Tanzania: $r = .84$.

Averaging across all thirty groups produced the following intercorrelation matrix:

	(1)	(2)	(3)
(1) Liking		.63	.54
(2) Social distance			.77
(3) Familiarity			

A simple algebraic method of factor extraction (Harman, 1960: 122) was applied to this matrix to determine whether a single factor could satisfactorily account for the pattern of correlations. The resulting loadings on the first factor extracted were .95 for social distance, .81 for familiarity, and .67 for liking scores. Since this unique single-factor solution produced reasonable factor weights for each variable, it provided strong evidence that all three variables were symptoms of a single dimension of intergroup attraction or friendship.[4] Once the existence of such a common source of variation was established for the three measures of intergroup relations, factor scores on this common dimension could be derived which would provide a combined index of attraction between each ingroup and outgroup included in the survey from each country. For this purpose, all the cell values in the 10 x 10 matrices of liking, social distance, and familiarity were converted to z-scores, multiplied by the appropriate factor loading, and summed to compute a factor score for each cell. The resulting matrices of intergroup attraction scores are reported in Tables 3.2-3.4. The reciprocity correlations reported for each matrix are consistently higher than those computed for the variables considered individually, averaging .64 ($p < .01$) across the three countries. This reflects the fact that factor scores cancel out sources of error or inaccuracy not shared by the three variables, thus producing a more reliable measure of the affective aspect of intergroup relations. This index of the favorability of attitudes between ingroups and outgroups was used in all subsequent analyses of intergroup attraction.

TABLE 3.2
INTERGROUP ATTRACTION RATINGS—KENYA

Ratings given to

		A	B	C	D	E	F	G	H	I	J
	A		+3.6	+2.5	+1.4	+1.4	-1.6	-2.8	-2.5	-0.9	+0.9
	B	+7.0		+5.0	+4.8	+0.2	-2.2	-2.3	-2.9	-2.9	-0.3
	C	+1.6	+5.9		+2.7	-0.3	-1.0	-2.1	-2.0	-0.4	+0.2
	D	+7.2	+0.1	+1.1		-1.0	-1.4	-1.7	-2.4	-2.0	+0.7
Ratings given by	E	-0.2	-1.3	-1.7	-0.9		-0.6	-1.3	-0.2	-2.5	+0.6
	F	+2.9	-0.2	-0.2	+0.2	+2.7		-0.8	-1.1	-2.9	+2.3
	G	0.0	-1.4	-1.0	-0.8	+0.1	+0.2		+6.7	-0.5	+1.5
	H	-0.2	-1.0	-1.3	-0.3	+1.0	+1.2	+4.0		+1.0	+0.4
	I	-3.4	-3.6	-3.3	+1.0	-3.7	-2.6	+3.4	+3.5		-2.8
	J	-2.7	-2.4	-2.4	+0.8	+4.9	+1.1	-0.8	-2.0	-0.7	

Reciprocity: r = .54

TABLE 3.3
INTERGROUP ATTRACTION RATINGS—UGANDA

Ratings given to

		A	B	C	D	E	F	G	H	I	J
	A		-0.6	+5.1	+5.3	+2.4	+3.0	-1.0	-2.4	-2.9	-5.2
	B	+1.0		+4.5	+1.9	+3.2	-0.9	-2.0	-1.0	-0.2	-4.8
	C	+0.2	+5.2		-1.5	+4.2	-2.9	-2.6	-2.6	-2.6	-3.0
	D	+7.6	-0.3	-0.7		-1.0	-1.2	-1.9	-3.2	-3.5	-3.7
Ratings given by	E	+3.5	+0.9	+3.4	-0.6		-2.2	-2.2	-3.7	-3.3	-3.1
	F	+5.8	+3.8	+5.2	+3.5	+2.4		-0.1	-1.2	-1.3	-4.2
	G	+4.9	-0.5	-0.6	+1.2	-1.7	-0.8		-1.3	-1.6	+0.5
	H	-0.8	-0.2	-0.8	-0.7	-0.5	-0.9	0.0		+7.1	-0.6
	I	-0.9	+0.6	-0.3	+1.0	-1.1	-1.5	+2.1	+5.2		-2.7
	J	-1.6	-2.5	-3.1	-2.5	-1.6	-1.9	+8.0	+1.3	+1.1	

Reciprocity: r = .62

TABLE 3.4
INTERGROUP ATTRACTION RATINGS—TANZANIA

Ratings given to

	A	B	C	D	E	F	G	H	I	J
A		+4.1	+0.4	+3.8	+1.0	-0.8	-1.2	-1.8	-3.3	-2.6
B	+3.1		+6.7	-0.7	+0.6	+1.6	+1.7	-1.1	-0.2	+0.4
C	+4.1	+9.1		+1.2	-2.7	+0.7	+1.2	-3.9	-5.1	-3.6
D	+3.4	+1.6	-1.2		+0.7	-0.3	-0.7	-1.8	+0.6	-1.5
E	+1.9	+1.0	-0.5	+1.7		+0.4	+0.7	-1.3	+4.0	-1.6
F	-1.5	-1.4	+0.2	-1.9	-2.1		+8.6	+0.5	-3.1	+0.5
G	-1.3	+0.4	+1.5	-2.0	-2.7	+8.3		+0.1	-3.3	+0.4
H	+2.0	-1.7	-2.3	-2.9	-2.2	+2.0	-1.8		-0.3	-2.0
I	+1.0	-2.7	-2.5	-2.8	+8.8	-3.3	-2.5	-3.3		-2.4
J	+0.6	-0.4	-0.7	-1.7	-1.3	+0.2	+2.1	-1.9	-2.5	

(row label: Ratings given by)

Reciprocity: r = .73

PATTERNS OF INTERGROUP ATTRACTION RATINGS

The reciprocity correlations are particularly relevant to one source of hypotheses regarding the pattern of attraction among acquainted groups— namely, the balance model of cognitive organization developed by Heider (1946, 1958) and extended by Cartwright and Harary (1956) and by New- comb (1953, 1961, 1963). One prediction generated from this theory is that of a tendency for a high degree of reciprocity in mutual attraction ratings between any two groups. This prediction is derived from the assumption that individuals and groups are primarily positive in their self-ratings. Therefore, for the set of relations between self and self, self and other, and other and self to meet the principles of psychological balance, the self-other and other-self ratings must be both positive or both negative (see Campbell and LeVine, 1968).

The correlations obtained between ratings given and ratings received in the attraction score matrices are consistently positive and significantly greater than .00, providing some support for the balance theory prediction. However, none of the reciprocity correlations approach a value of +1.00, as would be required for perfect balance. This is not unexpected, since the balance model predictions apply primarily to intergroup relations *as perceived by* a par- ticular respondent group. Thus, any inaccuracy in the perceptions of an ingroup regarding the attraction received from particular outgroups would have the effect of reducing the pattern of actual reciprocity. Newcomb's (1961) longitudinal study of interpersonal friendship indicated that the correspondence between actual, or objective, balance and perceived balance in interpersonal attraction ratings increased with prolonged interaction. In the matrices of intergroup attraction reported here, the pairs of groups along the diagonal are those for whom interaction, and therefore accuracy of per- ception, should be greatest. For these nine pairs in Kenya, the reciprocity correlation of attraction ratings is .83; for Uganda, .79; and for Tanzania, .94, all larger than the corresponding correlations for the full matrices. Thus, there is evidence that balance in reciprocal ratings is improved with increased intergroup contact.

Apart from reciprocity, the balance model has other implications for the pattern of outgroup attraction scores. The basic unit of analysis for balance theory is the triad of interpersonal (or, in this case, intergroup) relations. In order for a triad to be "balanced," the pattern of positive and negative attitudes among the three elements must be such that there is an even number of negative relations (i.e., either 0 or 2). A strict application of classic balance theory to multiple triads of individuals or groups leads to the prediction that elements of such sets will always fall into but two cliques (allowing for the possibility that one will be "empty"), with all positive relations within each clique and all negative relations between members of different cliques. However, the pattern of all negative relations in a triad (i.e., the case where the enemy of an enemy is an enemy) has always been handled equivocally in balance theory presentations, often being considered as "nonbalanced" rather than imbalanced (Newcomb, 1968). If such patterns are regarded as acceptable, the rigidity of the balance prediction is weakened enough to allow for multiple-clique outcomes (Davis, 1963, 1967).

The implication of the balance approach, then, is that the pattern of relations for any grouping of social units can be broken down into reasonably sized clusters which are consistently positive within and mutually hostile without. In order to test this in our data, the 10 x 10 matrices of intergroup attraction ratings, for the three countries, were subjected to cluster analyses. However, since all clustering procedures available to us required that the matrices of intergroup distance scores be in symmetric form, some transformation of our nonreciprocal ratings was required. For one analysis, a simple average of each pair of ratings was used which did not seriously distort the pattern of ratings, since there was rarely any large discrepancy in mutual ratings on the attraction index. A second analysis was done using the correlation between each respondent group's ratings of all groups (including a self-rating which was projected on the basis of self-evaluation scores)[5] and those of each of the other groups. This procedure produced matrices of symmetric similarity-of-rating scores which were appropriate to clustering analyses.

A clustering procedure developed by Warren Norman (1968), based on successive dichotomizations of the data matrix with the criterion of maximizing intercluster differences relative to intracluster similarity, was chosen as the most relevant for our hypothesis-testing interests.[6] The results of the cluster analysis for each of the types of data matrices are presented in graphic form in Figures 3.1 to 3.3 for ease of comparison.[7] The internal consistency values for all final clusters were acceptably high (alpha ranging from .469 to .999 for the mean attraction ratings and from .434 to .760 for the correlation matrices). For all three countries, the elements of the basic clusters were essentially the same for the rating and correlation data, although there was some variation in groupings at the higher levels. In one case (the Uganda correlation data), the matrix could be successfully dichotomized into two balanced clusters with all positive (or neutral) relations within cliques and predominantly negative (or neutral) relations between members of the different cliques. In all other cases, the data were broken down into multiple clusters with consistently positive relations within and predominantly negative relations between clusters. (Mixed patterns of positive and negative

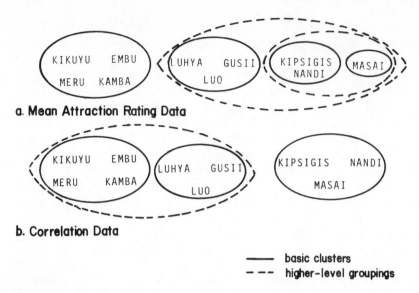

a. Mean Attraction Rating Data

b. Correlation Data

—— basic clusters
– – – higher-level groupings

Figure 3.1   Clustering of Ethnic Groups in Kenya

relations frequently occur between clusters which are included in the same larger grouping, but these are the only exceptions to consistent intercluster rejection.)

The obtained clusterings in all three countries reflect both historical-linguistic clusterings of ethnic groups and the nature of current political party alliances and district alignments (Edari, 1971). The influence of political factors is illustrated by comparing these data with those of another survey of inter-ethnic social distance ratings conducted in Kenya in 1966, just one year after the present survey (Mapp, 1972). The pattern of mean social distance ratings obtained in 1966 essentially replicated the Bantu/Nilo-Hamitic cluster-ings obtained here except that by 1966 the Luo had become an isolated group, reflecting the recent breakup of the Kikuyu-Luo coalition in the KANU party.

Despite such slight fluctuations in ratings, however, intergroup attraction patterns prove to be relatively enduring across time. Mapp (1972) found her social distance ratings in Kenya very similar to those obtained in Wilson's 1961 survey, and we have already reported above on the high comparability between our 1966 data and responses obtained in 1968. We have no compar-able data on temporal stability for Uganda and Tanzania, but the clusters obtained in those two countries correspond to traditional groupings with an extensive past history. Since the results of the cluster analyses of attraction ratings meet the criteria of objectively "balanced" sets of relations, cognitive

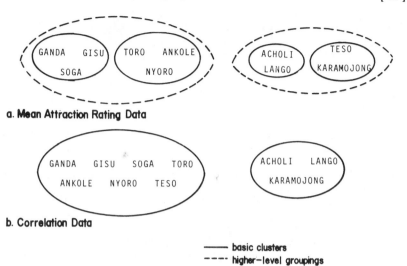

a. **Mean Attraction Rating Data**

b. Correlation Data

——— basic clusters
---- higher-level groupings

Figure 3.2   Clustering of Ethnic Groups in Uganda

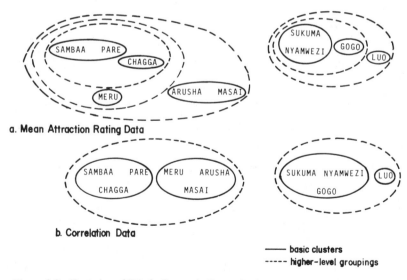

a. Mean Attraction Rating Data

b. Correlation Data

——— basic clusters
----- higher-level groupings

Figure 3.3   Clustering of Ethnic Groups in Tanzania

balance theory would preduct that they would be highly stable—even rigid—across time, barring major disruptive influences.

NOTES

1. All tabular materials that serve merely to document findings discussed in the text have been included as data matrices in Appendix D, numbered and ordered according to the chapter in which they are mentioned. It should be emphasized that the data matrices presented in Appendix D and throughout this volume are provided for the purpose of illustrating differential *patterns* of response across groups. Since scores are generally reported in terms of relative rather than absolute values, any individual rating is relatively uninterpretable. In order to focus attention on response patterns, these data matrices are presented without identification of ethnic labels.

2. The repeated finding of lower reciprocity coefficients among the Kenya groups than for the two other countries probably reflects political conditions existing at the time the survey was conducted. As discussed in Chapter 2, the period was one of political instability in Kenya, marked by recurring realignments of party coalitions. The same period, on the other hand, was one of relative political stability in Uganda and Tanzania.

3. As was mentioned in the preceding chapter, responses from the Kipsigis are regarded as highly atypical. The occurrence in this study of undifferentiatedly positive responses to outgroups by Kipsigis informants is in sharp contrast to the results of fieldwork by Daniels (1970) that indicated that Kipsigis males tend to make clear distinctions in their attitudes and perceptions regarding different neighboring groups. Examination of original interview protocols for the present study revealed that the same (Gusii-born) interviewer had conducted the interviews among both the Gusii and Kipsigis, and suggests that interview bias effects (evidenced also in the Gusii responses) were enhanced when the interviewer was an outsider among the Kipsigis. Thus, all results reported for the Kipsigis must be regarded with reservation even though they have not been deleted from any of the analyses. It should be noted that no other two groups in the survey were interviewed by the same interviewer.

4. It should be noted that, while this analysis indicates that liking and social distance share a common source of variance, the two measures can hardly be considered *identical* with a correlation of only .63 between them. This degree of relationship is consistent with that obtained by Triandis (1971) in various cross-cultural settings.

5. See Chapter 5.

6. Our sincere thanks to Dr. Norman of the University of Michigan for handling the data analyses for us. Appreciation also goes to Mr. Leighton Price and the Computer Institute for Social Science Research, of Michigan State University, for providing us with the intercolumnar correlation procedure and a hierarchical cluster analysis which was used to cross-validate the outcomes of Norman's dichotomous clustering program.

7. Since these clusterings are based on relative, rather than absolute, intergroup ratings, and since the results reflect well-known ethnic alliances, we felt presenting them with group labels would greatly enhance their meaningfulness without violating our position on protection of privacy.

Chapter 4

CORRELATES OF INTERGROUP ATTRACTION

The development of an index of intergroup attraction was the first step toward systematic analysis of situational determinants of affective intergroup relations. From each of the theories reviewed by LeVine and Campbell (1972), hypotheses were derived involving the characteristics of outgroups and the kinds of ingroup-outgroup relations that should be related to the degree of intergroup hostility. For a number of variables, different theories generate sometimes complementary and sometimes contradictory propositions, providing a basis for testing the relative predictive validity of the theoretical assumptions. Data analyses from the East African survey relevant to each of four such variables are considered in this chapter.

PHYSICAL DISTANCE

Geographical factors that affect the opportunity for contact and conflict between social groups provide an obvious potential source of variation in intergroup relations. Lewis Richardson's mathematical model of warfare emphasizes the positive relationship between physical nearness, in terms of common territorial boundaries, and frequency and magnitude of conflict between social units (Richardson, 1960; Wesley, 1962). The opportunity for conflict of interests between physically proximal groups is also a factor considered in realistic group conflict theory, leading to the prediction that intergroup hostility will be inversely related to distance.

A similar prediction is generated by frustration-aggression theory. The major implication of this latter theory for intergroup relations is that since the expression of frustration-aroused aggression against ingroup authorities would be disruptive of group functioning, social groups will develop mechanisms for inhibiting its expression at the intragroup level and for displacing such aggression onto other groups. The effect of such displacement should be greatest for those outgroups that are available for recognition, distinct enough to be released from inhibitions specific to the ingroup, and provide some provocation for intergroup conflict. Since all these criteria are likely to be met by neighboring outgroups, geographic proximity should be positively related to the extent of hostility expressed between groups.

On the other hand, physical proximity also provides opportunity for cultural exchange, trade, and other types of friendly social intercourse. To the extent that nearness is related to cultural similarity, consistency theories of interpersonal attraction predict a positive relationship between attraction and proximity. The functional theories of interpersonal relations (Homans, 1961; Thibaut and Kelley, 1959) stress the value of close physical contact in reducing the costs of interaction between groups and thus increasing the probability of positive attraction. Newcomb's theory of interpersonal attraction (Newcomb, 1956) includes a principle of propinquity: "Other things being equal, people are most likely to be attracted to those in closest contact with them." The results of an experimental study by Brislin (1968) support this principle in that laboratory groups playing a game against a group of experimental confederates were more likely to include "outgroup" members in sociometric choices the more visual contact and proximity they had during competition. It appears, then, that the effect of physical distance on intergroup attraction may be positive or negative, depending on what kind of ingroup-outgroup relations are promoted by geographical opportunity.

The effect of conflicting correlates of intergroup distance may be such that the overall relationship between proximity and attraction is nonlinear, rather than consistently positive or negative. The influence of conflict of interests, for example, may be most intense for groups with overlapping territories or shared borders and decreases in effect with greater distance, while the effect of friendly intercourse may be equally as strong for close nonadjacent groups as for immediately adjacent ones. The outcome of these effects combined would be a curvilinear relationship—an inverted U-curve—between distance and attraction such that intergroup friendship would be greatest between groups at intermediate distance and less for groups either closer or more remote. A contrasting curvilinear effect can be predicted from the perspective of frustration-aggression theory. While adjacent outgroups are most readily available as targets for displaced hostility, their very nearness also increases the chances for retaliation against expressed aggression. Thus, the combined effects of displacement and inhibitory tendencies may be such that the greatest degree of hostility is expressed toward visible but non-adjacent outgroups—those at intermediate distances—and less toward adjacent or remote outgroups. Different theoretical perspectives, then, provide us with four different predictions as to the relationship between physical distance and intergroup attraction, as summarized in Figure 4.1.

The positive linear relationship represented in part a of Figure 4.1 is derived from an emphasis on potential contact, cultural exchange, and low-effort interaction enhanced by physical nearness, while the contrasting negative relationship of part b is derived from an emphasis on the potential for conflict over resources and issues also enhanced by proximity. The two compromise predictions represent different composites of the preceding two, with part c derived from a cost-reward weighting analysis and part d from an aggression-inhibition-displacement perspective.

The data available to date on the effects of contact and proximity on the nature of intergroup relations show mixed outcomes. A series of experiments on the formation of attitudes as a function of familiarity with the attitude object (Zajonc, 1968) indicates that increased familiarity leads to more positive attitudes, at least toward objects with initially neutral connotation. However, research experience involving increased contact between members of initially hostile groups, such as racial subgroups in the United States, suggests that such contact improves group relations only under very specialized conditions (Amir, 1969). For the most part, such studies involve relations between subgroups that lack any distinct territorial boundaries. One exception to this is Mitchell's (1956) study of social distance among migra-

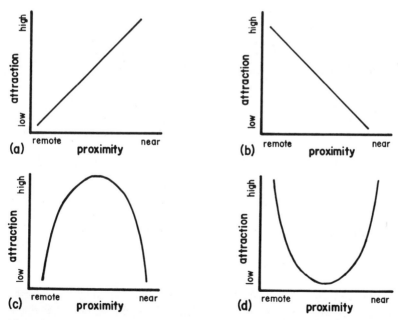

Figure 4.1   Alternative Relationships Between Proximity and Attraction

tory workers in the Zambian copperbelt, representing some twenty different tribes. His data clearly indicate a preference (in terms of lower social distance) for members of territorially adjacent tribes over those from more remote groups. It should be noted, however, that Mitchell's data came from respondents living at considerable distances from their homes and thrown together with total strangers, conditions under which a relatively familiar former enemy from one's home area might well become one's friend in coexile. Therefore, the results of the present study, based on interviews with respondents within their home territories, can further clarify the nature of the relationship between proximity and intergroup attraction.

It was somewhat problematic to devise a measure of intergroup distance which would adequately reflect the multiple factors represented in the various theoretical positions considered above. Any measure of linear distance between each pair of groups would have required some basis for determining a point within each territory from which such measurement would begin, and would not have taken into account geographical features or boundary conditions. For our purposes, a measure of proximity based on occurrence of territorial boundaries seemed more appropriate. In any one case, such a measure may not have been the most adequate indicator of functional intergroup distance, depending on factors such as territorial size, natural geographic conditions, and location of interviewees relative to border areas, but none of these potentially confounding factors was *systematically* related to the index of distance within any set of ratings.

Distance scores were assigned for each pair of groups, within each country, utilizing tribal maps provided by Good (1966). The highest level of proximity, 4, was assigned to adjacent groups, those sharing some common boundary regardless of the length of adjacent territory. The other three levels of distance were defined in terms of the number (disregarding size) of tribal territories intervening between the ingroup territory and that of the outgroup. Level 3 was assigned to groups separated by one other group, level 2 to those with two groups between, and level 1 to more remote groups (see Appendix B for all intergroup distance scores). Using this index, the intragroup correlation between proximity and attraction scores was obtained for the nine outgroup ratings within each respondent group and then averaged across the ten ingroups within each country, and across all thirty groups. (The distance-attraction correlation for each respondent group individually is reported in Appendix E.1.) The average correlations obtained were as follows: Kenya: $r = .54$; Uganda: $r = .68$; Tanzania: $r = .56$; overall: $r = .60$ ($p < .01$ for a t-test of the null hypothesis that $\bar{\rho} = .00$; d.f. = 29).

The results of this correlational analysis provide much more support for the hypothesis that geographical opportunity leads to friendly relations than that it leads to attitudinal hostility. In none of the thirty groups is the proximity-attraction correlation highly negative, as would be predicted from the latter hypothesis (although a few nonsignificant negative correlations do occur). However, the Pearson product-moment correlation, being a measure of degree of *linear* relationship between two variables, does not provide an adequate test of all the hypothesized relationships between distance and attraction. Any obtained correlation of less than 1.00 could reflect systematic nonlinear trends rather than just random variation. To assess whether this was the case with these data, the average ratings by ingroups for outgroups at each level of distance were computed, with the results (across all thirty groups) plotted in Figure 4.2.[1] It is clear from this figure that there is no evidence for curvilinearity: attraction scores are highest for adjacent outgroups, with ratings consistently decreasing with increased distance between ingroup and outgroup. The same essentially linear trend holds for the data averaged across the ten groups in each country considered separately. This does not mean, of course, that adjacent groups do not experience conflict and overt hostility, but rather that the effects of social contact and interchange are overriding as determinants of an attitudinal measure of intergroup attraction.

CULTURAL SIMILARITY

The implications of the principle of cognitive consistency for the patterning of intergroup relations have already been considered in Chapter 3. More basic to most of the models of cognitive consistency, however, is the relationship between interpersonal attraction and similarity of attitudes. The model is usually applied to the triad, $A_{\searrow_X \nearrow}B$, where A and B are two actors (groups in our setting, persons in Newcomb's [1961] study of friendship and values which we parallel at the group level), and X is some object or value toward which A and B are co-oriented. If X is regarded as an item of culture (a custom, belief, institution, or artifact), then the balance principle predicts that liking between A and B will occur when their valuing of X is similar—i.e., both are positive or both are negative toward it—and that disliking will accompany dissimilarity of attitude. Considering the many X's about which two social groups might be co-oriented, cognitive consistency clearly predicts that attraction between two groups will be positively related to overall cultural similarity.

In testing his own theory of cognitive organization, Rokeach (1960) applied this prediction to intergroup attitudes among religious denominations in the United States and found a strong positive relationship between belief dissimilarity and rejection. He found further that measures of intergroup mingling—shifts of church membership, denomination of college choices, and frequency of interfaith marriages—were directly related to similarity. Mitchell's (1956) study of social distance among tribal groups in Zambia also

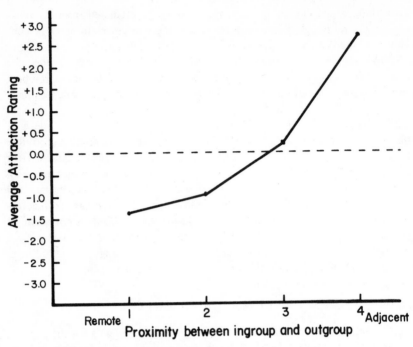

Figure 4.2   Frustration Generalization Gradients

indicated a strong relationship between cultural similarity (in terms of matri-lineal versus patrilineal organization) and intergroup social choice.

For most balance theorists (e.g., Newcomb, 1961, 1963), the relationship between similarity and positive affect is considered to be bidirectional; individuals and groups both seek friendship with similar others and become more similar to those they consider friends. Also, since balance is defined in terms of the cognitions of an evaluator, the relationship between liking and *perceived* degree of ingroup-outgroup similarity is expected to be greater than that between liking and some objective measure of intergroup similarity. However, Newcomb's (1961) findings strongly suggest that distortions of perception occur primarily during early acquaintance and that prolonged contact brings friendship choices more in line with actual similarity. The causal influence of actual similarity on interpersonal attraction is also sup-ported with results of experimental studies by Byrne (e.g., Byrne, 1969; Byrne and Nelson, 1965). When subjects in these experiments are presented with attitudinal information for hypothetical strangers, their attraction ratings for the stimulus persons are directly related to the manipulated proportion of attitude endorsements that are similar to those made by the subjects themselves. Projecting these results to the level of intergroup relations supports the prediction of a positive relationship between objective, as well as perceived, cultural similarity and intergroup attraction.

A different view of the effect of similarity on intergroup relations is provided by derivations from frustration-aggression theory (Dollard et al., 1939) related to the determination of targets of displaced hostility. Basic to the frustration-aggression model is the assumption that the probability of expressed aggression against a particular object is a joint function of the strength of frustration-aroused elicitation tendencies and the degree of inhibition against aggression toward that object. Both tendencies are assumed to generalize to other objects according to their similarity to the original source of arousal, but the gradient of generalization is presumed to be steeper (i.e., drop off faster) for inhibition than for elicitation. Thus, if the source of some frustration is such that the inhibition against expressing aggression toward it is greater than the elicited tendency to aggress, the aggressive expression should be displaced toward another target determined by the joint effects of generalized arousal and generalized inhibition, as in Figure 4.3.

Maximum displacement should occur at that point where generalized elicitation just exceeds generalized inhibition—namely, against targets which are of *intermediate* similarity to the source of frustration (i.e., neither so similar as to generate inhibition nor so dissimilar that generalized elicitation drops below 0). Extending this analysis to intergroup relations leads to the prediction of a curvilinear relation between similarity and attraction such that intergroup hostility is greatest between groups at intermediate levels of cultural similarity, while liking is greater for highly similar groups (which share sources of inhibition against hostility) and highly dissimilar groups (which bear little or no resemblence to ingroup sources of frustration).

The effects of similarity relative to generalization of ingroup responses can also be considered from a learning theory perspective. In contradiction to an aggression-displacement point of view, transfer-of-learning effects would suggest that hostility toward outgroups will be *directly* related to the permissibility of hostility expression within each ingroup. Those groups that suppress intragroup aggression will also exhibit low intergroup aggression, especially toward similar outgroups (predicting a positive linear relationship between similarity and attraction consistent with that predicted by cognitive balance models). On the other hand, groups within which expression of aggression is permitted or encouraged should exhibit greater intergroup aggression, particularly toward similar outgroups. (The apparent contradiction between this outcome and that predicted by balance theories is reduced when it is noted that application of the consistency principle is based on the assumption of positive self-regard and may not be expected to hold in cases where ingroup relations—parallel to self-regard at the group level—are negative.)

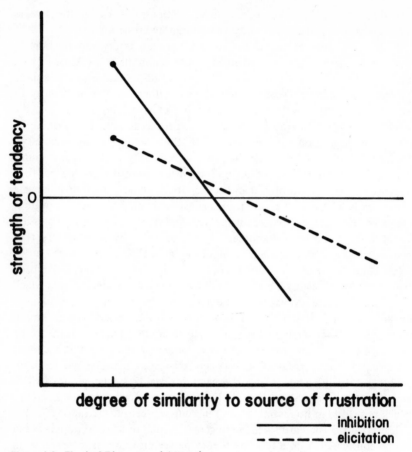

Figure 4.3 Physical Distance and Attraction

In order to obtain a measure of objective cultural similarity among the groups surveyed in this study, the ethnic groups in each country were classified into ethnic-linguistic clusters, and the degree of similarity within and between clusters was evaluated[2] on a three-point scale: high similarity, intermediate similarity, or low similarity (high dissimilarity). These evaluations were then used to derive similarity ratings between each pair of groups in each country, as reported in Appendix C.

The effect of similarity on intergroup attraction ratings was assessed by analysis of variance of all outgroup ratings (N = 270; nine ratings by each of thirty ingroups) differentiated according to level of similarity between ingroup and outgroup. The results of this analysis indicated a highly significant effect of degree of similarity (F = 14.7; p < .001, with 2 and 267 degrees of freedom). The mean ratings for each level of intergroup similarity are plotted in Figure 4.4. (This analysis was also done within each country with essentially the same results for each.) The positive effect of similarity on attraction is statistically reliable and clearly linear. Highly similar outgroups are significantly better liked than intermediate or dissimilar outgroups, as predicted by the balance principle of interpersonal relations. There is no evidence that outgroups of intermediate similarity to the ingroup are less liked than highly dissimilar outgroups, but the drop in attraction ratings between high and intermediate similar groups suggests that the latter may be regular targets of displaced hostility.

It can be seen from Appendix C that not all ingroups among those sampled had outgroups at all three levels of similarity. Therefore, the ratings of outgroups at each level were differentially influenced by the effects of specific ingroups. For this reason, the analysis of the relationship between similarity and attraction was repeated using the mean rating of outgroups at each level of similarity for the eighteen respondent groups with all three outgroup types. The results of this repeated-measures analysis of variance replicated those of the first analysis ($F = 38.4$; $p < .001$, with 2 and 34 degrees of freedom), and the means reported in Figure 4.4 reveal that the outcomes are essentially the same as those of the overall sample. The effect of similarity on attraction ratings is apparently highly reliable with or without control for ingroup effects.

Since ratings of objective cultural similarity may not correspond to ingroup's members' evaluations of the degree of similarity between their own group and others, a separate analysis of the relationship between friendship and similarity was made using a measure of *perceived* similarity between groups. Perceived similarity was obtained from responses to questions 58 and 59 of the interview schedule. Since these questions parallel those on liking of outgroups, the problems of obtaining an index of intergroup liking, discussed in Chapter 3, were also encountered in obtaining net similarity ratings. Again, the method of computing differences between actual and expected number of mentions was used for each intergroup rating and the net difference score used as the index of perceived similarity. The reciprocity correlations for this index ranged from .11 (Kenya) to .67 (Uganda) to .72 (Tanzania), averaging .54 across all three countries, revealing that group A's perception of similarity to group B may not always correspond to group B's perception of the same relationship. Thus, perceived similarity was measured from the point of view of each ingroup relative to each outgroup without regard for symmetry. These values were correlated with attraction ratings across the nine outgroups within each respondent group. The averages of the intragroup correlations (reported individually in Appendix E.2) were: Kenya: $r = .75$; Uganda: $r = .68$; Tanzania: $r = .78$; overall: $r = .74$ ($p < .01$, for t-test, d.f. = 29).

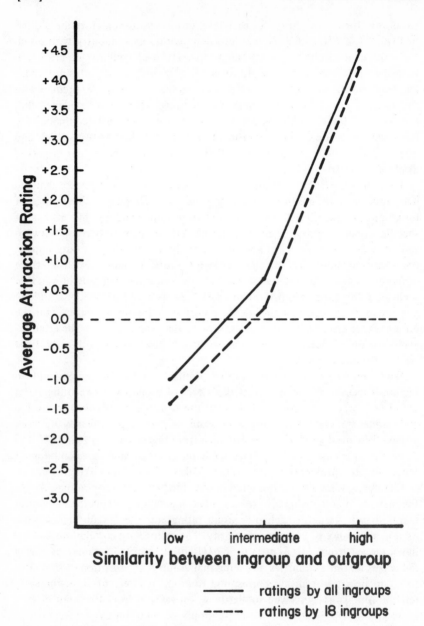

Figure 4.4   Objective Similarity and Attraction

As with actual similarity, the relationship between perceived similarity and friendship is clearly and consistently a positive linear one. In the latter case, the bidirectionality of the relationship is especially clear since ingroup members could adjust their perceptions of the similarity of outgroups according to their degree of liking for them as well as adjust liking to correspond to similarity. To the extent that perceived similarity corresponds to actual similarity,[3] the primary direction of causality may be from similarity to liking, but actual similarity may also be promoted by friendship involving prolonged intergroup contact. In either case, the balance proposition is strongly supported.

Another indication of the relationships among perceived similarity, objective similarity, and intergroup friendship was obtained by subjecting the matrices of similarity ratings (converted to symmetric matrices by use of average pair ratings) to dichotomous cluster analysis, for comparison with the clusters obtained from attraction ratings, presented in Chapter 3. The results of this analysis are reported in Figure 4.5. The comparability between similarity clusters and the attraction clusters reported in Figures 3.1-3.3 is marked, particularly for the symmetric attraction ratings in Kenya and Uganda. (The similarity ratings in Tanzania are so dominated by strong pairings that higher-order groupings are relatively uninterpretable.) The clusters also reflect the degree of correspondence between perceived and objective similarity ratings. For the most part, the perceived similarity clusters, particularly at the higher-level groups in Kenya and Uganda, follow historical language-culture grouping lines, and usually ethnic groups within the same clusters had received high or intermediate similarity ratings on the objective scale, while those in different clusters had received low similarity ratings. The exceptions to this correspondence usually reflect the effects of more current political alignments, which are only imperfectly related to traditional culture groupings.

Comparisons between attraction clusters (Figures 3.1-3.3) and these similarity clusters reveal some differential effects of current alliances and historical ties on the two indices. The most striking example is the Luhya-Gusii-Luo cluster of Figure 3.1, which reflects regional alliances that are not supported by historical roots of cultural similarity and are not represented in the perceived similarity clusters of Figure 4.5. In Uganda, the major perceived similarity clusters are split on the basis of Bantu-Nilotic culture groupings, but in Tanzania the splits are complicated by the differential alignments of the historically similar Meru and Arusha. Both groups are of mixed Bantu and Nilo-Hamitic heritage, but in recent years the Meru have identified more strongly with their Bantu neighbors while the Arusha have maintained more

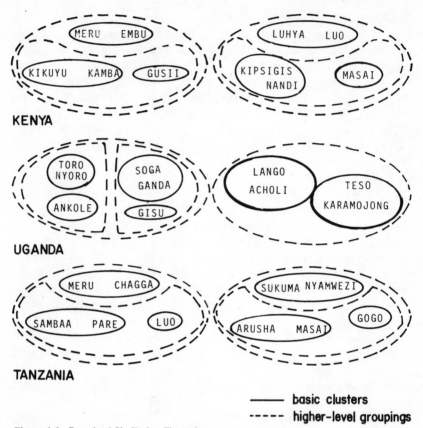

Figure 4.5 Perceived Similarity Clusterings

of the traditional ties with the Masai. Thus, in general, the correspondence between objective and perceived similarity reflects historical ethnic ties, but the deviations do indicate that perceived similarity may be manipulated to reflect or justify existing intergroup alliances and district alignments.

JOINT EFFECT OF SIMILARITY AND DISTANCE

Because of both theoretical and empirical association between intergroup similarity and proximity, their combined contribution to variance in intergroup attraction is of some interest. Across all thirty ingroups' ratings of outgroups (N = 270), the dyadic correlation obtained between similarity and attraction was .66, and between proximity and attraction, .43,[4] while a multiple correlation based on a linear combination of proximity and similarity ratings came to .69. Since both the similarity and proximity values made statistically significant contributions to the size of the multiple correlation (β-weights = .58 and .21, respectively), it is attempting to interpret this outcome as indicating that each variable influences attraction ratings to some extent independently of the effect of the other. However, because the multiple correlation is based on interrelationships among imperfect measures of the variables of interest (neither the three-point scale of cultural similarity nor the ordinal scale of physical distance reflects all relevant variations between groups on these two dimensions), at least three other interpretations of the combined effect are plausible. (1) The effect may be entirely one of similarity but measured imperfectly in such a way that the addition of the distance index enhances accuracy. That is, for any two pairs of groups with the same similarity ratings, the pair higher in proximity may be higher in *actual* similarity (either because opportunity for observation and contact promotes similarity or because cultural similarity influenced the settlement patterns represented by the index of proximity). In such a case, the apparent effect of proximity on attraction ratings would actually have been produced by a refinement of the measurement of similarity achieved when the two indices are combined. (2) Conversely, though somewhat less plausibly, the effect could be interpreted as one entirely of proximity for which the index of similarity enhances accuracy of measurement by reflecting extent of adjacent territory. (3) Alternatively, both the proximity and similarity ratings could represent imperfect measures, or symptoms, of some third factor (e.g., social interaction, military or economic alliance, or other forms of shared culture) which underlies the positive relationship to attraction (Brewer et al., 1970, for fuller discussion of this issue of interpreting multiple regression results).

Measures taken at a single time, with no adequate assessment of degree of measurement error or construct validity, provide no basis for objectively choosing among these four explanations of the joint effect of proximity and similarity on intergroup attraction (although the relatively low overall correlation between the two indices—r = .39—lends some credence to a two-effect interpretation). Fortunately, the theoretical positions under investigation do not require differentiating among the alternatives since the positive effects represented in all four interpretations are consistent with theories of intergroup attitudes based on principles of reinforcement and cognitive consistency and are contradictory to theoretical positions emphasizing conflict and displaced aggression, which would predict negative, or at least nonlinear, relationships with attraction for both variables. Thus, these correlational outcomes do provide differential support for some theoretical perspectives over others.

SOCIAL-ECONOMIC ADVANCEMENT

A third class of variables that enters into a number of theoretical analyses of intergroup relations may be identified broadly as the strength, power, or prestige of a particular social group. This dimension can be assessed independently of such variables as intergroup similarity and distance since the latter represent dyadic variables (that is, each is defined in terms of a relationship existing between two groups rather than as a characteristic of either group taken individually) while the former is usually defined monadically (that is, as a characteristic of a particular group considered individually). Of all the variables reviewed by LeVine and Campbell (1972), this one is probably most inadequately defined at the theoretical level. For one thing, the determinants of intergroup power are likely to vary considerably across regions and historical periods. Where intergroup relations are dominated by military conflict, resources for power will lie in population size, territory expanse, and material resources related to the arming and maintenance of military forces; where trade and economic competition dominate, power will be determined by availability of natural resources, artisan skills, and sociopolitical structures conducive to extrasubsistance economic production. In addition, theoretical perspectives differ on the issue of whether to conceptualize intergroup power in terms of objective conditions or subjective perceptions. Some economic and ecological determinists emphasize objective assessments of relative size, wealth, etc., of groups, which they see as affecting intergroup relations with or without the awareness of those involved, while other theorists place greatest weight on the group phenomenology, its collective awareness of the intergroup situation. Which view is taken can greatly affect not only what measures are considered relevant to the evaluation of intergroup power but also the historical time period to be taken into account.

Within the time period represented by the East African survey, intergroup variations in status or position within a "developing" economy provided the most salient index of relative intergroup power—a measure which we abbreviatedly refer to as "social-economic advancement."[5] Between-group variations on this dimension can be related to intergroup differences in overall ethnocentrism and to variations in attitudes toward outgroups from the point of view of any ingroup. The latter relationship is of interest here (the former to be considered in Chapter 5).

The potential effect of one group's economic success and prestige on its relations with other social groups is equivocal. On the one hand, advanced outgroups may be perceived as sources of threat or frustration, particularly by less-advanced groups, especially if economic advancement is associated with advantages in military or political efforts and in competition over scarce resources. In this case, high advanced outgroups would be targets of more resentment than low advanced groups according to the assumptions of realistic group conflict and frustration-aggression theories. On the other hand, reference group theory (e.g., Merton and Rossi, 1957) leads to the prediction that wealthy, successful outgroups will be admired and emulated by less-successful groups. In addition, to the extent that advancement is related to military or political power, frustration-aggression theory would predict that expression of overt hostility against such high advanced groups would be inhibited for fear of retaliation, and that such hostility would be displaced against weaker, less threatening outgroups.

The dimension of social-economic advancement in East Africa refers primarily to the process of urbanization (relation to centers of transportation, commerce, industry, and government administration), spread of formal education, and distribution of paid employment in a modern occupational structure. The complexity of obtaining objective descriptions of ethnic groups on such dimensions is illustrated by the analyses of modernization in Kenya by Soja (1968), which were based on statistics compiled between 1962 and 1965 in the thirty-six administrative districts of Kenya on twenty-five indices (including measures of ethnicity and density of population, literacy, relations to networks of transportation and communication, cash income, and participation in political organizations). Factor analysis of the intercorrelations among these twenty-five variables provided the basis for consideration of the dynamics of modernization (particularly of the precipitating role of spatial factors) and for assessment of district differences in development along the dimensions represented. A weighted sum of district scores on the twenty-five component variables—based on loadings on the first unrotated factor emerging from this analysis—provided an index of relative standing on a general developmental dimension (Soja, 1968: 77-84). Factor scores for ethnic groups on this dimension could be derived by averaging scores for home districts of each group. These values for the ten Kenya groups in our survey are presented in Table 4.1.

Using these factor scores as indices of relative advancement for the ethnic groups presents some problems. Most serious is the phenomenon of intra-ethnic differentiation in rate of modernization, particularly marked among the Kikuyu, Luo, and Kamba. Although the Kikuyu as a whole score very high on the developmental factor, the combined score masks considerable differences among the three home districts. Kiambu, with its proximity to the major urban center of Nairobi, is most developed and politically active, and scores highest on all modernization indices. Fort Hall, on the other hand, is more strongly traditional, while Nyeri represents an area intermediate in urbanization and levels of education. The Luo of Central Nyanza form a

TABLE 4.1
MODERNIZATION FACTOR SCORES–KENYA[a]

Ethnic Group	(Combined Districts)	Factor Score (Rank)
Kikuyu	Kiambu, Ft. Hall, Nyeri	200 (1)
Embu	(Embu)	307 (3)
Meru	(Meru)	341 (6)
Kamba	Machakos, Kitui	377 (8)
Luhya	Elgon Nyanza, North Nyanza	340 (5)
Gusii	(Kisii)	343 (7)
Kipsigis	(Kericho)	205 (2)
Nandi	(Nandi)	399 (9)
Masai	Kajaido, Narok	463 (10)
Luo	South Nyanza, Central Nyanza	314 (4)

[a]Values derived from Soja (1968: 128-129)
NOTE: Lower scores reflect higher standings on the developmental scale.

group second only to the Kiambu Kikuyu in measures of education and urban development, but the overall factor score assigned to the Luo is greatly affected by the contrasting conditions of modernization in South Nyanza, which is a fairly isolated agricultural district. (The two Luo districts are also marked by political contrast, Central Nyanza being the site of the formation of the KPU in 1966, while South Nyanza remained loyal to KANU.) Similarly, the combined Kamba score reflects a developmental rift between the primarily agricultural district of Machakos and the largely pastoral and less modernized Kitui district. For these groups, then, the average factor score may provide the most objectively "fair" index of relative advancement but does not necessarily represent the most visible segments of the respective ethnic groups. The tabled values provide more reliable indicators for the groups relatively homogeneous at intermediate levels of advancement—Meru, Embu, Luhya, Gusii—and for clearly peripheral groups such as the Masai. One major exception is the factor score for the Kipsigis which is based on district scores for Kericho, the population of which contains a large proportion of

Europeans and actually less than seventy-five percent Kipsigis. Just how much the Kipsigis as an ethnic group are associated with the high modernization status of Kericho District is uncertain.

Statistical analyses comparable to those of Soja (1968) were computed for Uganda districts by Jones (1971). As can be seen from Table 4.2, district units in Uganda correspond more closely to ethnic groupings than is true in Kenya, although the native population within home districts for Uganda groups is generally a lower proportion of total district population than for most districts in Kenya. However, Jones' indices do not incorporate proportion of European population but rather concentrate on variables reflecting spatial factors, such as access to urban centers, communication flow, trade and sales patterns, and on education and employment levels of the African population. Factor analysis of twenty-two such measures provided factor scores for each district on a general dimension of modernization (based on loadings on the first unrotated factor), which are converted to averages for ethnic groups in Table 4.2. In this case, ethnic variations correspond more closely to district scores with the exception of the Ganda, for which the average district score masks sharp differences between the highly modernized

TABLE 4.2
MODERNIZATION FACTOR SCORES—UGANDA[a]

Ethnic Ethnic Group	(District)	Factor Score (Rank)
Ganda	W. Mengo E. Mengo Masaka Mubende	79 (3)
Teso	(Teso)	123 (6)
Nyoro	(Bunyoro)	93 (4)
Toro	(Toro)	102 (5)
Ankole	(Ankole)	158 (9)
Soga	(Busoga)	54 (1)
Gisu	(Bugisu)	61 (2)
Acholi	(Acholi)	143 (7)
Lango	(Lango)	152 (8)
Karamojong	(Karamoja)	201 (10)

[a]Values derived from Jones (1971, p. 89)
NOTE: Lower scores reflect higher standings on the developmental scale.

Mengo districts (adjacent to the urban center at Kampala) and the more remote Mubende district.

Although the Kenya district data are somewhat equivocal in terms of ethnic differentiation, and although the two sets of modernization variables are not completely comparable, data from these two studies provide the best available objective indices of relative advancement among ethnic groups in Kenya and Uganda and are therefore used as the basis of determining whether any relationship exists between intergroup attraction and modernization. Within each respondent group, attraction ratings of outgroups are correlated with outgroup advancement scores (intragroup correlations appear in Appendix E.3). Among the Kenya groups, these correlations averaged to a value of .20[6] and, although the intragroup values were generally positive, they were relatively low and considerably more variable than those reported for distance and similarity. In Uganda, the positive relationship was somewhat stronger (r = .35) but the high variability of the intragroup correlation values (Appendix E.3) suggests that the relationship may have been determined largely by the strong correspondence between modernization scores and language-culture groupings in that country. Thus polarization of alignments relative to modernization is more marked in Uganda than in Kenya but is also confounded with other aspects of intergroup similarity.

Since compilation of the statistics necessary to provide equivalent indices of modernization for Tanzania[7] was beyond the scope of our survey, comparable analyses for objective advancement levels could not be done in the third country. In order to achieve further clarification of the effect of advancement across all three countries, a rougher index of relative advancement was utilized, in the form of rankings intended to correspond to ethnic reputations in urbanization and educational development. In each country, an advancement ranking of "3" was assigned to the most visibly advanced group, a ranking of "1" to least modernized groups (one each in Kenya and Uganda and two groups in Tanzania), and an intermediate ranking of "2" to all others (see Appendix A for rank values assigned to each ethnic group). Using these rankings, average attraction scores given to outgroups at each level of advancement were analyzed in each country, with the following results:

	High Advanced Outgroups	Intermediate Outgroups	Low Advanced Outgroups
Kenya:	M = +1.35 (S.D. = 3.56)	M = +0.03	M = -1.31 (S.D. = 1.26)
Uganda:	M = +2.19 (S.D. = 3.15)	M = +0.08	M = -2.96 (S.D. = 1.74)
Tanzania:	M = +1.48 (S.D. = 2.08)	M = +0.14	M = -1.42 (S.D. = 1.86)

Overall average ratings, across all 30 respondent groups, are reported in Figure 4.6.[8]

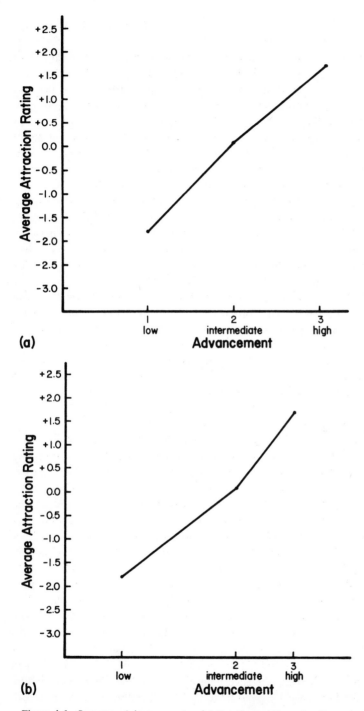

Figure 4.6 Outgroup Advancement and Attraction: Alternative Representations

Each of these analyses suggests a consistent linear trend, with high advanced outgroups receiving highest attraction scores. However, the aggregate means mask a considerable degree of variation in ratings. Reflecting this high variance, the mean trends correspond to correlation values (eta) of only .24 ($p < .10$) in Kenya, .40 ($p < .01$) in Uganda, and .28 ($p < .05$) in Tanzania. Most inconsistency occurs in attraction ratings for high advanced groups. Within each country, the variance of ratings for outgroups with rankings of "3" notably exceeds that for ratings of those with rankings of "1" (see above data). Thus, although there is no evidence for curvilinearity (in the sense that moderately advanced groups are generally more positively reacted to than more advanced groups), there is indication of ambivalence in reactions to the most highly advanced outgroups. The relationship between attraction for an outgroup and its level of social-economic advancement may vary considerably depending on whether the outgroup's success is perceived as a model or as a threat to the ingroup's way of life.

The methodology associated with the evaluation of monadic variables also makes interpretation of the advancement-attraction relationship difficult. Since each ethnic group was assigned a rating on the advancement variable which was invarient across all analyses, the advancement levels are confounded with the characteristics and reputations of the particular outgroups being rated. Within each country, the extreme points on the scale (levels 1 and 3) are each represented by only one outgroup,[9] making the advancement-attraction correlation for each ingroup highly dependent on its attitudes toward two particularly salient outgroups. This factor alone could account for the high variation of ratings across respondent groups. For these reasons, theoretical treatment of the advancement variable might be improved by considering it as a *relational* variable rather than as a monadic characteristic of each group. However, attraction toward advanced outgroups does not seem to be systematically related to the relative advancement of ingroups, according to results of analyses of the social distance data from this survey. Previous analysis (Brewer, 1968a, 1968b) of variance of mean social distance ratings from each ethnic group toward various categories of outgroups obtained no significant interaction between ingroup advancement and ratings of high- versus low-advanced outgroups (once the confounding effects of differential similarity were taken into account). Similarly, Sobel's (1970) analysis of demographic characteristics of respondents revealed no interaction between type of informant (classified on the basis of education, literacy, and occupation as traditional or transitional-modern) and outgroup advancement for average social distance ratings. While traditional respondents consistently held outgroups at greater social distance than did transitional respondents, within each ingroup both types of respondents were equally likely to rate high advanced outgroups somewhat more favorably than low advanced outgroups. Thus, differential attraction for advanced outgroups does not appear to be systematically related to objective measures of advancement of the respondent group.

Of course, advancement ratings based on statistical indices of modernization or on ethnographic evaluations do not necessarily correspond to subjective perceptions of outgroup characteristics by respondent groups. Reputational indices of advancement, obtained from responses to the trait attribution section of the interview, were also assessed in order to explore further the attraction-advancement relationship. For each ethnic group, a measure of reputational advancement was computed from net ratings received (from respondents across all outgroups) on achievement-related traits such as wealthy-poor, progressive-uncivilized, keen to advance-uninterested in advancement, intelligent-unintelligent, and hardworking-lazy (see Chapter 6 for further discussion of intergroup achievement ratings). These received ratings were then compared with objective advancement ratings assigned to each ethnic group and were found to be correlated .94, reflecting high agreement in the assignment of very high and very low advanced groups. The average intragroup correlations (reported individually in Appendix E.4) between attraction ratings of outgroups and their received achievement ratings were as follows: Kenya: r = .31; Uganda: r = .35; Tanzania: r = .33; overall: r= .33 (p < .01, t-test, d.f.=29). Thus, essentially the same level of relationship between outgroup advancement and attraction is obtained whether ethnographic evaluations or respondent ratings are used in the assessment of advancement. (In addition, as will be reported in Chapter 6, the nature of the relationship remains essentially the same when intergroup variations in achievement ratings are taken into account.)

OUTGROUP POPULATION SIZE

A more standardized index of intergroup power may be achieved by considering variations in population size as a major factor in allocation of resources. As with advancement on an economic dimension, the size of a social group could have either positive or negative effects on its relations with outgroups depending on whether the large group is perceived as a source of threat or help by smaller groups. Realistic group conflict theory and frustration-aggression theory stress the potential competition over land and resources posed by highly populous outgroups and predict that such groups would be targets of hostility (although frustration-aggression theory also provides for the inhibition of expressed hostility against large, strong outgroups). Reference group theory, on the other hand, emphasizes the rewards available to smaller groups for maintaining friendly relations with larger outgroups, especially as military allies. The intragroup correlations between attraction ratings and size of outgroups were computed based on population figures reported in Appendix A. The results provide somewhat more support for the reference-group hypothesis in that the average correlations were significantly positive: Kenya: r = .36; Uganda: r = .44; Tanzania: r = .33; overall: r=.37 (p < .01, t-test, d.f.=29). The size of these correlations was similar to those for advancement and equally variable across respondent groups (see Appendix E.5). Thus, either measure of intergroup power reveals an ambivalent effect on variations in intergroup attitudes. Further effects of population size and advancement on intergroup relations will be considered in the next chapter.

SUMMARY

The data reported in these last two chapters reveal striking parallels between analyses of intergroup attitudes and reviews of research on determinants of attraction at the interpersonal level (e.g., Berscheid and Walster, 1969). Numerous studies have demonstrated a strong relationship between physical proximity and friendship choices, as well as mate selection, and the nature of this relationship remains overwhelmingly positive despite some findings that proximity also provides opportunity for intensification of interpersonal conflict. Interpretations that have been advanced to account for this generally positive effect of proximity on attraction have included consideration of the lowered cost involved in interacting with those who are easily accessible (Thibaut and Kelley, 1959), enhanced opportunity for acquiring favorable information about the other which facilitates further interaction (Newcomb, 1956), and a tendency for propinquity to produce a "unit relation" between persons which is accompanied by positive affect in accord with principles of interpersonal balance (Heider, 1958).

Even more consistent in the literature on interpersonal attraction is the finding of a positive relationship between similarity of values and attitudes—or perceived similarity—and attraction for another individual, a relationship which has also been interpreted both in terms of the rewards associated with interaction with a similar other (Byrne, 1969) and in terms of the tendency toward maintaining cognitive balance (Heider, 1958; Newcomb, 1956). Together, these effects of proximity and similarity suggest a strong relationship between attraction for another person and feelings of *familiarity* with that person—familiarity promoted either by opportunity for extensive interaction or by knowledge of similarity which creates the potential for ease of interaction. Theoretically, familiarity should provide the basis for satisfying interpersonal relations both by serving the need for predictability in social relations and by satisfying the principles of "gestalt" perception (i.e., that elements with common properties, proximity, and other forms of shared variation "belong" together and are perceived as a unit; also explicated in the unit-affect relations principles of balance theory). A positive relationship between familiarity and attraction is also consistent with results of empirical research on the positive attitudinal effects of repeated exposure to an attitude object (Zajonc, 1968). However, an emphasis on felt familiarity as the major determinant of interpersonal attraction explains why contact per se does not always produce positive regard. Proximity under conditions which produce barriers to intimate forms of interaction may fail to promote any sense of familiarity despite extensive contact, while information which provides a basis for perceived similarity may enhance feelings of familiarity with another person in the absence of any direct contact. The focus on familiarity also explains occasional findings, supported in our data, that a known "enemy" (whose characteristics and patterns of interaction are familiar to the respondent) received higher attraction ratings than a remote or little-known target group with whom the respondent has experienced no prior conflict.

The literature on interpersonal attraction reveals an inconsistent relationship between status of a target person and attraction toward that person, paralleled in our data by attitudes toward outgroups at various levels of social-economic advancement, which may also be interpreted in terms of felt familiarity. The general weak trend toward positive attraction for high-status individuals or groups may reflect the fact that such persons represent values and life styles *known and accepted* by upwardly mobile respondents. That is, the effect of status may be mediated by perceived similarity, an effect which could be greatly attenuated by too large a disparity in status or by conditions which block the potential for upward mobility.

Since research on interpersonal attraction is frequently conducted by giving respondents information about target individuals without any actual contact with that person, it is not too surprising that those research results should be closely paralleled by data on intergroup attitudes where identification of group membership provides cues similar to the kinds of information on a particular individual provided by the experimenter in laboratory studies. Such parallels are likely to extend also to the relationship between attraction for target individuals (or groups) and perceived characteristics of those persons. While laboratory research on person perception generally indicates that positively evaluated characteristics are attributed to liked persons and negative characteristics to disliked others, this pattern of attribution is by no means highly consistent. One factor which seems to be related to how respondents perceive liked and disliked others is self-esteem, with low self-esteem respondents being generally more extreme and undifferentiated in their reactions to particular individuals or groups (e.g., Dittes, 1959). The analogy between self-esteem at the individual level and ethnocentrism at the group level is complex (LeVine and Campbell, 1972: ch. 9), but to the extent that ethnocentric regard for the ingroup can be seen as parallel to *defensive* self-esteem, we could expect such attitudes to be related to patterns of attribution of characteristics to outgroups in a manner similar to that found for interpersonal perception. The nature of that relationship will be explored in the following chapters.

NOTES

1. The presentation of this figure, like the use of the Pearson product-moment correlation, involves treating the clearly ordinal scale of physical proximity as if it represented an equal-interval scale. The regular rank ordering of the obtained data, however, suggests that use of this convention does not seriously distort interpretation of the nature of the relationship.

2. These evaluations were made by anthropologists Robert A. LeVine and Robert Daniels without knowledge of the obtained patterns of attraction ratings among the respondent groups.

3. An indication of the extent of correspondence was obtained by differentiating perceived similarity scores into high (> +2), intermediate (−2 to +2), and low (<−2), and comparing these with the objective ratings reported in Appendix C. For Kenya, sixty-one of the ninety ratings were identical; for Uganda, sixty-six; and for Tanzania, fifty-two, indicating a substantial but imperfect agreement between the two sets of ratings which is also reflected in the correlation of .56 between the two, computed across all thirty groups.

4. Note that these values are somewhat depressed from the intragroup average correlations reported previously since the effect of between-group variation in response level on the attraction measure has not been removed from the pooled dyadic correlation.

5. It should be understood that the use of this term does not imply an evaluative judgment, but refers to functional adaptation to an economic and political power structure imposed by European colonialism. In this sense, differential advancement is a dimension *recognized* by all respondent groups, though not necessarily equally subscribed to by all.

6. The sign of the obtained correlations has been reversed to indicate that the relationship between the two variables is positive although the advancement index was scored inversely.

7. Similar factor scores for Tanzania have been computed by Gould (1970) but based on small geographic units not readily translatable to our ethnic units. However, incorporation within ethnic regions of nodes of highly developed or underdeveloped areas (Gould, 1970: 167) was taken into account in assigning advancement rankings for Tanzanian groups.

8. In contrast to the measures of distance and similarity, evidence on the variable of advancement suggests that treating the three-point ordinal rating as an equal-interval scale is unjustified. The major difference occurs between least advanced groups and all of the others, suggesting that the scale would be more accurately represented by a wide interval between points 1 and 2 and a smaller interval between 2 and 3, as in alternative Figure 4.6b. In this presentation, the nature of the relationship, and its dependence on ratings at the two extremes of the scale (especially the consistently low values for outgroups at level 1), is somewhat more clear.

9. With the exception of Tanzania which had two groups assigned to level 1.

PART II

INTERGROUP PERCEPTION

Chapter 5

INGROUP SELF-REGARD AND ETHNOCENTRISM

From the perspective of an individualistic, hedonistic psychology, the process of inculcating loyalty to a social group is one of convincing the individual to identify the satisfaction of his or her basic wants and ego needs with the survival of the group and his or her continued membership in it. An emphasis on the perceived concomitance of ingroup and reward is apparent in Guetzkow's (1955) reinforcement analysis of ingroup loyalty and in Freud's interpretation of ethnocentrism as a form of narcissism at the group level (Freud, 1921, 1930). The paradoxical extreme of this identification of self-interest with that of the group occurs when the individual identifies with the social group to the extent that the individual sacrifices personal gratification for the sake of the survival or enhancement of that group:

> Finally, the apparently paradoxical behaviour of the individual who sacrifices his own interests for that of the group or who may even go so far as to offer up his own life so that his group may live, becomes less mysterious when we recall that the group itself has become part of the individual, through his identification with it. He dies that the group may live, that is, he dies for that which embodies his ideal self, whether in the abstract form of a social or moral ideal of a society, or in the more concrete form of a tribe, community, or nation, fatherland, or a motherland. His own physical death, and the extinction of his own egoistic gratifications, is not too great a price to pay for gratifying the demands of the very real self which is the group ideal or the embodied and personified group, the father or mother surrogate [MacCrone, 1937: 249].

Such extreme identification with the group is certainly not a universal characteristic of group membership, but some willingness on the part of group members to sacrifice or delay some forms of self-satisfaction for the maintenance of the social order is probably essential to the existence of social groups and provides the basis for a functional analysis of ethnocentrism.

THEORETICAL PERSPECTIVES ON INTERGROUP PERCEPTION

Ethnocentrism, as defined by Sumner (1906), is not a unitary concept. As discussed in the introductory chapter, it involves at least four different aspects of group behavior—ingroup integration, self-regard or hyperevaluation of the ingroup, hostile relations between ingroup and outgroups, and derogatory stereotyping of outgroup characteristics. As Sumner describes the syndrome, these four aspects are seen to be complementary: ingroup integration and solidarity is promoted by the tendency to exalt the ingroup and perceive its way of life as superior to that of other groups; hyperevaluation of the ingroup is maintained by contrast with distorted, derogatory perceptions of the customs and practices of outgroups which are also seen as threatening and hostile; in intergroup relations, the interests of the ingroup are considered paramount, which leads to hostility manifested in forms of aggression ranging from verbal expressions of dislike through types of exclusion (social distance) to overt violence. Theoretically, then, identification with the ingroup and dissociation from outgroups are two sides of the same coin.

The first prerequisite of such group identification is the delineation of the target group—the ingroup—with which the individual is to be identified. This implies differentiation of the ingroup from outgroups (which would otherwise be available targets of identification) and specification of the boundaries that separate them. As discussed by LeVine and Campbell (1972: ch. 7), the student of ethnocentrism in stateless, nonindustrial societies is faced with a great range of alternatives concerning types of boundaries, none of them entirely satisfactory for specifying pancultural units of ethnocentric sentiment and behavior. In such cases, a discussion of "what the most salient unit of ethnocentrism is" founders on the concept of ethnicity, which in the absence of hard and fast national boundaries, is ambiguous at best. For comparative study of nonindustrial societies, the concept of ethnicity and the various bases for ethnocentric identification need close examination and clarification.

Contrast in Perception

One concomitant of the definition of boundaries is the phenomenon of enhancement of contrast, or the perceived homogenization of differences within boundaries and exaggeration of differences across boundaries (see Campbell, 1956). In the differentiation of ingroup from outgroups, this is

likely to take the form of adulation of the ingroup and, in contrast, derogation of outgroups. The direction of this trend is described by Freud (1921
[1955] : 101-102):

> But when a group is formed intolerance vanishes, temporarily or
> permanently, within the group. So long as a group formation persists or
> so far as it extends, individuals in the group behave as though they were
> uniform, tolerate the peculiarities of its other members, equate them-
> selves with them, and have no feeling of aversion towards them. Such a
> limitation of narcissism can, according to our theoretical views, only be
> produced by one factor, a libidinal tie with other people. Love for
> oneself knows only one barrier—love for other, love for objects.

Even apart from overt hostilities between ingroup and outgroups, relative
adulation of the ingroup follows from socialization practices required for
inculcation of group norms and standards of behavior. While Sherif's main
emphasis is upon the development of the ethnocentric syndrome as a result of
competition between groups, he also emphasizes the relation between ingroup
adulation and intragroup coordination requirements:

> Stabilization of a system of reciprocities implies the demarcation of
> ingroup structure from other group structures. The ingroup thus
> delineated becomes endowed with positive qualities which tend to be
> praiseworthy, self-justifying, and even self-glorifying. Individual
> members develop these qualities through internalization of norms, and
> through example, verbal dictum, and a set of correctives standardized
> to deal with cases of deviation. Hence, possession of these qualities,
> which reflect their particular brand of ethnocentrism, is not essentially
> a problem of deviate behavior, but a participation in ingroup values and
> trends on the part of good members who constitute the majority of
> membership as long as group solidarity and morale are maintained
> [Sherif and Sherif, 1953: 299].

One of the most frequent occasions for the expression of opprobrium
toward outgroup customs is in the teaching of children. Frequently, the
image of the outgroup may be invoked as a bad example in the training of
children almost as much as the ideal ingroup model is invoked as a good
example. Sometimes this is done in such a manner as to implicitly threaten
the children with loss of ingroup membership or with treatment as an
outgrouper if they misbehave. Such aspects of the ethnocentric syndrome
have been given prominence in Levinson's concept of contra-identification
(Adorno et al., 1950: 146), in which a focused but negative cathexis is
developed toward a specific outgroup. Similar, too, are older psychoanalytic
concepts of the splitting of the father image into the good father and the bad

father, the latter (with its paternal origin repressed) being projected onto the outgroup, the former being generalized into the overidealized ingroup image.

Once begun, this process of differentiating ingroup and outgroups on an evaluative dimension may be perpetuated by individual members of the social group in accord with the principle of cognitive congruity (Osgood and Tannenbaum, 1955; Osgood, 1960). According to this principle, a consequence of self-regard is that anything associated with the self must be perceived as "good" or the individual suffers the psychological distress of cognitive inconsistency. Similarly, anything dissociated from the self must be regarded as "bad" to avoid inconsistency arousal. Putting the implications of this principle for intergroup relations simply, "If we are good, kind and fair and they are our enemy, then psycho-logic dictates that they must be bad, cruel, and unfair" (Osgood, 1960: 365).

Another psychological mechanism that can account for perpetuation of contrast in perception of ingroup and outgroup is the enhancement of self-esteem. Since conscious self-esteem is usually based on a comparative evaluation of the self with others, the distortions of information about the self (defense mechanisms) often involve distortions of information about others. Projection, the attribution to others of unacceptable behavior characteristic of one's own motives or actions, is one example of such a comparative distortion. Another example is the conscious (and exaggerated) belief in one's own superiority to others with a concomitant tendency to belittle them, in compensation for a low level of unconscious self-esteem. Both of these mechanisms involve enhancement of the contrast between self and others. Defining the ethnic unit as the group counterpart of the self suggests that similar mechanisms for maintaining positive self-regard will operate in intergroup perceptions.

From a frustration-aggression theory perspective, such cultural traditions would be required to further the two mechanisms of inhibition and displacement of aggression. If there were genuine provocations by the outgroups, these would be shared in common by ingroup members. And through a traditional preservation or fabrication of such offenses, a cultural tradition justifying displacement would develop. A tendency to portray the outgroup as animal or nonhuman, in similarity-generalization theory, would have the function of removing any generalized inhibitions to aggressive and exploitative actions. If we take the concept of an inhibition gradient less abstractly, we can see that it becomes a matter of specifying the conditions under which aggression must be inhibited or may be expressed. Within the ingroup, aggression in the form of punishment is allowed against the child or adult who behaves immorally. An outgroup with differing customs is indeed behaving in ways that the ingroup member has been taught are immoral and is therefore a target for legitimate, righteous aggression. With this background, we can define the socially institutionalized displacement mechanism as a verbal tradition leading ingroup members to perceive outgroups as the cause of frustrations and as maximally different from the ingroup.

Freud also explicitly stated that group narcissism is served by the displacement of aggression from ingroup to outgroup:

> It is clearly not easy for men to give up the satisfaction of this inclination to aggression. They do not feel comfortable without it. The advantage which a comparatively small cultural group offers of allowing this instinct an outlet in the form of hostility against intruders is not to be despised. It is always possible to bind together a considerable number of people in love, so long as there are other people left over to receive the manifestations of their aggressiveness. I once discussed the phenomenon that it is precisely communities with adjoining territories, and related to each other in other ways as well, who are engaged in constant feuds and in ridiculing each other—like the Spaniards and Portuguese, for instance, the North Germans and South Germans, the English and Scotch [sic], and so on. I give this phenomenon the name of "the narcissism of minor differences," a name which does not do much to explain it. We can now see that it is a convenient and relatively harmless satisfaction of the inclination to aggression, by means of which cohesion between the members of the community is made easier [Freud, 1930 (1961): 114].

The primary mechanism by which the displacement of aggression from ingroup to outgroup is facilitated is ingroup members' shared perceptions of outgroups that serve to blame the outgroup for ingroup troubles and promote distrust and fear of the outgroup. The focus of fear may be lacking for a few locally dominant ingroups whose ideology justifies aggression against outgroups without a defensive posture (e.g., Murphy, 1957), but in most cases perceived treachery and hostility from the outgroup are required for a sense of justified aggression. Serving this requirement, however, can lead ingroup members to emphasize the strength and power of outgroups to a point inconsistent with their own self-adulation. The potential psychological distress aroused by this inconsistency (relative to the principle of congruity cited previously) can be avoided by a process of differentiation whereby outgroup strengths are perceived as "bad," deriving from immoral practices, while ingroup strength lies in adherence to certain moral values. Interviews conducted with elderly informants among the Gusii of Kenya (LeVine and Campbell, 1964) provide an example of such a mechanism. Most of these informants had lived through a period of bitter conflict between the Gusii and the neighboring Kipsigis. In their interview responses, though obtained many years after the cessation of overt hostility, imagery of the Kipsigis is marked by repeated references to their treacherous practice of attacking at night, in contrast to the Gusii norms of daylight combat.

Group Differences in Ethnocentrism

The import of the discussion so far has been that, as long as boundaries differentiating social groups exist and loyalty is required within boundaries, ethnocentrism in the form of adulation of the ingroup and derogation of outgroups will be manifest. However, the degree of such ethnocentric self-regard may vary greatly across social groups. In small, stateless societies, the essential aspects of ingroup loyalty (e.g., prevention of member defection or loss of property to other groups, necessary coordination of ingroup activities, etc.) can be maintained through direct social control. Under such circumstances, we would expect less need for abstract, internalized identification with group norms to assure maintenance of the social order than in larger, politically complex societies or subgroups within them. In addition, the various elements of the ethnocentrism syndrome may not necessarily be closely related among all groups. Some groups, for example, may be high on hyperevaluation of the ingroup but maintain benevolent rather than hostile attitudes toward outgroups considered inferior. Conversely, some ex-colonial peoples seem to maintain a high degree of hostility toward the former colonial powers while conceding their cultural superiority. Contrast in the perception of ingroup and outgroup characteristics may reflect the recognition of real cultural differences, combined with a strong preference for the familiar, rather than hostile distortions of outgroup traits. The existence of interrelationships among these aspects of ethnocentrism is a matter for empirical study rather than a logical implication of the nature of the concepts involved.

MEASURING INGROUP SELF-REGARD

The aspect of ethnocentrism that received most attention in the preceding review is that of ingroup self-regard relative to outgroup derogation. The tendency to evaluate one's own group more highly than outgroups is postulated as a universal consequence of group membership. The more ethnocentric a group, the more its members will exaggerate the value of their own customs and behavior and the less willing they will be to recognize any other groups as similarly virtuous. Thus, the tendency toward self-regard reflects ethnocentrism when the ingroup self-evaluation is considerably more positive than "objective" perception would call for *and* when it is accompanied by inordinately negative evaluations of all outgroups.

From the results of the East African survey, it was possible to obtain an index of each respondent group's self-evaluation on the basis of responses to the trait questions in Section III of the interview schedule (items numbered 8-55). For the fifty respondents of each group the frequency of mentions of the ingroup and each of thirteen outgroups was tabulated for each trait. By considering responses to seven pairs of traits which were found to load highly on an evaluative dimension (see Chapter 6), intergroup evaluative ratings were obtained. Net evaluation scores for ratings of each ethnic group by each respondent sample were computed by summing the number of mentions of that group in connection with the seven positive traits (peaceful among themselves, peaceful with other groups, obedient, honest, clean, friendly, and handsome) and subtracting the total number of mentions to the corresponding negative traits (quarrelsome among themselves, quarrelsome with other groups, disobedient, dishonest, dirty, cruel, and ugly). The evaluative ratings thus obtained among the ten ethnic groups of each country are reported in Tables 5.1-5.3 with ingroup self ratings appearing along the main diagonal in each matrix.

Even a cursory inspection of Tables 5.1-5.3 reveals that all thirty ingroups rated themselves more positively than the average rating given to outgroups. However, this does not provide an adequate index of relative ethnocentricity of self-evaluation since the nature of the interview (requiring each respondent to name only one group in association with each trait) introduces an automatic negative correlation between number of self-mentions on positive traits and number of mentions of all outgroups combined to those same traits. A more satisfactory index is obtained by comparing self-evaluations with the evaluation given by each group to *any* outgroup, since undifferentiated negative perception of outgroups is most characteristic of ethnocentrism. Twenty-seven of the thirty respondent groups in this study gave higher ratings to themselves than to any other group; two groups (Bagisu and Karamojong of Uganda) gave one outgroup a rating higher than themselves; only respondents from the Arusha of Tanzania rated themselves less positively than their ratings of several outgroups.

Since self-ratings may be a function of actual ingroup superiority over outgroups on some characteristics, as well as distorted self-perception, each group's self-ratings should be considered in terms of the degree of overevaluation—i.e., the extent to which its members evaluate it more highly than the average evaluation received from outgroups. On this basis, all thirty respondent groups overevaluate themselves, with overestimates in net ratings ranging from +8 to +270.

Considering all the factors that may contribute to an ingroup's self-evaluation, an index of relative ethnocentrism was derived by comparing each ingroup's actual self-rating with an "expected" rating based on contributing factors. The expected rating for any ingroup may be considered the sum of

TABLE 5.1
EVALUATIVE TRAIT RATINGS—KENYA

Ratings given to

	A	B	C	D	E	F	G	H	I	J
A	+ 45	+ 16	+ 16	− 6	+ 22	− 28	− 29	− 22	− 81	+ 2
B	+ 22	+ 72	− 1	+ 11	+ 22	− 1	− 9	− 28	− 68	− 8
C	− 29	+ 67	+120	+ 17	+ 5	− 6	− 12	− 44	−104	+ 24
D	−154	+ 1	− 2	+274	+ 6	0	0	− 2	− 90	− 37
E	− 9	− 3	− 3	− 2	+ 78	+ 8	− 28	− 24	− 25	− 2
F	+ 20	+ 6	+ 2	− 3	0	+109	− 46	− 11	−151	− 29
G	− 8	0	− 3	− 1	+ 15	− 37	+245	+ 7	−168	− 25
H	− 3	− 6	− 6	− 3	+ 3	− 3	− 1	+ 24	− 5	− 1
I	− 46	− 5	− 10	+ 13	− 9	− 37	− 13	− 72	+137	+ 35
J	− 59	− 4	− 6	+ 10	+ 33	− 7	− 16	− 21	− 45	+ 60

Ratings given by

TABLE 5.2
EVALUATIVE TRAIT RATINGS–UGANDA

Ratings given to

		A	B	C	D	E	F	G	H	I	J
	A	+<u>248</u>	− 29	+ 18	−124	+ 3	− 8	− 8	− 27	− 31	− 81
	B	− 49	+<u>177</u>	+ 21	+ 19	+ 7	+ 15	+ 1	− 14	+ 6	− 89
	C	− 65	− 13	+<u>157</u>	+ 1	+ 38	0	− 6	− 24	− 1	− 27
	D	+ 69	+ 2	+ 17	+<u>161</u>	− 6	− 1	− 25	− 43	− 13	− 29
Ratings given by	E	+ 25	+ 6	+ 28	+ 4	+<u>120</u>	0	− 10	− 46	− 27	− 24
	F	+141	+ 7	+ 15	− 27	+ 5	+<u>136</u>	− 36	− 16	− 21	−180
	G	+ 71	+ 15	+ 7	− 8 ·	− 1	− 13	+<u>112</u>	− 25	− 17	− 56
	H	+ 55	− 3	+ 4	+ 6	+ 3	− 6	− 9	+<u>137</u>	− 46	−118
	I	− 6	+ 15	+ 23	+ 18	− 5	− 15	+ 12	+ 44	+ <u>63</u>	− 83
	J	+ 27	0	+ 1	+ 1	+ 11	+ 3	+ 50	− 18	− 4	+ <u>29</u>

TABLE 5.3
EVALUATIVE TRAIT RATINGS—TANZANIA

Ratings given to

	A	B	C	D	E	F	G	H	I	J
A	+ 72	+ 62	+ 39	+ 4	− 5	+ 16	+ 3	− 12	−122	− 5
B	+ 11	+110	+ 22	0	− 4	+ 72	+ 22	− 33	−195	− 33
C	− 4	+ 26	+203	+ 4	+ 2	+ 16	+ 3	− 24	− 43	− 12
D	− 16	+ 29	+ 8	+ 73	− 50	+ 42	+ 40	− 37	+ 4	− 12
E	+ 2	+ 31	+ 11	+ 18	+ 5	+ 43	+ 67	− 33	− 80	− 15
F	− 14	+ 3	+ 20	− 9	0	+159	+ 87	− 45	− 95	− 16
G	− 8	+ 13	+ 23	− 2	0	+ 47	+182	− 33	−112	− 40
H	+ 48	− 5	− 5	− 14	− 7	− 2	− 5	+ 87	− 46	− 8
I	+ 16	0	− 4	− 33	+ 40	− 34	− 21	− 1	+143	− 26
J	+ 12	+ 16	+ 6	+ 2	0	+ 14	+ 52	− 13	−152	+111

Ratings given by

three factors: (1) the general tendency of respondents to give positive self-evaluations (i.e., the mean self-rating of the ten groups of each country), (2) the ingroup's tendency to give positive ratings to any outgroup (the deviation of the ingroup's most positive outgroup rating from the mean of such ratings across ten groups), and (3) the relative evaluation received by the ingroup from outgroups (the deviation of the mean rating received by the ingroup from the overall mean rating given to outgroups by all ten groups). The difference between an ingroup's actual self-rating and its expected rating provides an index of ethnocentricity *relative to* the ten groups sampled in the same country.[1] For example, the expected rating for the Kikuyu of Kenya is 116 (the mean self-rating of Kenya respondents) with −1 (the difference between the Kikuyu rating of its most favored outgroup and the average rating of most-preferred outgroups by Kenya respondents) with −15 (the difference between the average rating received by the Kikuyu and the mean rating received by all outgroups), for a total of 100. The actual rating given by Kikuyu respondents to their own ethnic group is 45, yielding a deviation score of −55. The relative ethnocentricity scores thus derived for all groups in each country are reported in Table 5.4. It is interesting that the Arusha of Tanzania are the only peoples with an outstandingly low ethnocentricity rating since they represent a group currently going through a period of reevaluation and ambiguity with regard to their relations with and respect for the Masai (see Appendix A).

Self-Regard and Other Indices of Ethnocentrism

The tendency for ingroups to perceive themselves more favorably than they perceive or are perceived by outgroups represents only one of several aspects of the syndrome of ethnocentrism. Enhancement of self-regard may not necessarily be achieved at the price of negative affect toward outgroups. Several studies of national stereotypes suggest that positive imagery of respondents relative to their own nation (in terms of the ratio of favorable trait assignments to unfavorable ones) is accompanied by a similar (though less extreme) tendency toward net favorability in outgroup ratings (e.g., Buchanan and Cantril, 1953; Reigrotski and Anderson, 1959). Laboratory studies of competing work groups indicate that interaction among ingroup members is followed by significant increases in attraction toward the ingroup but also accompanied by slight *increases,* rather than decreases, of attraction ratings toward outgroups (Dunn and Goldman, 1966; Rabbie and Wilkens, 1971; Wilson and Miller, 1961). Thus, it appears that differential preference for the ingroup can be attained through enhancement of attraction toward the ingroup without any concomitant decrease in favorability toward out-groups.

Method artifacts in the present study make a direct comparison between

TABLE 5.4
ETHNOCENTRICITY SCORES

Kenya (Mean self rating = 116)

Ethnic Group	Relative Ethnocentricity
Kikuyu	−55
Embu	−66
Meru	−54
Kamba	156
Luhya	−49
Gusii	− 7
Kipsigis	139
Nandi	−63
Masai	76
Luo	−76

Uganda (Mean self rating = 134)

Ganda	111
Nyoro	67
Toro	15
Soga	15
Ankole	− 3
Gisu	−91
Teso	−45
Acholi	12
Lango	−53
Karamojong	−35

Tanzania (Mean self rating = 115)

Chagga	−62
Pare	−48
Sambaa	97
Meru	−33
Arusha	−126
Sukuma	−19

Ethnic Group	Relative Ethnocentricity
Nyamwezi	40
Luo	− 2
Masai	129
Gogo	11

ingroup evaluation and outgroup ratings impossible since the nature of the trait-rating task was such that any increase in the assignment of favorable traits to the ingroup automatically reduced favorability of ratings of outgroups.[2] However, favorability of self-perceptions could be compared with affective ratings of outgroups in the form of social distance scores, which were obtained independently for each outgroup. A theory of ethnocentrism would predict that ingroups high in self-regard would also be characterized by undifferentiated negative affect toward outgroups while less ethnocentrically biased groups would be generally more positive and discriminating in their ratings of outgroups. Correlations obtained between our index of self-regard and patterns of social distance responses do not support this prediction. The relationship between self-regard and *mean social distance* (i.e., the average rating across nine outgroups) proved to be highly variable from country to country (Kenya, $r = .22$; Uganda, $r = .21$; Tanzania, $r = −.72$) and statistically nonsignificant across all thirty groups.

The absence of any consistent relationship between the social distance and self-regard indices of ethnocentrism could be caused by the fact that mean social distance scores were subject to response bias differences (due to the confounding between respondent group and interviewer) and do not reflect differentiation of responses within groups. Therefore, an index of differential social distance was obtained based on the *product* of the mean social distance score and the standard deviation of social distance ratings for each ingroup. This index, too, proved to be unrelated to self-regard ($r = .05$, across all thirty groups). It appeared that ingroups with the highest self-regard values, rather than exhibiting undifferentiated negative reactions to outgroups, were somewhat more likely to show high preferential responses to some groups over others. This tendency is reflected in a positive relationship ($r = .22$) between the measure of each group's self-regard and the size of the intragroup correlation (reported in Appendix E.2) between perceived similarity and attraction ratings of outgroups. While this correlation is also quite low, it is in a direction contradictory to a simple interpretation of ethnocentric bias. It is consistent, however, with both balance theory and learning theory perspectives, in which positive self-regard would be extended to those perceived as similar to the self.

CORRELATES OF VARIATION IN SELF-REGARD

Whatever the relationship between an ingroup's self-regard and its orientation toward outgroups, the extent of hyperevaluation of the ingroup can be related theoretically to several facets of ingroup structure and intergroup status.

Social-Economic Advancement

The recognized differentiation among ethnic groups in positions relative to the developing economic and political systems of East Africa may be related to variations in ingroup self-regard. The direction of such a relationship is a matter of theoretical controversy. Guetzkow's (1955) analysis of ingroup loyalty stresses that successful or advantaged groups, which offer their members greater rewards for membership, will exhibit more ingroup solidarity and less tendency to admire or emulate other groups. A similar prediction is derived from Freud's (1921) view of ethnocentrism as a form of narcissism at the group level which would be most likely to occur among successful ingroups for whom group narcissism provides more gratification than do other available narcissistic outlets. However, neo-Freudian theories of self-esteem emphasize the unconscious need of unsuccessful individuals to enhance their self-perception by indiscriminate derogation and rejection of others. Applied to the group level of interaction, this would imply that less successful ingroups would be characterized by general hostility and distorted negative evaluations of outgroups while groups higher in self-esteem should be more capable of objective recognition of ingroup and outgroup attributes. Thus, psychoanalytically based approaches to intergroup relations produce conflicting predictions about the effects of ingroup success on intergroup perceptions.

One other theoretical orientation with psychoanalytic origins, frustration-aggression theory, provides yet another perspective on the ingroup advancement-ethnocentricity relationship. To the extent that economic advancement is related to the development of more complex social and political institutions, requiring greater coordination and discipline among ingroup members, high advanced groups would be characterized by more frustration-producing restraints on individual members than would less advanced groups. Since the direct expression of aggression aroused by such frustrations would be incompatible with the maintenance of ingroup integration, such groups have more need for mechanisms for reducing or displacing that aggression, as through the idealization of the rewards of ingroup identification and derogation of outgroups as targets of displaced hostility. Thus, frustration-aggression theory leads to the prediction that high advanced groups will be characterized by greater self-regard relative to outgroups than will less advanced groups.

The predicted relationship between societal complexity and increased ethnocentricity is also consistent with an evolutionary or functional approach to the study of social institutions. From this perspective, it would be predicted that a complex social group would require mechanisms for indirect social control over its members that would substitute for the direct social pressures available to ensure group loyalty in simpler societies. Ethnocentric idealization of the ingroup relative to outgroups would serve as such a mechanism by preserving group identification in the absence of more personal loyalties. This analysis of the function of ethnocentric self-regard suggests a bidirectional causal relationship between ethnocentrism and ingroup advancement. On the one hand, the conditions associated with social-economic advancement enhance the value of ethnocentric group identification, but on the other hand, the self-regard aspects of ethnocentrism may *produce* ingroup advancement, since the existence of ethnocentric loyalty makes possible the development of complex social institutions. Whichever causal direction is chosen for emphasis, a positive relationship between advancement and ethnocentricity is predicted.

Testing these hypotheses by differentiating the thirty East African ethnic groups according to three levels of social-economic advancement (see Appendix A) revealed no systematic relationship between an ingroup's advancement and its index of ethnocentricity. The average ethnocentrism rating for the three high advanced groups was −2.0, for the twenty-three intermediate advanced groups, −8.4, and for the four low advanced groups, +45.0. Only the low advanced groups were fairly consistently high in ethnocentricity; the other groupings were erratically high and low, and there were no statistically significant differences among the respondent groups based on level of advancement. Thus, although there is some evidence that the least successful ingroups are characterized by relatively indiscriminate positive self-regard,[3] the effects of increasing levels of advancement are ambiguous. Apparently, the potentially competing effects of economic advancement on ingroup self-regard operate differentially across different social groups. For one thing, the relationship between a group's advancement and urbanization of its population produces confounding effects in East Africa, where living in urban centers often means prolonged contact with members of other ethnic groups. Edari (1971), in a study conducted in Kenya, found that to the extent that urban living produced informal contacts between ethnic groups, social distance between those groups was reduced. Thus, the relationship between ethnocentricity and ingroup advancement in this area may be mediated by differential effects of urbanization on intergroup relations.

The relative advancement ratings of groups used in the preceding analysis were based on group reputations and not on measures obtained from the individual respondents who provided the ethnocentricity ratings for each ingroup. Based on reports of occupation, education, and literacy, Sobel (1970) computed a factor score for each respondent on an index of traditionality-modernity. Mean factor scores for each respondent sample were also computed (reported in Appendix B) and were found to be imperfectly related to the reputational advancement ratings of the ethnic groups (not surprisingly, given the nonrepresentative sampling procedures used in selecting respondents for this survey). Therefore, the relationship between ethnocentricity and ingroup advancement was reassessed using the mean respondent modernity score as the index of relative advancement for each ethnic group. The correlations in different countries proved to be highly erratic (Kenya, $r = -.08$; Uganda, $r = .68$; Tanzania, $r = -.60$) and nonsignificant overall ($r = .06$), thus supporting the previous finding of no systematic relationship between ingroup advancement and level of self-regard.

Population Size

The size of the population of any social group has potentially conflicting effects on its internal structure and status relative to other groups. On the one hand, large populations place pressures on land and other natural resources, increasing the probability of conflict of interest between the ingroup and neighboring outgroups and increasing the complexity of intragroup coordination. On the other hand, large population size is related to the probability of group success, particularly in military ventures, and to the visibility and prestige of the ingroup among outgroups. These two aspects of population size lead to different predictions regarding the effect of population on ingroup ethnocentricity. Stressing the opportunity afforded by large populations for internal frustration and conflict between groups, realistic group conflict theory and frustration-aggression theory predict a positive relationship between ingroup size and ethnocentric hostility, promoted by overevaluation of the ingroup. On the other hand, the attenuation of narcissistic gratification associated with attempts to identify with a large group may reduce ingroup solidarity and ethnocentrism. However, if group size is correlated with success and prestige, identification with the large group should be rewarding and ethnocentrism increased.

Using the population figures cited in Appendix A, the correlation between total population size and ingroup ethnocentricity was computed for the ten respondent groups in each of the three East African countries. The correlation again proved to be variable across countries, being slightly negative for groups in Kenya and Tanzania ($r = -.18$ and $-.07$, respectively) but moderately positive in Uganda (r = .58, not significantly different from .00 with only nine degrees of freedom). Across all thirty groups, the correlation reduced to close to .00.

It is possible that the failure to obtain any consistent relationship between ingroup size and ethnocentricity is due to the fact that total population size could be associated with either success or poverty, depending on its distribution relative to land and other natural resources. Population density, number of people per square mile of tribal territory, should be related more directly to the negative pressures of population size and therefore may be more consistently related to ethnocentrism. The correlation obtained between density and ingroup ethnocentricity was negative for each of the three countries computed separately, and −.32 (p < .10) across all thirty groups. Thus, there is no evidence that high population density is associated with high ethnocentrism and a consistent trend indicating that the relationship between the two variables is negative.

Interpretation of this negative trend is problematic since it may be related to the effects of natural selection on the migration of peoples, leading to greatest concentration of population in areas rich in arable soil and other natural resources. An inspection of the demographic data provided in Appendix A reveals that the groups with the highest population densities are those in territories with more than adequate annual rainfall and mixed farming economies while the low-density groups have insufficient rainfall and often pastoral economies. This suggests that the effects of selection have operated such that it is low population density that is associated with meager resources and a frustrating ecological environment, while densely populated groups are more prosperous and economically secure. In addition, the conditions of high-density population would be likely to produce both pressures and opportunity for migration to urban centers where contact with members of other ethnic groups might tend to reduce ethnocentric perceptions.

Geographic Location

Apart from availability of scarce resources, another environmental factor that may affect a group's ethnocentrism is its location relative to other social groups. If, as assumed by realistic group conflict theory, intergroup hostility is primarily a function of competition over scarce resources and other conflicts of interest, then isolated groups should be characterized by less ethnocentric hostility than groups surrounded by potentially competitive outgroups. A similar prediction can be derived from frustration-aggression theory since farther removed groups are less able to displace frustration-aroused aggression onto outgroups. However, centrally located groups have more opportunity for positive intergroup contacts and, to the extent that this is related to intergroup friendship (as indicated by the results of analyses discussed in Chapter 4), should be characterized by less ethnocentric hostility than isolated groups with minimal opportunities for such contact.

The geographical location of each of the ten ethnic groups surveyed in each East African country, relative to the other nine groups in the same country, was indexed in two ways: (1) a *total distance index* was computed from the sum of distance ratings (based on adjacency or number of intervening tribal territories between each pair of groups) for each group relative to the other nine; (2) a *proximity index* was based on the number of outgroups, out of the nine, adjacent to each ingroup. The correlation between each of these indices and ingroup ethnocentricity was computed across the ten groups in each country. The correlation between total distance and ethnocentricity was consistently negative for the three countries and −.37 (p < .05) across all thirty groups. The proximity-ethnocentrism correlation was consistently positive but only .22 (p > .10) across the thirty groups. In either case, there is some evidence that more isolated groups are characterized by less ethnocentric self-perception than centrally located respondent groups. However, geographic location relative to others seems to be an imperfect measure of intergroup contact, distance ratings being correlated only .58 with the measure of intergroup familiarity. Other factors, such as distance of groups from urban centers, differential tendencies of ethnic groups to migrate to urban areas for jobs, appear to be additional determinants of intergroup interaction. For this reason, the relationship between familiarity and ethnocentrism was considered separately from physical distance.

Average Familiarity with Outgroups

Familiarity with outgroups is predicted to be negatively related to ethnocentrism to the extent that familiarity is associated with extensive positive, equal-status interaction between members of different groups (e.g., Newcomb, 1956; Deutsch and Collins, 1951). The relationship between these two variables is probably bidirectional, since groups low on ethnocentrism are likely to be more open to intergroup contact, and contact in turn promotes liking and decreased ethnocentrism. It is always possible, of course, that "familiarity breeds contempt," particularly if it provides opportunities for selective observations that reinforce negative stereotypes. The latter is more likely to occur when interaction is limited to restricted contexts, whereas more extensive contact should promote more accurate intergroup perception and reduced perceived dissimilarity (Amir, 1969).

Among the groups surveyed for this study, the correlation between mean familiarity of ingroup respondents with all nine outgroups in the same country and ingroup ethnocentricity was consistently negative for each of the three countries, amounting to $-.31$ (p $<$ .10) across all thirty groups. The nature of the relationship between familiarity and ethnocentricity was more clearly revealed by an analysis of variance of mean familiarity scores of respondents grouped according to degree of ethnocentrism. The three groups from each country lowest in ethnocentrism had significantly higher total familiarity with outgroups (M = 119.4) than moderately or highly ethnocentric groups (M = 77.6 and 84.4, respectively) (F = 3.91, p $<$ .05 with 2 and 27 degrees of freedom). Thus, there is evidence that extensive contact with outgroups is associated with low ethnocentrism, but, beyond that, decreasing contact is not consistently related to increasing ethnocentricity.

Since measures of ingroup evaluation (net mentions of the ingroup to positive traits versus negative traits) and average familiarity with outgroups were available for individual respondents as well as for groups, the relationship between ingroup self-regard and familiarity was also analyzed on the individual level. The correlation between each respondent's evaluative rating of the ingroup and average familiarity score across thirteen outgroups was computed both within and between ethnic groups. The average intragroup correlation was $-.08$ and intergroup (N = 1,500) was $-.09$, which was statistically significant (with such a large N) in the expected direction but not impressively high. The fact that the individual-level correlation was so much smaller than the intergroup correlation could be a function of the restriction in variation in ingroup-evaluation scores for individuals. However, it could also reflect the possibility that, due to intragroup communication, the evaluation of the ingroup relative to outgroups is less affected by individual familiarity with outgroups than by the degree of familiarity across all group members.

Received Attraction

Another variable which is expected to be bidirectionally negatively related to ethnocentrism is the extent to which an ingroup is positively regarded by all outgroups. Groups low in ethnocentrism should provoke less hostility among outgroups and, conversely, the objects of friendly relations should manifest less hostile ethnocentrism in return. For each respondent group, an indication of positive regard was obtained from the mean social distance rating received by that group from the nine outgroups in the same country. The correlation between this received attraction rating and ethnocentrism was slightly negative among the groups of Kenya (r = $-.01$) and Tanzania (r = $-.26$) but positive in Uganda (r = .49). Overall, the relationship between received friendship and ethnocentrism (r = .10) was not significantly different from .00. Perhaps this lack of relationship reflects inaccuracy of most ingroups in perceiving the extent to which they are positively regarded by outgroups, making the objective measure of received attraction psychologically irrelevant.

On the other hand, there is the possibility that ethnocentric self-regard is curvilinearly, rather than linearly, related to received attraction and other indices of intergroup status. This might be the case if the index of self-regard reflected *either* a relative security or sense of well-being associated with membership in well-liked or advantaged ingroups, *or* a compensatory self-esteem mechanism for members of relatively disadvantaged or low-status ingroups. Some support for curvilinearity is found in the mean ethnocentricity scores for ingroups at different levels of received attraction from outgroups. Groups with positive social distance ratings (eight groups with average received ratings of 5.0 or better) average +35.0 in self-regard values; groups with neutral social distance ratings (fifteen groups with received mean ratings between 4.0 and 5.0) average −29.2; and groups held at negative social distance (seven groups with mean ratings less than 4.0) average +19.9. Such a dual interpretation of ethnocentricity could account for the relative inconsistency in relationships between self-regard scores and other measures of ethnocentricity or indices of status.

NOTES

1. The relativity of these scores should be kept in mind, particularly since they are being reported with ingroup identification. All the groups in this survey give ratings that are positively ethnocentric in the sense that they regard themselves more highly than they regard or are regarded by outgroups. A negative ethnocentrism score merely means that a particular group is *less* ethnocentric in this regard than are other groups in the same country. It should also be kept in mind that the relative values within each country reflect not only ingroup differences but also some differences in the nature of the set of outgroups being rated by each ingroup in terms of similarity, contact, etc. However, some evidence of the validity of this measure of ethnocentrism is provided by the agreement between the high score of the Baganda obtained in this study and the findings of a study by Klineberg and Zavalloni (1969). Using a different sample of respondents (college students) and very different measuring techniques, these investigators found that Baganda students consistently expressed more tribal orientation than respondents from other ethnic groups in their Uganda sample.

2. It should be noted that, although this method can be criticized as enhancing the ingroup-preference effect, it does have the advantage of isolating such biases from a generalized positive response set often elicited in interview situations. In the more commonly employed methods of trait attribution, where respondents are free to apply items from a given trait list to any of the groups being rated, an informant has the option of assigning favorable traits across the board and thereby not reveal any differential

preferences. In our case, where the assignment of a trait to one group precluded its assignment to any other, consistent choosing of the ingroup relative to any favorable traits (as opposed to allocating favorable responses evenly) reveals the preference pattern more clearly (as does the method of ranking generally, in comparison with rating techniques).

3. While this suggests some support for a hypothesis based on enhancement of self-esteem, this result is highly confounded by the fact that the low advanced groups in this study differ greatly from the other surveyed groups on a number of dimensions.

Chapter 6

INTERGROUP ATTRACTION AND PERCEPTION

Interpretation of the measure of self-regard discussed in the preceding chapter rests on the assumption that imbalanced attribution of favorable characteristics to members of a group reflects positive attraction and an implicit willingness on the part of the respondent to be identified with that group. Such a presumed relationship between attraction and favorable attribution is predicted from the tenets of cognitive consistency theory. The consistency motive constrains the individual to respond favorably to any entity that he or she perceives as being positively linked with him- or herself and, conversely, to evaluate negatively any entity that he or she actively rejects from association with him- or herself.[1] Extending this principle to the realm of intergroup relations, the individual who is positively identified with an ingroup should hold perceptions of outgroups that are consistent with the nature of relations between the ingroup and each of the other groups. Friendly relations should be accompanied by attributions biased in the direction of evaluatively positive traits, and unfriendly relations should be accompanied by negatively biased trait attributions. Such predictions are also inherent in a functional analysis of ingroup adulation and outgroup derogation for maintaining intergroup boundaries and preserving stability of group membership. In this context, an examination of the relationship between intergroup attraction and evaluative content of group perceptions can shed light on the function of stereotyping in intergroup relations and on the role of ethnocentric preference for the ingroup in mediating patterns of intergroup perception.

Most of the available literature on intergroup stereotyping provides little systematic investigation of the relationship between content of stereotypes and preference for the groups being rated (see Brigham, 1971). The traditional procedure for obtaining ethnic stereotypes (Katz and Braly, 1933), through selection of a specified number of traits from an adjective checklist, is not suited for a balanced elicitation of positive and negative trait characteristics. Estimates of favorableness of traits are usually obtained, if at all, by post-hoc ratings by respondents (e.g., Taft, 1959; Vinacke, 1949, 1956; Ziegler et al., 1972) or by judgments on the part of the investigators (e.g., Buchanan and Cantril, 1953; Lambert and Klineberg, 1967), either procedure being likely to contaminate favorableness judgments with ratings of preference. One recent study (Brigham, 1972) that did obtain independent judgments of trait favorability, found correlations ranging from .30 to .40 between measures of racial prejudice and mean favorability of traits attributed to blacks by white college students. The size of this correlation lends some support to the contention that trait-attribution and attitude measures may tap different, though overlapping, dimensions. Existing research on stereotyping does, however, suggest a systematic relationship between content of stereotypes and prevailing functional relations between ethnic or national groups. Results from the UNESCO survey of national stereotypes (Buchanan, 1951; Buchanan and Cantril, 1953), for example, indicate that ratings of "friendliness" of other nations reflect primarily existing governmental alliances. That such ratings reflect, rather than precede, changing patterns of intergroup relations is illustrated in studies of changes in American images of Germans and Japanese prior to and during World War II (Dudycha, 1942; Meenes, 1943) and of variations in ethnic stereotyping by Indian university students related to the 1959 Sino-Indian border dispute (Sinha and Upadhyay, 1960). Thus, available evidence points to a relationship between attraction and evaluative content of intergroup perceptions in that content of stereotypes is subject to influence by situational factors that affect intergroup attraction.

AFFECTIVE CONTENT OF INTERGROUP PERCEPTIONS

The interview schedule for the East African survey contained two measures of intergroup perception, one open-ended (the free response sentence-completion items of Section II of the interview) and one structured (the trait list of Section III). The characteristics included in the structured trait list were selected for their potential evaluative connotation as well as for ease of translation across languages. However, since literal translation of items does not guarantee comparability of affective meaning, patterns of responses to the trait items were examined in order to identify clusters of traits that represented common dimensions of response *across all respondent groups.* For this purpose, factor analysis of the intercorrelations among outgroup ratings on the forty-eight traits, plus responses to the liking-disliking and similarity-dissimilarity questions, was employed. Since interest was focused on patterns of response to different traits independent of ingroup differences in response bias relative to particular outgroups, a rating score for each outgroup on each trait was computed as the difference between the total number of mentions of the outgroup by the ingroup in association with that trait and the mean number of mentions of that outgroup by the ingroup across all traits. The intercorrelations among these deviation scores produced a 52 x 52 matrix of correlations, each based on an N of 390 (thirty ingroups' ratings of thirteen outgroups each).[2] Principal axes factor analysis and orthogonal rotation of factors extracted from this matrix produced three interpretable bipolar factors, accounting for forty percent of the total variance. The clusters of traits with highest loadings on each rotated factor were examined to determine the nature of the dimension being represented by each.

The first factor was interpreted as an evaluative factor with particular emphasis on peacefulness and cooperativeness, as indicated by Table 6.1.

TABLE 6.1
FACTOR 1

Positive loadings	*Negative loadings*
Peaceful among themselves (.39)	Quarrelsome among themselves (−.59)
Peaceful with other groups (.59)	Quarrelsome with other groups (−.71)
Obedient (.44)	Disobedient (−.73)
Honest with others (.48)	Dishonest with others (−.38)
Gentle (.61)	Brave (−.61)
Friendly (.48)	Cruel (−.67)
Clean (.38)	Dirty (−.44)
Religious (.55)	Hot-tempered (−.56)

The second factor was represented by a cluster of traits related to socio-economic advancement and achievement, interpreted as a "dynamism" factor (see Table 6.2).[3]

TABLE 6.2
FACTOR 2

Positive loadings	*Negative loadings*
Pushy, keen to advance (.71)	Uninterested in advancement (−.43)
Progressive (.78)	Uncivilized, backward (−.61)
Wealthy (.61)	Poor (−.45)
Proud (.57)	Lacking pride (−.42)
Smart (.72)	Stupid (−.60)
Clean (.50)	Dirty (−.52)
Hardworking men (.31)	Lazy men (−.43)
Hardworking women (.46)	Lazy women (−.43)
Thrifty (.68)	
Lacking generosity (.67)	
Backbite (.64)	

   The third factor was interpreted as an attraction factor dominated by liking and perceived similarity, along with a component of physical attractiveness (see Table 6.3). The emergence of this third factor, orthogonal to the first evaluative factor, provided initial evidence of an unexpected independence between evaluation and attraction as aspects of intergroup relations.

TABLE 6.3
FACTOR 3

Positive loadings	*Negative loadings*
Liked (.80)	Disliked (-.63)
Similar (.77)	Dissimilar (-.61)
Light-skinned (.28)	Dark-skinned (-.45)
Handsome men (.34)	Ugly men (-.52)
Beautiful women (.36)	
Friendly (.47)	

   Most of the forty-eight items in the structured trait list were included in the first three factors, but a few traits formed isolated clusters with no relation to any of the major factors. These isolated traits involved specific behavior patterns, such as sexual restrictiveness and use of magic, and some physical characteristics—strength and effeminancy. For the most part, however, the results of the factor analysis made it possible to place each trait along at least one bipolar dimension of affective meaning common to all respondent groups.

   On the basis of the factor analysis results, unweighted factor scores were constructed for three affective dimensions. Each factor score was computed from the sum of responses to bipolar traits with high loadings on the same factor (the members of each trait pair being scored either positively or negatively depending on direction of factor loadings). Factor scores on the evaluative dimension have already been presented in the preceding chapter (Tables 5.1-5.3) in the form of matrices of intergroup ratings. Trait pairs with high loadings on the dynamism dimension were divided into two subclusters on the basis of secondary factor loadings. The first cluster included pairs of traits with highest loadings on factor 2 and a connotation of activity or achievement, scored either positively (progressive, keen to advance, smart, wealthy, hardworking men and women) or negatively (uncivilized, uninterested in advancement, stupid, poor, lazy men and women). The second subcluster was composed of two pairs of highly intercorrelated traits with moderately high loadings on factor 2 and small loadings (in the opposite direction) on factor 1. Based on direction of loadings on the second factor, two of these traits were scored positively (brave, proud) and two negatively (gentle, lacking pride) and combined into a factor score, for convenience labeled "potency" (or "arrogance").

Summary statistics of the ratings on each dimension received by each of the thirty survey groups from the nine outgroups in their own countries are given in Table 6.4. In addition to providing data on intergroup differences in average received ratings, these statistics provide information on the degree of agreement among outgroup ratings for each ingroup on different dimensions, and on the relationships among those dimensions. For all three factors, the greatest variation in ratings occurs for those given to the most visible outgroups within each country—the Kikuyu and Masai in Kenya, the Ganda and Karamojong in Uganda, and the Chagga and Masai in Tanzania—reflecting the extremity of ratings assigned to these particular groups by some outgroups. In most cases, however, the variation of achievement ratings is less than that of evaluative ratings, suggesting that intergroup perceptions on the former dimension are somewhat more objectively determined than those on the latter (a conclusion supported by the positive correlation between total achievement ratings and outside ratings of advancement, discussed in Chapter 4). This outcome corresponds to Druckman's (1968) finding that more bias in intergroup ratings occurs for traits involving "liking" than for those involving "respect."

Differences in objectivity among the three dimensions are also revealed in differential correlations between self-ratings and received ratings for the respondent groups in each country. For evaluative ratings, the average correlation, across all three countries, is .41, while for the potency ratings it comes to .61, and for the achievement ratings, .74. Thus, although there is some evidence for a systematic direction of bias in self-attributions on achievement and potency traits, self-ratings on these dimensions are clearly not as distorted as are evaluative self-ratings.

It is clear from the data in Table 6.4 that no consistent linear relationship exists between a group's evaluative rating and its achievement rating. In every country, the most negatively evaluated group is also the one with the lowest average achievement rating, but in only one case is the group most highly rated on achievement also the most positively evaluated. This suggests again (as in the discussion of attraction and advancement in Chapter 4) that a certain amount of ambivalence characterizes the reaction of ingroups toward more advanced outgroups, the same ambivalence being reflected in the relationship between average achievement and potency ratings. In all three countries, the highest potency ratings are given to the most advanced and least advanced outgroups. Since potency is somewhat negatively correlated

TABLE 6.4
MEANS AND VARIATION OF OUTGROUP TRAIT RATINGS
(N=9, ratings received by each group)

Ethnic Group		Evaluation Mean	S.D.	Achievement Mean	S.D.	Potency Mean	S.D.
Kenya	A	−29.5	50.9	104.3	63.4	12.0	7.6
	B	8.0	21.8	0.2	6.0	−4.5	6.8
	C	−1.4	7.0	5.3	8.7	0.3	3.9
	D	4.0	8.1	−9.0	17.4	−5.3	9.6
	E	10.8	12.4	−9.5	13.8	−3.9	8.5
	F	−12.3	16.0	−0.1	14.6	−3.0	4.8
	G	−17.1	14.0	−8.3	8.3	−1.2	2.2
	H	−24.1	22.0	−18.0	15.9	0.5	2.5
	I	−81.9	51.0	−88.2	69.2	18.0	15.7
	J	−4.5	22.4	−10.2	13.9	6.7	17.6
Uganda	A	29.8	60.3	74.5	25.6	24.9	14.9
	B	0.0	13.2	−19.0	23.4	−4.0	8.6
	C	14.9	8.6	−19.4	19.4	−7.8	7.3
	D	−12.2	41.6	5.0	9.8	−1.5	4.3
	E	6.1	12.4	−25.7	13.8	−7.2	5.4
	F	−2.8	8.6	−0.8	3.7	−4.4	7.2
	G	−3.4	22.9	10.2	16.1	−3.0	5.9
	H	−18.8	24.6	8.0	12.2	2.9	3.6
	I	−17.1	15.3	6.4	6.5	2.0	7.4
	J	−76.3	47.8	−68.3	26.6	10.1	7.7
Tanzania	A	5.2	18.6	54.2	41.1	.12.2	14.6
	B	19.4	19.4	−9.3	5.4	−11.0	16.8
	C	13.3	13.3	−7.4	3.8	−6.5	3.7
	D	−3.3	13.5	−4.7	10.3	−2.7	4.2
	E	−2.7	21.4	−9.2	15.9	−0.4	3.4
	F	23.8	29.4	31.2	33.4	−2.0	2.8
	G	27.5	34.1	−2.9	11.8	−8.0	8.3
	H	−25.7	13.4	3.2	4.1	2.1	2.9
	I	−93.4	57.1	−63.0	19.7	35.7	11.5
	J	−18.5	11.2	−55.0	22.2	−6.1	7.3

with evaluation (apparently pride and bravery are equated with arrogance and disdain) this curvilinear relationship reflects the degree of negativity common to the perceptions of very high and very low advanced outgroups.

The greater variation of ratings on the evaluative dimension than on achievement suggests that the former may be more affected by variations in intergroup relations than are the latter. Another indication of this differential effect is found in the relationships between ratings of outgroups on these two dimensions and intergroup attraction scores (obtained from Tables 3.2-3.4). The average intragroup correlations (reported in Appendix E.6-E.7), within and across countries, were as shown in Table 6.5. To some extent, all of these correlations are deflated because self-ratings tend to reduce variation in outgroup ratings on trait ratings but do not affect the attraction scores.[4] However, this cannot account for the fact that achievement is consistently less positively related to liking than is evaluation. Since correlations do not provide unequivocal evidence for direction of causality, this may be interpreted to mean that the perception of outgroup achievement is more objectively determined, less subject to distortion, than that of evaluative attributions, or it may be that ambivalence associated with perceived achievement of outgroups is responsible for the imperfect linear relationship with liking. Probably both effects are operating.

In order to determine more clearly the relationship between affective content of perceptions and factors related to intergroup attraction, some measure of the degree of bias or misperception in the ratings of each outgroup by each ingroup was required. The method of deriving "halo" scores, described by Guilford (1954: 284) was again utilized for this purpose since it provides a measure of intergroup ratings above or below expected values based on the ratee's average received score (matrix column means) and the rater's average response tendency (matrix row means). The intergroup rating matrices on all three dimensions were converted to halo scores (recorded in Matrices D.6.1-D.6.3 in Appendix D). In reading these matrices, it should be kept in mind that the cell values do not reflect the direction of actual net ratings but the direction of *bias* in the rating of one group by another relative to the ratings given that group by all respondent groups combined. Thus, although the net evaluation of the Kenya group I by group E (Table 5.1) is negative, the halo score (Matrix D.6.1) is quite positive because the group E respondents tend to be less negative in their evaluation of group I than are other respondent groups.

One type of information provided by the halo score matrices is an indication of degree of bias in self-ratings, the values recorded in the main diagonal of each matrix. For evaluative ratings, these self-bias scores are consistently positive and, with only three exceptions, are more extremely positive than any rating given to or received from other groups.[5] The greater

TABLE 6.5

	Attraction and Evaluation	Attraction and Achievement[a]
Kenya:	$\bar{r} = .36*$	$\bar{r} = .34*$
Uganda:	$\bar{r} = .65**$	$\bar{r} = .39*$
Tanzania:	$\bar{r} = .56**$	$\bar{r} = .33*$
Overall:	$\bar{r} = .53**$	$\bar{r} = .35**$

*p $<$ .05 (by t-test)
**p $<$ .01 (by t-test)

a. Note the similarity between these values and the correlations reported in Chapter 4 between attraction and average achievement ratings.

objectivity of achievement ratings is again reflected in the lower (though consistently positive, except for group G of Uganda) self-bias scores, and in the fact that several ingroups are less positively biased in their ratings of themselves than in their ratings of some outgroups. Potency ratings, on the other hand, reveal an opposite pattern. On this dimension, the majority of self-bias scores are in the negative direction—ingroups rate themselves as less potent (brave, proud, arrogant) than expected from outgroup ratings. Thus, the syndrome of ethnocentrism is revealed not only by the biased attribution of positively valued traits to the ingroup but by the denial of negatively evaluated attributes in self-ratings.

VARIATIONS IN EVALUATIVE BIAS TOWARD OUTGROUPS

Considering the evaluative "halo" scores as measures of bias in the evaluation of each outgroup relative to other groups, these scores were analyzed according to various possible sources of such bias. The first factor considered was distance between the respondent group and the outgroup being evaluated. For each ingroup, the mean bias in evaluation was computed for adjacent outgroups, one-removed outgroups, and more remote outgroups. The results of the analysis of variance of these mean ratings, across the thirty groups, were not statistically significant ($F = 1.54$, with 2 and 58 degrees of freedom). The nonsignificant effect of distance indicates that physical closeness between groups does not exert a systematic biasing effect on overall evaluative ratings as it does on attraction ratings (see Chapter 4). The analysis of bias scores for the ten respondent groups within each country produced nonsignificant results for all three countries, but in each case the trend of ratings was such that the least negative bias was directed toward remote outgroups and the most negative toward one-removed outgroups. However, this result may have been an artifact of the method of data collection; since all ingroups tended to name their own group most frequently in response to positive traits, any tendency by an ingroup not to name remote outgroups at all would give them fewer negative ratings relative to other outgroups. Thus, there is no reason to interpret the obtained trend as a slight perceptual bias in favor of remote groups.

Mean bias scores were also analyzed according to the level of objective similarity between groups, comparing ratings of highly similar outgroups with those of intermediate and low similarity (but only for the eighteen ingroups who had outgroups available at all three levels of similarity). Again the results ($F = 1.73$, with 2 and 34 degrees of freedom) revealed no significant effects, although in this case the trend was clearly in favor of high similar outgroups (mean bias = -0.9) over intermediate (M = -11.4) and low (M = -13.2) similar groups, despite the fact that the artifactual effects of any response tendencies against naming dissimilar groups would have operated in the opposite direction. In addition, the effect of similarity may have been masked because outgroups classified as highly dissimilar were generally the same for each ingroup within one country, which meant that *relative* rating scores had a tendency to cancel out. In order to correct for this, the similarity effect was reanalyzed in reverse, using the ratings received by the eighteen ingroups from outgroups at each of the three levels of similarity. The results of this analysis were statistically significant ($F = 10.83$; d.f. = 2/34; $p < .01$), but the effect of similarity was nonlinear in that, while ratings from high similar groups ($M = +2.4$) were significantly more favorably biased than ratings from less similar groups, outgroups at the intermediate level of similarity gave more unfavorably biased ratings ($M = -20.9$) than did highly dissimilar outgroups ($M = -14.4$). Thus again, a factor that is highly significantly related to intergroup attraction ratings proved to have considerably less systematic influence on degree of bias toward favorability in trait ratings of the same groups.

The third variable explored for potential effect on evaluative bias was intergroup contact or familiarity. The UNESCO studies of national stereotypes (e.g., Reigrotski and Anderson, 1959) established contact between nations as a major determinant of content of stereotypes, particularly of the number of favorable traits attributed to other nations. In general, it was found that nationals with high levels of contact with other nations showed less bias toward high favorability in ratings of their own nations, greater willingness to attribute favorable traits to members of other nations, and greater correspondence between their attributions to the ingroup and attributions received from members of other groups (an effect also reported by Triandis and Vassiliou, 1967). Analyses of the East African data reported in Chapter 5 provided some corroboration for a negative relationship between average intergroup contact and degree of ethnocentric bias in ingroup evaluative self-ratings, although the relationship was quite small at the individual level. Similarly, some support was found for a relationship between intergroup contact and convergence between self-attributions and attributions received from outgroups. Comparing the ten respondent groups having the highest average familiarity with outgroups (mean familiarity scores greater than 1.15) with those ten having the lowest (mean familiarity scores less than .80) revealed consistent differences in the correlations between self-ratings and received ratings on all three dimensions of trait attribution, as reported in Table 6.6. These differences support the potential effectiveness of increased intergroup contact in reducing discrepancies between an ingroup's self-imagery and its reputation among outgroups, although the effect is less

TABLE 6.6
CORRELATIONS BETWEEN SELF RATINGS AND RECEIVED RATINGS
AS A FUNCTION OF AVERAGE CONTACT WITH OUTGROUPS

	High-Contact Groups	Low-Contact Groups
Evaluative Ratings	$r = .33$	$r = -.03$
Achievement Ratings	$r = .79$	$r = .53$
Potency Ratings	$r = .70$	$r = .56$

dramatic than that reported by Reigrotski and Anderson (1959) for European national stereotypes.

As contact with outgroups in general has some effect on evaluative content of ingroup ratings, extent of contact with specific outgroups may be expected to have a systematic effect on evaluative ratings consistent with the relationship between familiarity and liking of outgroups. For each ingroup in the East African sample, all outgroups were categorized as high (mean acquaintance score > 1.5), medium (between 0.5 and 1.5), or low (mean < 0.5) on the measure of familiarity. With this categorizing system, seventeen of the thirty respondent groups had outgroups at all three levels of familiarity and the mean evaluative bias scores of these groups toward outgroups at each level were analyzed. The results indicated a nonsignificant trend ($F = 1.38$, with 2 and 32 degrees of freedom) in favor of high familiar outgroups. In this case, again, an artifact resulting from a general tendency not to name low familiar outgroups in response to trait questions may have suppressed the effect of familiarity. However, other studies (e.g., Triandis and Vassiliou, 1967) have also demonstrated that extensive contact does not necessarily enhance the average favorableness of stereotypes of outgroup members, whatever its effect on attraction for that outgroup.

The low relationship between factors intimately related to intergroup attraction and bias in evaluative ratings of the same groups is reflected in a low correlation between intergroup bias scores and attraction ratings ($r = .33$, averaged across all thirty groups). Although most groups give highly negative evaluative ratings to outgroups that are generally disliked, *differential* ratings do not seem to correspond to patterns of attraction. Cluster analyses of average evaluative bias scores also revealed no consistent patterning of responses corresponding to those obtained for attraction ratings (see Chapter 3) and perceived similarity (see Chapter 4).

The failure to identify sources of bias in evaluative ratings at the group level of analysis led to consideration of differences among individual respondents as the basic source of variation in evaluative ratings of outgroups. Reigrotski and Anderson (1959) found that, among respondents within a particular nation, systematic differences in imagery of specific outgroups appeared as a function of the respondent's personal contact with that outgroup. Among French respondents, for example, the ratio of favorable to unfavorable trait attributions to Germans was 27:10 for those with high scores on a measure of contact with Germany, in comparison with a 14:10 ratio for those with no personal contact.

A similar measure of individual contact, or familiarity, with each outgroup was available for comparison with net evaluation ratings among respondents within each group in the East African sample. Correlations between familiarity and evaluation scores for all outgroups were computed within each respondent group (each based on an N of 650 representing fifty respondents' ratings of thirteen outgroups each) and averaged across groups. The resulting correlations were very low for all three countries (Kenya, r = .02; Uganda, r = .12; Tanzania, r = .12), and the overall average correlation of .08 (p > .05) provided no evidence for a favorability bias in outgroup evaluation based on familiarity on the individual level. Again, this may reflect the point made in Chapter 5 that individual familiarity is relatively unimportant in determining ingroup-outgroup attitudes in comparison with intergroup familiarity. On the other hand, individual *social distance* ratings may reflect each respondent's perception of what the ingroup's norms are relative to each outgroup and thus provide a better indication of how attraction mediates evaluation. Average intragroup correlations between individual social distance ratings and net evaluation of each outgroup were consistently positive (Kenya, r = .09; Uganda, r = .20; Tanzania, r = .20) and statistically significant across all thirty groups (r = .17, p < .05). However, the degree of relationship proved surprisingly low at the individual level as at the group level.[6]

In general, the data on favorability of attributions to outgroups suggest that evaluative bias is either nonsystematic or determined by idiosyncratic relations existing between particular groups rather than by the general factors related to attraction. Comparisons between the East African data on patterns of intergroup attraction and other data on national stereotyping support the latter possibility. Buchanan and Cantril (1953) reported that attributions of "friendliness" and other evaluative traits to outgroup nations were most strongly related to post-World War II political alliances and only slightly related to more enduring factors such as shared boundaries or common language. This pattern led them to emphasize the role of stereotypes as symptomatic rather than causal factors in international relations, but it presents a reverse picture from the kinds of relationships obtained in this study for attraction ratings. For the latter, while transient political and economic role relationships exert some influence, by far the greater proportion of variance is accounted for by long-term effects of cultural similarity and physical proximity. These differences in patterns of variation support a view taken by Pepinsky and Patton (1971: 20) that while *content* of stereotypes may well reflect actual changes in the state of intergroup relations, feelings of affection and rejection are less modified by circumstances. Such differences in modifiability may reflect the pattern suggested by Ehrlich (1973) that the different components of prejudice—stereotypes, personal distance, and affective responses—have quite different developmental growth rates, with acceptance of negative stereotypes occurring more rapidly, for example, than behavioral rejection.

NOTES

1. As has been mentioned previously, this analysis is based initially on an assumption of positive self-regard on the part of the responding individual. Following the symbol system of Rosenberg and Abelson (1960), these relations could be diagrammed: $\underset{\text{self}}{\oplus} + \underset{\text{entity}}{\oplus}$ and $\underset{\text{self}}{\oplus} - \underset{\text{entity}}{\ominus}$, respectively. Technically, any such pattern of associated entities is consistent, or "balanced," if it contains an even number of negative signs.

2. Note that since ingroup self-ratings were not included in this matrix, identification of an evaluative factor was achieved independently of biases in self-assignments. This avoided any circularity in the assessment of ingroup evaluations relative to favorableness of the traits assigned.

3. The emergence of these first two factors is consistent with other cross-cultural analyses of dimensions of affective meaning obtained by Osgood and his associates (Osgood, 1962). Typically, factor analyses of bipolar adjective ratings produce an evaluative factor, accounting for the largest proportion of common variance, and second and third factors interpreted as the "potency" and "activity" dimensions of affect (sometimes combined into a single "dynamism" factor, as is the case here). The dominance of relational qualities in the evaluative factor for traits applied to ethnic groups is consistent with other recent analyses of the structure of stereotypes based on content analyses (Ehrlich, 1973) and on multidimensional scaling (Jones and Ashmore, 1973). The validation of this pattern of factor extraction in the present set of outgroup ratings supports a distinction between two dimensions of intergroup affect—evaluation and respect—as identified in Druckman's (1968) simulation study of intergroup relations and consistent with Triandis' (1964) distinction between "respect" and "friendship" as components of intergroup attitudes.

4. This attenuation effect is especially problematic for interpretation of positive evaluation scores because the method used for obtaining these trait ratings required each respondent to name only the *one* group most characterized by each trait. Since in most

groups a large proportion of respondents tended to name their ingroup in association with any positively evaluated traits, positive ratings for outgroups reflect responses from those few informants who were not highly biased in favor of the ingroup, and one might expect these responses to be less systematically related to attraction ratings of outgroups than would the responses from the entire group. (This problem does not affect evaluative ratings on the negative side of the scale. Since few respondents named their ingroup in connection with unfavorable traits, negative outgroup ratings are more representative of the entire group of informants.) The bias ratings on the evaluative dimension, reported later in this chapter, reduce this problem somewhat since scores are reported in terms of *relative* favorability (i.e., relatively *less un*favorable ratings would be scored as positive) but responses of nonethnocentric informants are still somewhat overrepresented on this scale.

5. The evaluative halo scores for self-ratings were considered as a measure of ethnocentrism but were rejected in favor of the modified index reported in Chapter 5 because of the influence of two factors: (1) the necessary negative correlation between extremity of ingroup self-ratings and average ratings given to outgroups, and (2) the inflation of column means—received ratings for each group—due to the inclusion of self-ratings. However, since values on both indices are determined largely by the pre-ponderance of positive attributions in self-ratings for each group, the ethnocentrism scores and evaluative halo scores are highly correlated ($r = .94$ across all thirty ingroups).

6. These values are fairly consistent, however, with the correlation of .29 between social distance ratings and evaluative content of stereotypes of Negroes obtained in a study by Ewens (in 1969, as reported in Ehrlich, 1973: 104).

Chapter 7

CONTENT OF PERCEPTIONS OF OUTGROUPS

The relatively low degree of systematic evaluative bias in attributions of traits to various outgroups is consistent with Peabody's (1967) emphasis on the relative importance of descriptive, or denotative, aspects of trait ratings over their evaluative connotation. Lambert and Klineberg (1967) also reported a fairly low degree of evaluative content in children's imagery of foreigners, and found that intragroup consensus on evaluative dimensions of outgroup ratings followed a pattern quite different from that of consensus in descriptive content of stereotypes. Similarly, Gardner et al. (1968) reported that among bipolar ratings of French Canadians by English Canadian students, the cluster of traits that represented the prevailing stereotype of the outgroup proved to be factorially orthogonal to an evaluative-attitudinal item cluster. More recently, Aboud and Taylor (1971) found that *role* concepts carried greater weight than ethnic identification in trait ratings by both French and English Canadians, particularly among respondents with a high degree of contact with members of the other ethnic group. This finding was replicated by Feldman (1972) in stereotype attributions to racial groups. All of these results suggest that any systematic effects of the nature of intergroup contact and role relationships may be reflected in the *descriptive content* of outgroup stereotypes rather than in their evaluative tone. The purpose of the present chapter is to explore those multiple sources of bias that may influence the content of intergroup perceptions.

OUTSIDER'S JUDGMENTS

LeVine (1966) hypothesizes that the perceptions of group characteristics from any nonmember observer are likely to be influenced by the following factors: duration of observation, limitations of interaction (the observer can only report on the attributes corresponding to the behavioral domains in which interactions with the group take place), loyalistic biases due to friendly or unfriendly relations between his or her own and the perceived group, similarity between his or her own culture and that of the other (which prevents perception of their behavior as distinctive) or dissimilarity between the two cultures (which leads to perception of global contrasts and striking incompatibilities), personal motives and anxieties, and preconceptions derived from the beliefs of his or her own group concerning the other group.

This last category of bias shifts consideration from the perceptions of an individual observer to those of an entire group. According to LeVine's analysis, the sources of bias that determine what beliefs about characteristics of outgroups will be transmitted within a particular ingroup are similar to those that affect individual perceptions: extent of contact or remoteness, loyalistic biases related to the history of amity or enmity between the groups, limitation of opportunities for observation due to functional specialization of intergroup contact, and degree of cultural similarity which affects the probability that particular attributes will be noticed and commented upon. Several of these factors are likely to merge under conditions where intergroup differentiation is closely associated with differentiation of function within a particular economic or political system. One recurrent pattern to which LeVine (1966) refers is a tendency toward ethnic specialization when numerous groups are being incorporated into a modern division-of-labor economy. Such specialization may have its roots in nothing more intrinsic than differences in nearness to ports and railroads, but it comes to be reflected in intergroup images because of the restriction in the nature of contact between groups induced by limited role relations. An ethnic group specializing in physical labor ends up being characterized as strong, stupid, improvident, while one associated with trade is stereotyped as grasping, deceitful, clever, and sophisticated.

Examples of the operation of such biases are available from the content of specific trait attributions obtained in the East African survey. The Kikuyu, for instance, as a whole are heavily overpopulated and may not be the wealthiest of the Kenya ethnic groups on a per capita basis. However, many Kikuyu who reacted to homeland poverty by emigrating into other areas have been characterized by prosperous trading and modern wealth. On the basis of contact with these latter Kikuyu, a majority of the other Kenya respondent groups surveyed frequently name the Kikuyu as most "wealthy," "thrifty," "keen to advance," and "intelligent." The Luo, on the other hand, are known to remote groups primarily as migrant laborers, particularly railroad workers. Among these groups, the Luo are characterized as "hard-working," "spend-thrifty," "proud," and "physically strong." Highland groups neighboring the

Luo, however, see them in their more traditional role as poor farmers (their area having less adequate rainfall than the highlands), and informants from these groups frequently name the Luo as most "lazy" and "physically weak."

The perceptual biases suggested by LeVine were based on an anthropological perspective. Campbell (1967) has demonstrated that the same principles of intergroup perception can be derived from psychological learning theory. In the latter analysis, the perception of a particular stimulus, or attribute, is treated as a response disposition which, according to Hullian learning theory (Spence, 1956), is a function of stimulus intensity (V), drive (D), incentive (K), and habit or familiarity (H). This formulation provides a perspective for summarizing the results of much research on how perceptual thresholds are affected by the drive state of the perceiver and the value or familiarity of the stimulus. It has been demonstrated that the more drive-relevant the stimulus, the greater its associated reward value, and the more familiar it is, the more likely it is to be responded to (or the lower its perceptual threshold) and the more likely it is to be misperceived as present when it is not (see Postman, 1953). These research results represent the effects of the "intrapsychic" determinants of response (D, K, and H) which may be regarded as "projections" of the personality of the perceiver. When D, K, and H are collectively very strong, then a "projective" perception may occur even though V is very weak or the stimulus very inappropriate.

The experimental literature on perception shows that the same factors determine both lower perceptual thresholds and "covaluant errors" (perceiving the stimulus to be present when it is not—e.g., Postman et al., 1948; Postman, 1953). Research relating degree of anti-Semitism and accuracy of judging from photographs which persons are Jewish provides a relevant example. Anti-Semites judge more photos to be of Jews than do non-anti-Semites, both when the picture is in fact of a Jewish person and when it is not (Allport and Kramer, 1946; Carter, 1948; Lindzey and Rogolsky, 1950; Elliot and Wittenberg, 1955; Scodel and Austrin, 1957; Himmelfarb, 1966). The diagnostic or projective nature of the perceptual response is the same under both circumstances.

More neglected in research on perception is the obvious fact that perception is also a function of V, stimulus strength. In threshold studies, length of exposure, brightness of stimulus, and clarity of focus all affect frequency and certainty of perception (e.g., Wyatt and Campbell, 1951). If we take the stereotypes or images which persons or groups have of each other and regard them as response dispositions, this analysis suggests that such perceptions can at one and the same time reflect both the nature of the group being described and, projectively, the character of the group doing the describing. This frees us from the either-or analysis of stereotypes in which, when interpreting stereotypes as symptoms of the preoccupations of the stereotype-holder, one implicitly regards the outgroup being stereotyped as a "living inkblot" whose characteristics are independent of the stereotype content (e.g., Ackerman and Jahoda, 1950). In the terms of Zawadski's (1942) analysis, the "well-deserved reputation" theory of stereotypes and the "scapegoating" theory can both be appropriate in the same setting (Allport, 1954).

In many instances, the relative strength of various stimuli is obvious—in general, the more physical energy in a stimulus, the stronger the V. However, a great deal of experimental research indicates that a still more appropriate statement of stimulus strength is in terms of *relative* physical energy, in contrast to previous stimulation or other parts of the stimulus field (Helson, 1964; Campbell and Kral, 1958). Helson has referred to this as the law of adaptation level: effective stimulus strength depends upon its degree of departure from the adaptation level for that stimulus modality established by prior stimulation or other parts of the present stimulus field. A stimulus intensity below the adaptation level can be as stimulating as one above it. Thus, rats can be conditioned to respond to the turning off of an otherwise continuous sound as well as to the turning on of a sound; thus, the same saline solution can taste salty on one occasion and sweet on another, depending on what saturation the mouth has previously been adapted to.

The implication of this adaptation-level principle for intergroup perception is that there will be an effect of cultural similarity on which outgroup attributes are likely to be noticed. The greater the differences between groups on any particular culture trait, the more likely that trait is to appear in the stereotyped imagery each group has of the other. This implies that attributes of a group which in some intergroup contexts would go totally unnoticed may become the object of vivid imagery by other groups in a cultural context in which they stand out.

While the above points illustrate the "grain of truth" content of intergroup stereotypes, it would be wrong to assume that the degree of difference perceived between groups is an accurate reflection of actual differences. The homogeneity with which either ingroup or outgroup members have the trait in question, and the amount of overlap between groups, is usually misperceived. This corresponds to pervasive cognitive processes noted in perception research as the enhancement of contrast through homogenization of differences within gestalt boundaries and exaggeration of differences across boundaries. (This effect can be derived directly from elementary considerations of stimulus generalization in learning theory [Campbell, 1956].) Extension of the principle to intergroup perception leads to the prediction that differences between ingroup and outgroup, if sufficient to be noted, will be exaggerated in the mutual stereotypes each holds of the other.

To the extent that perception is a function of D, K, and H determinants, we would expect that the direction of perceived differences between ingroup and outgroup would reflect the nature of intergroup relations. In the service of hostility, all differences can be opportunistically interpreted as despicable; a difference in almost any direction can be anathematized. Thus, an outgroup can be hated as too shrewd or too dumb, as too lazy or too pushy, as too forward or too reclusive, as too emotional or too reserved (Merton, 1957). If stereotypes are divided into two components—the evaluative (reflecting D, K, and H determinants) and the descriptive (reflecting V)—the preceding analysis leads us to expect latent agreement in the reciprocal stereotypes of two groups. Agreement should occur in the descriptive content of the mutual images but not necessarily in the direction of evaluation. A good example of this is found in Bruner's (1956) description of the mutual stereotypes held by the Hidatsa Indians of the Dakotas and the local "Yankee" ranchers. The Hidatsa characterize themselves as generous and unselfish and the Yankees as stingy and selfish, whereas the Yankees perceive themselves as thrifty and provident and the Hidatsa as improvident spendthrifts. In this case, a genuine culture difference is being reported in a different light by each group. An extension of this principle has been applied by Peabody (1967) to group perceptions in the Philippines.

A number of other implications of the basic learning theory formula can also be applied to intergroup perception. As a function of increasing V, the more opportunities for observation, and the longer the exposure, the larger should be the role of real differences in intergroup stereotypes. This also implies that nearer outgroups, and outgroups with which most interaction occurs, will be more accurately stereotyped, while the more remote and less well-known the outgroup, the more the content of the stereotype will be determined by intrapsychic or projective factors. The content of intergroup interaction also would be expected to affect V strength such that those trait differences involved in interaction will be most strongly and accurately represented in mutual stereotypes. The "social reality" to which stereotypes in part refer focuses upon the nature of intergroup interaction, the content of which may be a purely arbitrary product of historical circumstances.

TRAIT ATTRIBUTIONS AS A FUNCTION
OF INTERGROUP CONTACT

The analyses reported in Chapter 6 revealed that intergroup factors such as similarity and distance do not exert consistent biasing effects on overall evaluation of outgroups. The preceding discussion, however, suggests that these factors will affect the *specific* traits attributed to outgroups to the extent that they determine the nature of contact and interaction between ingroup and outgroup members.

The two methods of eliciting trait attributions used in the present study permit assessment of these effects for comparison with other research using either the checklist or the free-response approach to obtaining stereotypes. The trait list provided in questions 8-15 of the interview schedule is similar to the adjective checklist procedure used in most studies of stereotyping among American college students since Katz and Braly's (1933) classic study (with the exception that the attribution of any trait is here limited to one ethnic group). The free-response method of trait elicitation represented in interview questions 6-7 (the items, "What is the best thing about _____" and "What is the worst thing about _____") is similar to the technique employed by Lambert and Klineberg (1967) to obtain children's images of eight specified reference groups.

Trait-List Assignments

From the trait-list responses, differential stereotyping of the East African groups was examined by identifying those traits that were attributed to each ethnic group by at least ten percent of respondents (a) from all near outgroups (adjacent and one-removed), (b) from all distant outgroups, (c) from all similar outgroups, (d) from all dissimilar outgroups, (e) from near and similar outgroups, (f) from distant and similar outgroups, (g) from near and dissimilar outgroups, and (h) from distant and dissimilar outgroups. Differences in patterns of trait attributions to all groups from these different types of outgroups were examined to provide evidence for general effects of various sources of bias on the content of intergroup perception. A summary of the attribution patterns for each group individually appears in Appendix F.[1]

In general overview, it was found that traits such as "peaceful" and "honest," which were most often attributed by respondents to their own ingroups, were attributed to others primarily by similar outgroups. "Quarrelsome," on the other hand, was most often attributed to any particular group only by *near and dissimilar* outgroups, suggesting that such groups were the most likely to have experienced hostile interaction with the target group. In general, most of the attributions given to any ethnic group were made by *similar* outgroups, for whom the target was a high-probability response. Besides those mentioned above, the traits most frequently attributed to any group only by similar outgroups were "backbite," "independent," "obedient," "brave," "handsome," and "not thrifty." The varied nature of these traits suggests that intergroup similarity affects the saliency of perceived outgroup characteristics rather than their evaluative content.

The effects of differential contact were frequently evident in the nature of traits assigned to specific target groups by varying outgroups. For instance, the Kikuyu were often mentioned as "sexually loose" by remote outgroups who knew them primarily through contacts in urban centers where displaced

Kikuyu women are frequently employed as prostitutes. In contrast, groups nearer to the Kikuyu, who were familiar with traditional Kikuyu values, frequently named them as "most sexually strict." A similar contradiction has already been mentioned in the perception of the Kenya Luo as "hard-working" by distant outgroups and as "lazy" by near outgroups. In other cases, contradictory perceptions were not so obvious, but there were differences in which characteristics of particular groups were noticed or reported by various outgroups. For example, the Gusii, who have frequently engaged in internecine warfare, were mentioned as "quarrelsome among themselves" only by outgroups that were near and dissimilar, whose own loyalty structures preclude internecine warfare.

Perceptions of skin color, cleanliness, and beauty were frequently associated with the relative progressiveness of ethnic groups. The Ganda, for example, who are not reported by outside observers to be particularly light-skinned, were frequently mentioned as "light in skin color" by distant and dissimilar outgroups who know them only by reputation as prosperous traders. The Ankole, on the other hand, who are only moderately economically advanced, were mentioned as "light-skinned" only by their immediate neighbors. And the Masai, who are objectively quite light, were not mentioned as light-skinned by any outgroups.

In many cases, differences in perception reflect differences in standards of judgment or frames of reference. It has already been mentioned that similar groups most frequently named each other as "handsome," reflecting, quite likely, ethnocentric standards of beauty. In Tanzania, the Masai were considered "poor" by most outgroups but were named as "most wealthy" by near and similar outgroups who share the Masai traditional standard of wealth in terms of cattle. In several instances, the same group (particularly the Kikuyu or Ganda) was mentioned as both "progressive" and "conservative" by near and similar outgroups, suggesting that these two traits were evaluated on different dimensions, the former according to modern economic advancement and the latter according to the maintenance of traditional institutions and values within home areas.

The effects of culture contact and similarity on intergroup perception were evident in the common attributions of traits to the three pastoral groups—the Masai of Kenya and Tanzania, and the Karamojong of Uganda. The dissimilarity between these groups and the predominantly agricultural groups in the rest of the survey was reflected in their widespread reputations as "independent and unruly," "cruel," and "hot-tempered," traits attributed to the pastoral groups by outgroups in all three countries. According to the results of a personality-assessment study by Edgerton (1965), pastoral societies are more likely than agriculturalists to value independence of action for males and to express aggression directly and freely. Such differences between agricultural and pastoral groups are clearly reflected in the trait attributions found in this study.

Free-Response Trait Assignments

Since the open-ended questions designed to elicit perceptions of each outgroup were included in the interview before the list of traits specified by the interviewer, the content of responses to the former items provides uncontaminated information as to the saliency of various types of attributions in intergroup perception. The responses to the open-ended questions were recorded verbatim by the interviewer and were then reduced to a three-digit code according to a coding system which made fine distinctions among responses in order to minimize coder discretion (for instance, the response "they are clean" was coded 1.1.1, while "they are neat" had a different code number, 1.1.3.). Out of 42,000 possible responses (combining "best trait" and "worst trait" questions), 37.8% were "don't know" answers. To some extent, this high frequency of refusals to respond reflected the lack of knowledge on the part of many respondents about remote outgroups. However, since "don't know" responses were not consistently related to personal acquaintance of respondents with the target outgroup, the high percentage of such responses may also indicate that summary characterizations of outgroup members were not particularly salient for our respondents, at least not in the sense of being readily accessible in this spontaneous response format.[2]

"Don't know" responses provide information not only about the general level of saliency of stereotypic trait perceptions but also about differences among ethnic groups as response targets. As already indicated, the total number of "don't knows" assigned to any group was related to the degree of acquaintance between that group and others. Across the three countries, the average correlation between "don't knows" and the average acquaintance score *received* by each target group was −.70 (i.e., trait responses were more likely to be assigned to groups that were generally well known than to those less well known). Similarly, large groups were less likely to receive "don't know" responses, the average correlation between population size and received "don't knows" being −.61. Geographic location of groups also had some effect, although "don't know" responses were related not so much to the geographical isolation of groups as to their position relative to the best-known ethnic groups. Groups like the Embu and Meru, who are both near and similar to the well-known Kikuyu, received many more "don't knows" than groups more distant from such central societies.

An interesting tendency appeared in the pattern of "don't know" responses in that they were more frequently given to the "worst trait" open-ended question than to the "best trait" question. Of the 2,296 "don't knows" given by the Kenya respondents, for example, fifty-seven percent were in lieu of negative traits; similarly, fifty-three percent of the 3,499 Uganda "don't knows," and fifty-nine percent of the 3,295 Tanzania "don't knows," were in response to the negative trait question. This bias against negative responses appeared in the ratings of all but three of the thirty respondent groups, but it was strongest in the ratings given by members of each group to their own ingroup. "Don't knows" were relatively rare in response to ingroup questions, but of the 280 that did occur, 247 (eighty-eight percent) were in response to the request for "worst traits." This tendency of ingroup members not to associate negative characteristics with their own group is clearly related to the previously given definition of ethnocentrism in terms of biased self-regard. Therefore, the correlation was computed between each group's ethnocentrism rating (as given in Chapter 5) and its net frequency of ingroup "don't know" responses (negative "don't knows" minus positive). Across the three countries, the average correlation between these two indices was .42, which was significantly greater than .00 and fairly high considering the restricted range of the net "don't know" index.

Apart from the pattern and frequency of "don't know" responses to the open-ended questions, another indication of the lack of saliency of responses referring to personality characteristics of outgroups is the frequency of content responses (9.2% of total responses) which related to the outgroup's agricultural productivity or other traditional skills. Another 1.1% of the total open-ended responses referred to observable cultural similarities or differences between ingroup and outgroup in practices regarding circumcision, bodily mutilations, dowries, and food habits. A little less than 50% of the open-ended responses referred directly to perceived personal traits of outgroup members, these ranging from physical appearance, work habits, and use of witchcraft, to relations with other groups, cooperation, self-respect, honesty, intelligence, and social progressiveness. In general, the patterns of these responses corresponded closely to the trait attributions elicited in the trait-list section of the interview.[3]

Because the amount of contact between respondents and outgroup members was anticipated to be the most reliable determinant of the *content* of outgroup perceptions, comparisons were made between free responses regarding each target group from respondents who were personally familiar with members of that outgroup and from those who were unacquainted with the outgroup. However, the number of "don't knows" and impersonal responses assigned to relatively unknown ethnic groups made such comparisons meaningless in many cases. A few groups in each country—the Kikuyu, Masai, and Luo in Kenya, Chagga and Masai in Tanzania, and Ganda and Karamojong in Uganda—had reputations widespread enough to make comparisons among different types of respondents possible. For those groups, open-ended trait responses were tabulated among outgroup respondents at each of six levels of familiarity with the target group (see Chapter 3 for description of the familiarity scale) ignoring ingroup identification. Agreements in attribution among five percent or more of the respondents in each familiarity category were recorded, and comparisons were made among these shared attributions.

For each of the seven widely known ethnic groups, there were some characteristics that were frequently mentioned by respondents at all levels of familiarity. Informants ranging from those with no personal acquaintance with the Kikuyu to those who lived in Kikuyu territory for an extended period all showed agreements in characterizing the Kikuyu as hardworking and industrious, well-educated, and "jealous of other groups." Similarly, the Kenya Luo were characterized by all levels of informants as proud, seeking education, and practicing magic or witchcraft. Respondents of different familiarity levels agreed that the Kenya Masai are good at herding cattle and other livestock; that the Ganda are sociable to other groups and yet despise or look down on others, and tend to be proud; that the Karamojong are good cattle herders and like fighting; that Chagga are well educated, good in agriculture, and proud; and that the Tanzania Masai are good with cattle, like fighting, and are conservative and primitive. In general, there appears to be an impressive amount of cross-respondent validation for these attributions, although several characterizations could represent biases shared by familiar and unfamiliar outgroupers reflecting the nature of contacts between agricultural and pastoral societies. Most, however, probably reflect real (though selectively perceived) group differences that have been transmitted from those with personal contact with the outgroup to those without such contact.

The major difference between high-familiar respondents (i.e., those with familiarity scores of 3 to 5, representing extensive personal contact with members of the particular target outgroup) and low-familiar informants was evident in the frequency of stereotypic responses. Although respondents in the high familiar category were always fewer, there were consistently proportionally more agreements among the responses of low-familiar informants than among those of the highly familiar. For instance, although respondents with extensive contact with Kikuyu showed some agreements in the three characteristics listed above, the less familiar respondents had proportionally more agreements and included other traits such as "good businessmen," "clever," "rich," "dirty," "unfriendly to others," and "quarrelsome." For the Kenya Luo, least familiar respondents alone concurred in mentioning "intelligence," while those with only partial familiarity (i.e., with contact with Luos outside their own territory, primarily with urban Luo) showed high agreement in characterizing them as "extravagant" or "wasteful" and as "respectful to their women." Among the few respondents high in familiarity with the Kenya Masai, there were some who concurred with the description of Masai as cattle herders, but only those personally unacquainted with the Masai mentioned "bravery" or "fighting other groups" as salient characteristics. Similarly, only low-familiarity respondents characterized the Tanzania Chagga as "progressive" and "civilized."

The tendency for respondents low in familiarity with the target group to produce more stereotypic responses than high-familiar respondents is somewhat inconsistent with findings of other research on intergroup stereotypes. Vinacke (1956) reported that among ethnic groups in Hawaii, higher familiarity (assessed in terms of an estimated probability of direct contact between respondent groups and respective outgroups) was associated with *greater* uniformity of trait assignments. Similarly, Taft's (1959) analysis of ethnic stereotypes in Australia produced a high positive correlation between respondents' self-ratings of acquaintance with other ethnic groups and the uniformity of stereotyping of those groups (measured in terms of the minimum number of different traits required to include fifty percent of all trait assignments made). More recently, Triandis and Vassiliou (1967) reported that Americans' stereotypes of Greeks were more uniform (in terms of less variability of semantic differential ratings) among maximum-contact respondents (living in Greece) than within the minimum-contact group (although this same pattern of increased clarity of stereotyping with increased contact did not appear in Greeks' ratings of Americans).

The difference between previous findings and those of the present study may have several sources. In the first place, the present analysis has been restricted to those target groups that have widespread reputations among outgroups regardless of relative personal acquaintance. (In this respect, the ratings are parallel to those of Greeks rating Americans in the Triandis and Vassiliou study, as opposed to the Americans' ratings of Greeks.) It has already been reported that stereotyping was very low for less well-known groups.[4] In the second place, it is probable that uniformity of stereotyping among respondents familiar with the target group reflects real group differences within the arena in which the contact takes place. Any restriction of that arena of contact should enhance uniformity of perceptions. It is likely that the measures of intergroup acquaintance used in the reported studies previous to this one reflected primarily limited or truncated contact, such as that restricted to market settings, educational institutions, or political arenas. In the present study, such limited sorts of acquaintance with outgroup members would have been characteristic only of respondents classified as low (or possibly, intermediate) in level of familiarity with the target group.

High-familiarity respondents included only those with extensive personal contact with the outgroup, in settings less conducive to uniform experience with outgroup members.

The highest level of familiarity is, of course, represented when informants respond to questions about their own ingroups. Among the seven target groups considered here, there was a great deal of variation in the willingness of the fifty respondents from each to make characterizations of their own group. The Kikuyu, for instance, produced relatively few shared self-attributions, although there were a few repetitions of the traits "hard-working," "proud," and "jealous of other groups." The Kenya Luo, too, generated a low frequency of ingroup-respondent agreements, except to concur with their widespread reputation in the practice of magic and witch-craft. Among the other ingroups, the frequency of agreements in self-attributions was considerably higher but these only occasionally intersected with the most frequent attributions from outgroupers and were often unique in content. For example, although the Ganda informants showed a high frequency of agreement (twenty-six percent) with their reputation among outgroupers as "proud," the rest of their self-descriptions were unique in content—friendliness, politeness, good manners, and cooperativeness. The Karamojong, too, concurred with their reputation among outgroups as cattle herders and stock thieves but also frequently mentioned themselves as "friendly and sociable with other groups" (twenty-four percent) and "brave" (ten percent). The Chagga showed high frequency of agreement with their reputational attributions as good agriculturalists, well-educated, and proud, but also frequently named traits such as "highly civilized" and "progressive." The Chagga were also unique in their frequency of admission of negative traits such as untrustworthiness (ten percent) and a tendency to drink too much (eighteen percent). The Masai, on the other hand, in both Kenya and Tanzania, showed very little agreement with their reputation among out-groupers but, on the contrary, frequently characterized themselves as "generous" (twenty-seven percent), "friendly," "kind," "gentle," and "warm-hearted."

The seven groups included in this analysis represent both extremes of the social-economic advancement dimension described in Chapter 4. Some interesting patterns of reputational stereotypes emerge as a function of this advancement factor. Advancement-related traits do not appear much in the free responses, except that the Chagga and Kikuyu are both universally perceived as well-educated, but all three high-advanced ethnic groups are universally stereotyped as "proud" or "jealous of other groups," and in all three cases the ingroup respondents show a high percentage of agreement with these attributions. Such consistency of perception in the free-response situation, replicated in all three countries, probably reflects the saliency of economic and political factors in intergroup perceptions, particularly among informants who are not personally acquainted with the outgroup.

The greatest differentiation among informants of different familiarity levels occurred in the attribution of negative traits (in response to the open-ended question "What is the *worst* thing about _____?"). It has already been pointed out that, in general, the frequency of "don't knows" was greater in response to this negative question than to the positive version, and that this was particularly true for informants responding about their own ingroups. (Among the Ganda informants, for example, thirteen characterized their ingroup as "too proud" while twenty-three [fifty-six percent] responded that they "didn't know of any bad thing" about the Ganda.) In the characterizations of outgroups, different patterns of negative and positive responses were found for different types of informants. Among respondents highly familiar with each target outgroup, the frequency of agreements, or shared stereotypes, was generally greater for positive characteristics than for negative ones, and the frequency of "don't knows" was greater in response to the negative question than to the positive. Less familiar respondents reversed this pattern and tended to give "don't know" responses more frequently when asked for positive traits. Less than half the "don't know" responses (forty-seven percent) given by informants of low familiarity were in lieu of negative characteristics, while most of those from high-familiarity respondents (sixty-five percent) were in response to the negative question, a statistically significant difference in proportion ($\chi^2 = 13.12$, p $<$ .01).

In sum, these tabulations suggest that the content of intergroup perception is largely a function of the frequency and type of contact between ethnic groups and the degree of personal acquaintance of the individual informant with members of each target outgroup. Respondents with little or no familiarity with an outgroup apparently rely on reputational stereotypes based largely on economic or political relations among groups, while respondents that are better acquainted with outgroup members tend to be more idiosyncratic in their attributions, probably as a function of personal experience with particular outgroupers. The evidence here suggests that familiarity does not necessarily tend to bias perceptions in the direction of positive evaluation but rather that it introduces more variety and complexity of perception.

NOTES

1. Identification of target groups has been omitted from Appendix F (and order of presentation scrambled) because it was not felt to be essential to the purpose here of investigating patterns of attribution that appear irrespective of the group being rated.

2. There is little evidence that response refusals represented a reluctance on the part of respondents to apply labels to other groups since in the next section of the interview, for which the interviewer provided trait names, the percentage of "don't know" responses dropped to 11.0%.

3. The differences that appeared in types of responses to the open-ended and structured rating tasks correspond to those reported by Ehrlich and Rinehart (1965) in a methodological study of the effects of response format on obtained stereotype attributions. In ratings of various ethnic groups, Ehrlich and Rinehart found more target groups described under more trait clusters in the closed format (checklist) than in the open format of response elicitation. The closed format also promoted use of emotionality terms that never appeared in open-ended responding, while the open format generated frequent reference to physical characteristics or qualities seldom included in checklists of traits. Such differences in response patterns obtained as a function of response format probably reflect differential saliency of trait ascriptions and should moderate the importance attached to stereotyping obtained under closed response formats unless cross-validated by data in other response modes.

4. Appendix F also reveals how often high-frequency trait assignments came from near and similar outgroups, rather than from remote, dissimilar groups. Berry (1970) has pointed out that a functional analysis of stereotypes leads to a prediction that high visibility of outgroups should generate *both* greater uniformity of stereotypes (because the higher probability of interaction creates a need for efficient summary representations of outgroup characteristics) *and* greater differentiation (because of potential variability of individual contact experiences). Although the trait response format of the present study did not permit a quantitative test of this hypothesis, the total trait ascriptions to highly visible outgroups did produce both greater variety and more frequent agreements than those ascribed to less well-known groups.

PART III

CONCLUDING PERSPECTIVES

Chapter 8

REPUTATIONAL ETHNOGRAPHY AND IMPLICATIONS
FOR A THEORY OF ETHNOCENTRISM

The evidence provided in the preceding chapter for the influence of differential contact and intergroup similarity on perception of outgroup characteristics suggests that any attempt to assess actual group differences in traits requires multiple sources of information—i.e., validation of observations across different sources of bias. The rationale behind this suggestion is that of reducing uncertainty by diagnosing the same construct from independent points of observation, through a kind of "triangulation" described in more detail elsewhere (Campbell, 1959, 1964). Given that any single observation (such as a trait attributed to group A by respondents in group B) is understood to be a function of the characteristics of both the observer and the observed, it becomes impossible to separate the subjective and objective components with only the one report. However, when observations from several vantage points can be focused on the same entity, then it becomes possible to disentangle these components. Considered from this perspective, the matrix of data in Appendix F becomes an expanded version of the multiple-ethnography paradigm suggested by Campbell (1964: 331):

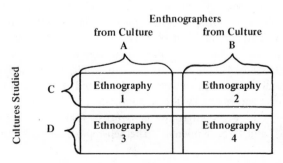

In the general model, two observers (ethnographers) from different cultures each report on a third and fourth culture. Among the four resulting ethnographies, attributions appearing in 1 and 3 not shared by 2 and 4 can be attributed to perceptual biases of ethnographer A, the common features in 2 and 4 not appearing in 1 and 3 to those of ethnographer B. In the other direction, consistencies in ethnographies 1 and 2 not shared with 3 and 4 (and vice versa) can be identified as "objective" characteristics of the respective cultures under observation.[1] (Attributes common to all four ethnographies are inherently ambiguous, interpretable either as shared biases of the ethnographers or as shared traits of the societies studied. Similarly, attributions appearing in only one ethnography cannot be unambiguously interpreted as either an interactive bias on the part of one observer or a "blind spot" on the part of the other.) As an expansion of this matrix, Appendix F can be read as thirty cultures (rows) studied by observers from five different perspectives (including the ingroup).[2] Attributes appearing repeatedly within one column—such as attributions of "peaceful" from ingroup observers and from similar outgroupers—can be identified as systematic observer biases unrelated to the group being observed. On the other hand, unique attributes appearing across a particular row (as summarized in column 2 of Appendix F) can be associated more confidently with the observed group.

Within this matrix, the most impressive convergent validation is obtained when a unique attribution of a specific trait to a particular group is agreed upon by outgroup respondents varying in distance and similarity to the target group and by the ingroup members themselves. In the data of Appendix F, such cross-group agreement was attained in several instances. The Kenya Luo, for example, were named as "lacking in thrift" by respondents from all types of outgroups and by the Luo themselves. Physical characteristics were often consensually validated, as with the universal perception of the Luo, Acholi, and Lango as "dark-skinned" and the Toro and Chagga as "light-skinned" and "beautiful."

Economic differences were often reflected in consensually validated stereotypes. The widespread reputations of the Kikuyu and the Ganda as economically and socially advanced showed up in agreements across outgroups, and in self-reports, on such traits as "intelligent," "pushy," "progressive," "wealthy," and "thrifty." The analyses of the open-ended trait responses reported in Chapter 7 also provided examples of mutually shared stereotypes associated with the more economically advanced ethnic groups.

The cultural differences between pastoral and agricultural groups were reflected in the agreement by the Karamojong and the Kenya and Tanzania Masai with the cross-outgroup consensus that they were "brave," "uncivilized," and "hot-tempered." The self-reports of Karamojong respondents also agreed with multiple outgroup attributions of the traits "dirty," "cruel," and "lacking in wisdom." Other examples of cross-group attributions validated by ingroup self-perception included a reputation for "interest in witchcraft" and "powerful magic" among the Luo, Kamba, and Sambaa; "pride" and "cleanliness" for the Chagga, Ganda, and the Kenya Luo; "strength" for the Acholi, Lango, Karamojong, and Sukuma; "friendliness," "honesty," and "lacking pride" for the Nyamwezi; and "dirty" and "poor" for the Gogo.

Another form of validation of intergroup differences is obtained when there is latent agreement between ingroup and outgroup perceptions, as when the Gogo refer to themselves as "conservative" while outgroups describe them as "backwards," or when the Ganda self-report includes "thrifty" while their outgroup reputation involves "lacking generosity." Such latent agreements are most likely to occur when real differences between groups along some dimension are perceived from different perspectives by ingroup and outgroup members. They are more likely to be elicited in interview situations where flexibility of descriptive and evaluative dimensions of responses is promoted rather than in the context of restricted bipolarity characterizing the trait list and open-ended questions used in this interview.

A somewhat more equivocal form of cross-group validation of trait attributions occurs when multiple outgroups, with varying sources of bias, agree on the attribution of a particular trait which is not confirmed, or is contradicted, by ingroup self-perceptions. Particularly if the trait is a negative one, the ingroup disagreement may be attributed to loyalistic bias or to an ethnocentric basis of judgment. However, it could be that the attributing outgroups share some peculiar experience with the ingroup that colors their perception. For instance, in Uganda, seven of the nine outgroups, varying in distance and similarity to the Ganda, named the Ganda as highest on the trait description "they appear to be friendly but backbite and are two-faced, hypocritical." The Ganda did not agree with this attribution, but the cross-outgroup validation is impressive except for the possibility that the consensus represents a shared bias resulting from the history of political alignments in Uganda rather than a real behavioral difference. This suspicion is buttressed by the fact that the two politically inactive groups did not share the consensus.

Since the data presented in Chapter 6 provide strong evidence for an evaluative bias in self-perceptions, and since apparent shared biases among groups differing in distance and similarity to any target group are difficult to detect, most cases in which ingroups fail to confirm cross-outgroup attributions can probably be accounted for by loyalistic bias. One common example resulted from an overwhelming tendency (twenty-nine of thirty groups interviewed) for ingroups to describe themselves as most "peaceful" and/or "honest with other groups," and in no case to name themselves as "quarrelsome" or "dishonest." Most attributions of quarrelsomeness or dishonesty were made by near and dissimilar outgroups whose perceptions could easily be accounted for by their history of relations with the target group. Some groups, however, were named as "quarrelsome" or "dishonest with others" by all types of outgroups, a consensus which suggests some real behavioral bases despite the lack of ingroup validation.

A similar example is found in the perception of industriousness among various groups. In most cases, ingroups describe their own men and women as "hardworking" and in few cases did self-perceptions include "lazy." However, multiple-outgroup attributions concurred in perceiving several of the target groups as "lazy." In these cases, the ingroups may have been using a different or unique dimension of judgment from the one on which they were being evaluated by outgroups, as when the cattle-oriented Karamojong name themselves as "most wealthy" while their nonpastoral outgroups concur in their description of the Karamojong as "poor." In many other such cases, loyalistic bias may reflect ethnocentric value systems that mark real differences between a particular ingroup and most of its outgroups. This may account for the fact that most Gusii and Kamba respondents named their own groups as "strong" despite cross-outgroup agreement that they were "most weak," or that Kenya and Tanzania Luo described themselves as "handsome" in contradiction to multiple-outgroup perceptions of them as "unattractive, ugly men."

Stereotypes that occur with high frequency, or salience, in the imagery of a specific group among the members of a particular ingroup are likely to reflect real differences between those two groups on certain dimensions of behavior or values, though probably represented in exaggerated form. However, where these images are not confirmed in mutual stereotyping or by observations from other outgroups, interpreting them as arising from real differences, rather than from other potential sources of bias, requires additional information and consideration of the context in which the stereotypes were elicited. Open-ended response forms would seem to offer the best opportunity for eliciting perceptions of highly salient group differences, but the nature of the free-response data obtained in this study suggests some methodological problems with this technique. The occurrence of convergent responses among informants, within or between groups, was relatively rare, even for cases where important cultural differences are known to exist. One such case, involving perceptions of the Kenya Luo, can serve to illustrate the methodological difficulty.

Within the culture area represented in this study, the Luo differ from their predominantly Bantu neighbors relative to the practice of circumcision and its role in male initiation to adult status. Traditionally, all Bantu groups, as well as the Nilo-Hamitic Kipsigis, Nandi, and Masai, practiced circumcision in connection with male (and female) initiation, and the absence of this practice among the Luo was conspicuous and related to considerable derogatory imagery. The nature of this imagery, and its widespread occurrence, can be illustrated through responses obtained from ethnographic interviews in several Kenya groups:

From Gusii respondents (a Bantu group neighboring the Luo) (LeVine and Campbell, 1964):

> Gusiis didn't dislike Luos very much; only despised them because they were uncircumcised [p. 82].

> Gusiis used to tell their children not to be like Luos who are uncircumcised [pp. 90, 95, 103].

> We only told them [Gusii children] never to be like Luos and when they grew up they cried for circumcision lest they be like Luos [p. 119].

> We called them Abagere and Abaisai because they were uncircumcised and [so] we did not intermarry. . . . The only bad custom Luos had was that they never got circumcised, otherwise we would intermarry with them [p. 92].

> We [Gusii] called them Abagere . . . because they were rather childish, for they were never circumcised [p. 105].

> Our girls were circumcised. But later our girls were spoiled and got married by the uncircumcised Luos which was rather ridiculous [p. 100].

> They [Luos] refused to be circumcised and Gusii told them [you] better stay away from us, since you are not circumcised [p. 113].

From Kipsigis respondents (Nilo-Hamitic, nonadjacent neighboring group) (summarized by Daniels, 1970):

> When judging the masculinity of outsiders the Kipsigis base their views primarily on whether or not the outgroup practices circumcision comparable to that of the Kipsigis [p. 209]. . . . Thus an uncircumcised Luo man, not being fully a man . . . falls into the category of *lagok,* women and children [p. 217].

From Embu respondents (remote Bantu group) (Saberwal, 1964):

> Embu circumcised girls [and we] would tell them that if they were afraid of being circumcised, they'd be taken to Njue [Luo] country where there are no circumcisions [p. 29].

Beyond the Masai were Jaluo; they [Embu] used to hear that the
Kavirondo people in that area didn't get circumcised [p. 31].

In contrast to this consensus in reputation of the Luo obtained in ethnographic interviews, the survey responses from members of the same Kenya
groups contained no references to circumcision or related characteristics
(although this did receive one mention from Luhya respondents and fourteen
from the Masai). This difference in response pattern could be related to
differences in interview settings, types of respondents, or nature of interviewers. The ethnographic data reported above were all obtained from interviews with elderly male informants for whom traditional cultural practices
may have assumed an importance not represented among the younger, more
modernized survey respondents. On the other hand, the difference may have
been less a function of respondent values than of interviewer effects. The
ethnographic interviews were conducted (with or without native interpreters)
by anthropologists who, as "outsiders" to the culture, required detailed
explanation of customs and values already familiar to natives of the area. The
survey interviews, in contrast, were conducted by ingroup natives to whom it
may have seemed unnecessary—even insulting—to mention obvious differences that "everybody knows." Thus, the rarity of references to Luo circumcision in the survey data could reflect either the lack of importance of this
dimension of group difference or its importance being so obvious as to be
taken for granted. In either case, this example highlights the necessity of
taking into account the·context of response elicitation in interpreting free-
response data.

Another context effect that can influence the kind of responses obtained
to open-ended interview questions is that of "external anchoring" or
"contrast effects" produced by the particular range of groups considered for
rating (see Diab, 1963). It is conceivable, for example, that including the
Masai among the groups to be judged focused attention on a different type of
response (or "displaced" the ratings given to other groups) from what would
have been obtained had the Masai been excluded. The most obvious anchor
effect operating in the East African study is the inclusion—in all three
countries—of groups representing both extremes of a political-economic
development dimension. This context may account for the heavy concentration on economic role-related imagery in much of the stereotype data. That
such economic differences were largely effected by arbitrary factors such as
geographic location does not, of course, negate the possibility that they now
represent real group differences in behavior and values. Whether cause or
effect, differential expectations regarding economic and political opportunity
can be related to child-rearing practices, value decisions, and commitment to
alternative life styles, which are reflected in intergroup imagery.

ETHNIC STEREOTYPES AND SOCIAL CHANGE

The issue of validity of economic-related intergroup perceptions rests on a conception of ethnic change derived from the old hypothesis (stated by Myrdal, 1944, as the "principle of cumulation") that the perception of groups by other groups (as images or stereotypes) and the objective qualities of groups influence each other. Though the East African social-structural setting differs considerably from the American racial situation which Myrdal was describing, a similar process of mutual influence of stereotype and actual group qualities seems to have occurred there. In the colonial period in Africa, pacification and the establishment of superordinate order was followed by the expansion of internal trade and the development of urban centers which fostered the mingling of people from diverse ethnic groups among whom contact and communication had previously been very limited.

In the absence of pronounced racial differences, stereotypes in these new settings were formed on the basis of the behavioral distinctiveness of groups as perceived by other groups. Some of these perceived behavioral distinctions could have been based on differing cultural traditions confronting each other in interpersonal relations—differences in language, food habits, dress and adornment, deference and courtesy, recreational behavior, etc. On these bases, some groups may have come to be seen in negative terms (e.g., as "dirty" people or sorcerers) and marriage or other social contact with them avoided, thereby reinforcing the original differences. With other groups, similarities in language and culture were given opportunity for recognition so that they came to regard each other as "brother" and to welcome social contact. In this latter case lies the incipient basis for the formation of the "ethnic blocs" of which Geertz (1963) has written.

Other sources of behavioral distinctiveness between groups developed in the structural transformation of autonomous ethnic units into a larger socio-economic order. This transformation (discussed in detail by Fallers, 1963) involved the development of a new series of socioeconomic differentiations— into occupations, status groups (based on income, education, and access to power), and central versus peripheral positions with respect to modernizing influences (in part a rural-urban difference). The recruitment of pre-existing groups into this new structure rarely resulted in a perfect correspondence between social role and ethnic identity, but social perception often leveled the inconsistencies and sharpened the rough congruence into group stereotypes.

Thus, some groups came to be known in terms of those occupations with which they were associated by others—as trader, teacher, clerk, policeman, manual laborer, political organizer, etc. Perhaps most important among these ethnic reputations were those that related most closely to status evaluation, modernity, and urbanism. On the one side, there were groups that came to be known as wealthy, intelligent, hardworking and ambitious, advanced and progressive. These were groups with whom contact and even intermarriage were generally regarded as desirable (as was indicated in the analysis of attraction ratings), although their privileged position in society also gave rise to resentment that could be politically crystallized. On the other side, there were groups that acquired reputations as thieves and prostitutes, or as backward and illiterate peasants or herdsmen capable of no more than menial work. Social contact with the latter came to be regarded as undesirable in the cities and among the literate throughout the country.

In these patterns can be seen the basis of an interactive spiral between the objective qualities of groups and the manner in which they are perceived by others. In those African areas where large-scale ethnic interaction began during the colonial period, actual differences in traditional customs and ethnic differentials in recruitment into modern social roles gave rise to stereotypes that influenced interaction, with groups coming to be seen as desirable or undesirable companions and marriage partners. This conception of the ethnic situation could lead to a series of predictions concerning the new ethnic blocs that would be formed as a function of perceived similarities in traditional culture and modern status differentiations, *if* we assumed that the patterns of ethnic recruitment into modern statuses were static. It is clear, however, that these patterns of recruitment are susceptible to change and in some cases have changed either during the colonial period or shortly after, due to the expansion of educational opportunities, the establishment of universal suffrage, and the loss of ethnic favoritism in government employment by colonial officials. In some places, groups that once formed the "colonial aristocracy" have fallen relative to parvenus from the more peripheral areas of the country. On the other hand, some groups that had an early advantage in education, employment, and politics have managed a "snowballing" career of cumulative status.

Insofar as earlier differentials in ethnic access to opportunities for status enhancement are perpetuated in patterns of recruitment (particularly in education), then earlier stereotypes and incipient ethnic blocs are likely to be stabilized. However, insofar as recruitment patterns are changed—either by government policy or by ethnic differentials in seeking and taking advantage of existing opportunities—then stereotypes and incipient ethnic fusions are likely to change accordingly, either in terms of a progressive blurring of ethnicity or a change in actual and perceived ethnic alignments.

The relationships between ethnic identification and political/economic role systems bear on the discussion in the preceding chapter regarding the differential responsiveness of descriptive and affective components of intergroup perception to conditions of social change. If these two aspects do change at markedly different rates (or in response to different social conditions), then a period of transition would be expected to produce certain inconsistencies, or shifts in patterns of response along different dimensions of intergroup perception. Results of the East African survey reveal just such a pattern—systematic variations in affective responses to outgroups were found to overlap only partially with variations in evaluative content of stereotypes, which was, in turn, largely independent of other dimensions of intergroup perception. No assessment of overt hostility between groups was included in the survey data, but informal examination of the history of intergroup conflict in the area suggests that this is yet another dimension only poorly correlated with affective measures. The conditions under which these various aspects of intergroup relations would be expected to converge has important bearing on the conceptual validity of ethnocentrism as a unitary and universal syndrome of human groups.

ETHNOCENTRISM AND CLARITY OF INTERGROUP BOUNDARIES

Since the demarcation between "ingroup" and "outgroup" is essential to the concept of ethnocentrism, the assessment of ethnocentrism is inextricably tied to the perception of group boundaries. Only recently has the anthropological literature begun to come to grips with the problematic nature of the boundedness of ethnic groups, particularly in small, stateless societies (Levine and Campbell, 1972: ch. 7). In brief, the traditional assumptions of well-bounded ethnic communities have been challenged by anthropological data documenting (1) frequent cases of territorial interpenetration of ethnic groupings, (2) the existence of continuity, rather than discontinuities, in regional variations in cultural and linguistic characteristics, (3) inconsistencies among peoples in a region in assignment of ethnic labels and intergroup demarcations, (4) high levels of formal and informal social contact and interaction across ethnic communities, and (5) cases of shifts of ethnic identification on the part of individuals or groups within particular regions. Given these findings, it becomes essential to consider any data on intergroup attitudes with respect to what referents the respondent is using in drawing distinctions between his or her own group and the labeled outgroups.

The systems theory approach to the study of social groups (e.g., Berrien, 1964, 1968; Miller, 1965) conceptualizes boundaries in terms of discontinuities in the frequency or quality of the flow of communication or information among elements of a system. From this perspective, group boundaries need not be defined in terms of any physical barriers or markers, but rather in terms of those subjective judgments on the part of group members that facilitate or limit the frequency and ease of interaction with other individuals. The centrality of such judgments to ethnic identification is illustrated in the present data by the dominance of attributions of peaceful and cooperative intent in descriptions of ingroup characteristics. In both the trait-list and open-ended response data, qualities such as "peaceful," "friendly," and "honest" were universally attributed to respondents' own ethnic groups and rarely to outgroups (with the exception of those of overlapping ethnic identity). Thus, it appears that the perception of belonging to the "same" group is marked by a ready assumption of friendly relations that does not extend to members of "other" groups.

Other researchers have also identified differential feelings of trust, familiarity, and personal security as characteristic of the distinction between ingroup and outgroups. Enloe (1973: 39) defines the basic function of ethnicity as that of informing an individual "where he belongs and whom he can trust," while in his analysis of local communities in urban settings, Suttles (1972: 4) notes that the delineations between neighborhood groups frequently reflect "preoccupation with personal safety and the need to get a quick fix on the relative trustworthiness of fellow pedestrians, residents, and 'trespassers.' " Thus, an individual's anticipated interactions are guided by an understanding of the rules of inclusion that indicate who is "one of us" and who is not. Understanding and application of these rules will inevitably be subject to the vagaries of personal learning experience, language usage, and judgment context. Recent research in social judgment has demonstrated marked changes in response patterns with shifts in the salience of different dimensions of judgment (e.g., Eiser, 1971b; Cohen, 1971). Such research indicates that the boundaries of conceptual groupings and the inclusion of particular stimuli within a conceptual category are dramatically affected by which dimension of judgment is made salient within the judgment context. Similarly, the boundaries of social groupings may be drawn with respect to multiple bases of differentiation that may not necessarily converge in the sense of including the same individuals within the boundaries across all dimensions.

Boundary Convergence

To some extent, the coincidence of group boundaries may occur as a function of natural covariation among various dimensions of intergroup relations. For example, between groups where territorial boundaries are based on restricted accessibility (i.e., physical distance or geographical features), concomitant limitation of contact is likely to produce recognizable boundaries along dimensions of social mores, language, economic exchange, and intermarriage. However, relations between such groups are not likely to be characterized by frequent warfare. On the other hand, between groups where territorial boundaries are more arbitrarily drawn, they are less likely to coincide with interaction boundaries but more likely to converge with warfare boundaries.[3] Boundaries may also coalesce as a function of threat of invasion or penetration from some external agent. Initially unbounded networks of interpersonal interactions may be transformed into bounded units by virtue of some common hostile force; that is, a cultural unit gains identity by first being defined as a target of expansionist interests by some other group. In such cases, convergent boundaries of interaction, perceived cultural differentiation, and symbolic or ideological identification may rapidly develop, concomitant with the demands of common defense. Similar processes may operate whenever previously unbounded local groupings recognize some common interest in political or economic spheres, leading to the development of "ethnic blocs" and redefinition of group loyalties.

LeVine and Campbell (1972: ch. 7) make a case for an "evolutionary drift" toward coinciding intergroup boundaries as a function of a principle of least effort and of the necessities of group survival. To the extent that efficiency of group decision-making and coordination is facilitated by sharp definition of group membership (i.e., clear recognition of who is subject to the consequences of group action), well-bounded groups may have a selective advantage over less-bounded groupings relative to capacity for mobilizing and coordinating individual effort in support of group endeavors. The potential circularity of the notion that successful coordination is related to sharpness of boundaries of participation is reduced somewhat if one assumes that efficiency of coordination in new activities is enhanced by convergence with already existent systems of coordinated effort, so that selective pressure for coincident boundaries will be operative within physical or social environments that require a high degree of joint effort to meet the needs of individual and group survival.

The anthropological evidence cited at the beginning of this section suggests that, in the absence of such strong selective pressures, convergence of boundaries may be the exception rather than the rule, and that whatever cognitive bias may exist toward coincidence in bases for differentiation of persons can be overcome by institutionalized sustained ambivalence in intergroup relations. Pairs of ethnic groups that are characterized by frequent military confrontation and also by high rates of intermarriage provide the more dramatic examples of nonconvergent systems in which the rules of inclusion for social interactions involving familial and affinal obligations are markedly different from those involving warfare. In such cases, the lack of convergent boundaries may operate as an adaptive asset, preventing the disruptive effects of all-inclusive military mobilization and making possible a flexible combination of the advantages of large-scale coordination of effort on some activities and smaller-scale coordination on others.

Other conditions that would promote disjunction of group boundaries are those associated with widespread and rapid social change, particularly those involving economic and political systems that alter conditions of survival and patterns of coordinated activity. Even in areas where ethnic group relations may have evolved into stable, well-bounded systems of interaction, forces of change imposed by external agents may not prove sensitive to existing patterns of group differentiation. In such cases, new rules of inclusion-exclusion may be developed relative to roles and activities associated with the new conditions, while old rules are maintained in traditional spheres of activity, thus producing a complex pattern of overlapping but noncoincident systems in which identification of group boundaries shifts with different dimensions of intergroup relations. Under such conditions, individuals are likely to exhibit opportunism in their patterns of interaction and alliance, being free to shift perceptions of group loyalty in order to maximize advantages of differential group identification in different realms of activity.

Enhancement of Contrast

The decision rules regarding inclusion-exclusion that define the boundaries of social groups are primarily functional distinctions and do not of themselves account for the investment of affect that is associated with judgments differentiating ingroups from outgroups. In order to relate the process of group differentiation to the evaluative aspects of ethnocentrism, we must take into account available evidence regarding the effect of identification of boundaries on perceptions of related characteristics of stimuli within and across boundaries.

It has been repeatedly demonstrated in research on social judgment that superimposing a rule of categorization on an otherwise continuous series of stimuli produces an "enhancement of contrast" effect (e.g., Clarke and Campbell, 1955; Eiser, 1971a; Tajfel and Wilkes, 1963), that is, a tendency to rate stimuli within categories as more similar (assimilation) and those between categories as more different (contrast) than they would be rated in the absence of the category boundary. As a result of this enhancement effect, the existence of boundaries leads to perceived discontinuties between sets of stimuli that do not correspond to objective measures of attributes. (Suttles [1972], for example, has demonstrated that residents' "cognitive maps" of urban neighborhoods are characterized by sharper boundaries than exist in terms of spatial or physical features.) Further analysis of this phenomenon indicates that the polarization effect occurs most reliably on rating dimensions that are made salient by the nature of the superimposed categorical boundary. Particularly relevant are experimental studies of group game-playing (e.g., Wilson et al., 1965; Dion, 1973) which indicate that evaluative biases in favor of ingroup members are most pronounced on dimensions or traits *relevant* to the game situation.

In his development of the accentuation theory of social judgment, Eiser (1971b; Eiser and Stroebe, 1972) has suggested that the polarization of judgments characterizing the enhancement of contrast effect is a function of the degree of correlation between differences among stimuli in the attribute being judged and differences on the superimposed classification dimension. Extending this argument suggests an additive effect of bounded systems such that "if the systems are congruent with each other they should reinforce each other (and hence lead to increased polarization) whereas if they are incongruent with each other, they should inhibit or cancel each other out (and hence lead to decreased polarization)" (Eiser, 1971b: 448).

Applying this effect to the realm of intergroup attitudes, we would expect the consistent polarization of affect associated with the classic ethnocentrism syndrome to be characteristic only for those social groups in which multiple criteria for intergroup differentiation converge. In general, the data from the East African survey do not represent such a pattern, in that ratings of outgroups by a particular ingroup tend to be neither highly polarized nor consistent from one rating dimension to another. It is interesting that the major exceptions to this result occur in ratings of and by the Masai (Kenya and Tanzania) and Karamojong (Uganda), groups for which (relative to other groups in the survey) boundaries based on traditional patterns of interaction, cultural similarity, and participation in modern political and economic systems all do tend to converge. As a consequence, whatever bases for distinguishing between "us" and "them" are made salient by any particular judgmental context, these groups are more likely than others to have correlated attributes.

Determinants of Boundary Convergence

If the presence of ethnocentric attitudes is associated with the degree of coincident boundedness among social groups, then any factors that can be related to increased convergence of boundaries should provide the best predictors of ethnocentrism in intergroup relations. A number of such factors that would tend to increase or decrease the probability of coincident boundaries have already been discussed in this chapter and generally fall into two classes—pressures arising from internal structural needs and those deriving from external sources.

Internal features most relevant to boundary formation are those associated with the development of centralized decision-making and related individual loyalty structures. The far end of the continuum is represented by highly politically centralized societies with concomitant clarification of boundaries necessary to identify those who are subject to the decision outcomes of the political system. As LeVine (1972: 6) describes this pattern:

> The growth of differentiated political institutions, and particularly of the state with its centralized leadership for making, administering, and enforcing decisions, tends to stabilize military loyalties and make opportunistic alliances more difficult. The state operates so far beyond the sphere of face-to-face relations, affecting so many primary groups that its demands . . . must be explicitly formalized, and this sets in motion the boundary-setting process of recognizing who is subject to the demands and who is not. Those who are subject to its demands must be convinced that they are getting something in return, hence the development of ideologies of uniqueness, superiority, contrast with inferior outsiders, etc.

In addition, the regulation of intergroup contact by centralized gatekeeping institutions facilitates homogenization of ingroup imagery of outgroups and formation of bases of intergroup differentiation along lines coincident with patterns of political alliance. Thus, both clarification of ingroup membership and systematization of intergroup relations contribute to the coalescence of group boundaries characteristic of centralized states.

Apart from these variations in internal structure that correlate with convergence of social boundaries, pressures for greater boundedness may be generated by external agents. Existence of a common threat is frequently cited as a source of ingroup integration (e.g., Coser, 1956; Sherif et al., 1961; Burnstein and McRae, 1962), but even apart from threat, any type of differential treatment from outside agents may be sufficient to coalesce group identity. In his analysis of local communities in urban settings, Suttles (1972) gives particular emphasis to the role of relations with external organizations in originating and maintaining community boundaries. Results of laboratory studies (Rabbie and Horwitz, 1969) indicate that, while mere assignment of individuals to different group labels is not sufficient to create ingroup-outgroup distinctions, differential treatment of groups by the experimenter does produce disjunction in perceptions of own-group versus outgroup members. This effect can lead to a self-fulfilling prophecy phenomenon in intergroup relations in which perceptions by outgroups that an aggregate of individuals constitutes a social group produces differential treatment which in turn produces a correlation between "similarity" and "common fate" that enhances group identification (Campbell, 1958).

Interethnic relations in pluralistic societies reflect complex interactions of these internal and external mechanisms of boundary formation. Ironically, the requirements associated with development of a centralized political system frequently create the conditions that sharpen lines of subgroup differentiation which were only vaguely drawn in the past. As Enloe (1973: 20, 28) puts it, "Modernizers who penetrate social barriers inadvertently generate . . . ethnically based mobilization. . . . [Thus] it is one of the ironies of modernization that it combats ethnic loyalty while it stimulates ethnic awareness." Where such enhanced awareness of ethnic identity leads to politicization of ethnic groups, the demands of internal coordination combine with forces of external origin to enhance the coalescence of intergroup boundaries. As variation across societies in political structure is reduced, ethnocentrism may yet become the universal syndrome Sumner envisioned. The potential homogenization of the political context in which intergroup relations occur highlights the importance of collecting and maintaining data from different points in time and social development in order to prevent a "historo-centric" version of social science theory.

NOTES

1. When dealing with dispositional traits, of course, one cannot assume that the characteristic is correctly identified in terms of the underlying disposition or intent but rather that it refers to some distinctive behavior pattern of the target group members, particularly in relations toward outgroupers.

2. The analogy to Campbell's model is not perfect since the same observers actually recur in different columns of the Appendix F matrix, but the similarity holds up with respect to each row or each column considered singly.

3. Note, in either case, the territorial boundary may be equally well recognized by respective group members. It is not the clarity of specific boundaries that is at issue here, but the extent of convergence with other dimensions of intergroup differentiation.

Chapter 9

RESULTS REVIEWED

In the preceding chapters, responses obtained from our East African survey have been analyzed and cross-analyzed from a variety of perspectives. Although each chapter focused on a single response dimension, results from multiple measures, multiple respondent samples, and multiple levels of analysis were presented, much of them in essentially undigested form. By staying so close to raw data, we have been able to examine in some detail several variations in measurement and analysis strategies, to discuss points of intersection between specific aspects of our findings and results of prior research on intergroup perception, and to explore the advantages and limitations of approaching correlational data with a hypothesis-testing orientation. As a result, however, the reader who has borne with us thus far may well feel an acute need for a summary of findings at a level of abstraction that ignores variations in sampling and unit of analysis. The purpose, then, of this concluding chapter is to provide such a concise review in the form of summary statements of results and their relevance to the conceptualization of ethnocentrism with which we started.

SUMMARY PROPOSITIONS

The major findings from the survey can be summarized in the following ten propositional statements:

(1) Measures of liking-disliking, social distance, and personal familiarity between groups all tap a common bipolar dimension of intergroup affect that can best be represented in terms of the desirability of close interpersonal relationships between members of the different groups—sort of the group counterpart to interpersonal attraction at the individual level. Under condi-

tions where patterns of actual intergroup interaction have had an opportunity to stabilize, responses on this global affective dimension tend toward mutual reciprocity, the direction and intensity of ratings given by one group to another corresponding closely to those received from that same group. These mutual ratings also exhibit a high degree of stability across time, despite variations in political and economic alliances.

(2) Within ethnic groups, there is a high degree of agreement among respondents as to where various outgroups stand on this affective dimension. Although variations among respondents in education and urbanization have some effect on absolute ratings given, the relative attractiveness of various outgroups remains constant across ingroup members. At this global level, informants apparently respond to outgroups categorically, giving ratings that reflect generalized intragroup norms little influenced by variations in specific personal experiences with outgroup members.

(3) Attraction toward outgroups covaries most strongly with factors associated with opportunity for intergroup contact—particularly with cultural-linguistic similarity and geographic proximity. As a result, the individual respondent's "cognitive map" of psychological distances among groups appears to be an integration of cultural and geographic distances. The resulting mutual attraction ratings among ethnic groups can be divided into clusters that exhibit properties of cognitive "balance"—the set of relations within clusters being all positive and the set of relations between clusters primarily negative or neutral.

(4) Clusters of mutual attraction ratings tend to correspond closely to *traditional* patterns of intergroup relations. Most positive ratings of desirability or attractiveness are expressed toward outgroups that have an extensive history of contact and interaction with the ingroup. It is equally true, however, that behavioral indices of overt conflict tend also to be positively related to proximity and opportunity for interaction. Thus, while there is considerable evidence for the existence of "balanced" relationships *within* the affective domain, there is also evidence for inconsistency *between* the set of relations obtained on the affective measure and those that would be derived from some behavioral measures. Despite a relatively recent history of overt conflict among ethnic groups in our survey sample, respondents apparently feel psychologically closer to a "familiar enemy" than to a little-known stranger.

(5) The relationship between attraction ratings and the power/status of outgroups is somewhat ambiguous. While psychological distance is uniformly high toward outgroups regarded as low in social-economic status, affective responses toward high-status groups are marked by high variance suggestive of approach-avoidance conflict. On the one hand, high-status groups represent a

model of a desired state, at least for respondent groups that share the social value system reflected in the status hierarchy. On the other hand, high-status groups provide visible targets for resentment and blame from those lower in the status hierarchy. The balance of attraction toward the most advanced groups is confounded by cultural similarity and conditions of rivalry. For the most part, those that are similar to high-status groups show a more positive correlation between attraction and status than those at greater cultural distance. However, where similarity is great enough to generate close competition over economic resources and power, the relationship is less positive. Less ambivalence and greater uniformity, however, characterize ratings of high-status groups on measures of perceived strength and achievement. Thus, the results of this study support those of numerous others indicating that "respect" and personal attraction are independent dimensions of positive regard.

(6) Although some variation exists among ingroups in extent of positive self-regard, respondents from almost all ethnic groups in the survey rank their own group as highest on positively evaluated characteristics, and without exception rate their ingroup more favorably than it is rated by any other respondent group. Traits most marked by this biased self-perception are those connoting friendly, peaceful, and trustworthy interpersonal relationships. Less ingroup bias is obtained with trait ratings related to achievement, strength, wealth, or beauty. Thus, the facet of ethnocentrism that comes closest to universality is the tendency to regard own-group members as more honorable and trustworthy than others. The degree of positive self-regard on this dimension is not linearly related to ingroup status, being equally high for those groups held in high and low regard by other groups in the survey sample. The least (though by no means minimal) ethnocentric self-perception is exhibited by groups of intermediate status, who also tend to be geographically and culturally close to larger and more visible outgroups. These findings suggest a dual interpretation—and corresponding dual function—of ethnocentrism. Ethnocentric self-perception may reflect high self-esteem associated with achievement and positive regard from others, or a defensive self-esteem associated with rejection and/or threat.

(7) While positive characteristics, particularly trustworthiness, are uniformly ascribed to ingroups, the relationship between evaluation of outgroups and their affective distance from the ingroup is complex. Although disliked outgroups are generally distrusted and negatively evaluated, outgroups given positive attraction ratings are not consistently assigned positively evaluated characteristics. As a result, a clustering of intergroup relations derived from net evaluative ratings overlaps only partially with those derived from attraction measures. Particularly outgroups that are geographically close may be

simultaneously liked (held in low social distance) but distrusted and assigned negative trait characteristics. Further, while ratings on the affective dimension appear to be rather stably linked to long-term intergroup relations in traditional spheres, specific evaluative trait ratings appear to be more affected by contact in the arenas of modern economic and political activity.

(8) Evidence for a cognitive differentiation between global attitudinal responses, mediated by long-term cultural stereotypes, and specific ascriptions, mediated by personal experience, has frequently been noted in the social science literature, particularly from political surveys revealing a disjunction between attitudes toward government policies or institutions in general, and specific programs or agencies in particular (e.g., Katz et al., 1975). Such findings indicate that attitudes toward institutions or groups cannot be summarized on a single dimension of acceptance-rejection. Adequate representation of the patterns of intergroup perception obtained in the present study would require at least a three-dimensional space, with axes representing bipolar judgments of trust-conflict, attraction-repulsion, and admiration-disrespect. Analysis of the content of responses from the survey would locate ingroup-outgroup pairs (i.e., the perception of a particular outgroup by a given ingroup) in almost all sectors of this conceptual space.

(9) Assuming that the ingroup occupies a fixed reference point (usually in the positive sectors) in conceptual space, the distance between the ingroup and any specific outgroup will depend on which dimension of judgment is made salient and on what is the relevant basis of differentiation between ingroup and outgroup. A dimension correlated with some distinction (boundary) between the two groups should generate more polarized responses than a dimension associated with little basis for distinction between ingroup and outgroup. High familiarity between groups is conducive to increased differentiation among ratings on different judgmental dimensions while lack of contact generates little differentiation since there is no discontinuity between judgments mediated by normative expectations and those mediated by personal experience.

(10) Ethnocentrism as conceived by Sumner (1906) represents an extreme variation in the pattern of intergroup relations—one in which the ingroup, and close allies, are represented in one sector of conceptual space, at the positive pole of all dimensions, and all other outgroups are located in the opposing sector. For this pattern to occur, there must be a convergence of boundary-defining mechanisms such that all bases of distinction between "us" and "them" are highly correlated. The social and environmental conditions likely to promote such coincidence of boundaries include existence of physical and psychological barriers to direct personal contact between individual group members, presence of environmental threats to survival that necessitate a high

degree of internal coordination and self-sacrificing group loyalty, or the existence of legal/economic discrimination based on ethnic identity.

Results of the present study indicate that convergent ethnocentrism is not a necessary or universal pattern of intergroup relations in a pluralistic society. What remains to be determined is whether or not it represents the most *stable* variation—whether group distinctions that coincide with others become rigid-ified so that a drift toward convergent boundaries represents an irreversible trend in the nature of intergroup relations. Theories of cognitive consistency, and other homeostatic models of human motivation, postulate just such a "strain toward symmetry" (Newcomb, 1953) in the cognitive representation of interpersonal relations. Sets of perceived relations that do not generate consistently positive, or consistently negative, links between the self and a given social object are presumed to be unstable, motivating a selective information search that will serve to bring the configuration into a balanced— and stable—state.

Persistent findings of enduring inconsistencies between attitudes assessed at different levels of abstraction cast doubt on the motivating force of cognitive inconsistency. Recent theorists (e.g., Cohen, 1971) have suggested that consistency-seeking is limited to unidimensional responding, and that the presence of inconsistency in one dimension merely motivates a shift of attention to a different judgmental dimension in which the salient informa-tion can be accepted without contradiction. Hence, one has the capacity for mobilizing uniformly negative sentiments, matched by an equivalent capacity for unmitigated positive affect that can be mobilized when the response contingencies change.

In the preceding chapter, it was suggested that the absence of convergent boundaries between social groups may have adaptive significance, permitting flexibility in adapting patterns of alliance to correspond to differing func-tional requirements. A similar view has been expressed by Triandis (1972: 351): "In a more general sense we might define the ingroup as the set of people with whom a person believes that it is appropriate to cooperate to achieve a particular goal. This means that for every group goal there may be a different ingroup." This perspective suggests that the demands of a multi-ethnic society would promote a cognitive flexibility of individuals that permits mobilization of alternative sympathetic responses in ways that avoid costly approach-avoidance conflict.

Results of a survey conducted by Berry and Annis (1974) among Canadian Indians provide at least indirect support for the functional significance of such cognitive complexity. Assessing individual differences in "psychological differentiation" by means of measures of ability to make figure-ground and self-other distinctions, Berry and Annis found that indices of acculturative stress (e.g., psychosomatic symptoms, feelings of marginality or deviance, and negative attitudes toward Euro-Canadian society) were significantly lower for informants scoring high in differentiation (both perceptual and social) than for those scoring low. In the context of cultural pluralism, individual adjustment is apparently enhanced by the ability to respond differentially to discrepant stimulus cues. Social science theory must correspondingly adapt its concepts of ingroup, outgroup, and ethnocentrism to match the potential complexity of individual cognitive systems.

REFERENCES

Aboud, F. E. and Taylor, D. M. "Ethnic and role stereotypes: their relative importance in person perception." Journal of Social Psychology, 1971, 85, 17-27.

Abrahams, R. G. *The peoples of greater Unyamwezi, Tanzania.* London: International African Institute, 1967a.

– – –. *The political organization of Unyamwezi.* Cambridge, Eng.: Cambridge University Press, 1967b.

Ackerman, N. W. and Jahoda, M. *Anti-Semitism and emotional disorder.* New York: Harper, 1950.

Adorno, T. W., Frenkel-Brunswik, E., Levinson, D. and Sanford, R. *The authoritarian personality.* New York: Harper, 1950.

Allan, W. *The African husbandman.* Edinburgh: Oliver & Boyd, 1965.

Allport, G. W. *The nature of prejudice.* Reading, Mass.: Addison-Wesley, 1954.

– – – and Kramer, B. M. "Some roots of prejudice." Journal of Psychology, 1946, 22, 9-39.

Amir, Y. "Contact hypothesis in ethnic relations." Psychological Bulletin, 1969, 71, 319-341.

Austen, R. "Ntemiship, trade and state-building: political development among the Western Bantu of Tanzania." In D. F. McCall, N. R. Bennett and J. Butler (eds.) *Eastern African history.* New York: Praeger, 1969.

Baker, S. J. K. "Bunyoro–a regional appreciation." Uganda Journal, 1954, 18, 101-112.

– – –. "The geographical background of Western Uganda." Uganda Journal, 1958, 22, 1-10.

Banow, H. "Status reversal and political reaction: a case study of the Masai." EAISR Conference Papers, January, 1965.

Beattie, J. H. M. *Bunyoro: An African kingdom.* New York: Holt, Rinehart & Winston, 1960.

– – –. *The Nyoro state.* Oxford, Eng.: Oxford University Press, 1971.

Berrien, F. K. "Homeostasis in groups." General Systems, 1964, 9, 205-217.

– – –. *General and social systems.* New Brunswik, N.J.: Rutgers University Press, 1968.

Berry, J. W. "A functional approach to the relationship between stereotypes and familiarity." Australian Journal of Psychology, 1970, 22, 29-33.

– – – and Annis, R. C. "Acculturative stress: The role of ecology, culture, and differentiation." Journal of Cross-Cultural Psychology, 1974, 5, 382-405.

Berscheid, E. and Walster, E. H. *Interpersonal attraction.* Reading, Mass.: Addison-Wesley, 1969.

Bogardus, E. S. "Measuring social distances." Journal of Applied Sociology, 1925, 9, 299-308.

– – –. *Immigration and race attitudes.* Lexington, Mass.: D. C. Heath, 1928.

Brewer, M. B. "Social distance among East African tribal groups." Ph.D. dissertation, Northwestern University, 1968a.

———. "Determinants of social distance among East African tribal groups." Journal of Personality and Social Psychology, 1968b, 10, 279-289.

———, Campbell, D. T. and Crano, W. D. "Testing a single-factor model as an alternative to the misuse of partial correlations in hypothesis-testing research." Sociometry, 1970, 33, 1-11.

Brigham, J. C. "Ethnic stereotypes." Psychological Bulletin, 1971, 76, 15-38.

———. "Racial stereotypes: measurement variables and the stereotype-attitude relationship." Journal of Applied Social Psychology, 1972, 2, 63-76.

Brislin, R. W. "Contact as a variable in intergroup interaction." Journal of Social Psychology, 1968, 76, 149-154.

Bruner, E. M. "Primary group experience and the process of acculturation." American Anthropologist, 1956, 58, 605-623.

Buchanan, W. "Stereotypes and tensions as revealed by the UNESCO international poll." International Social Science Bulletin, 1951, 3, 515-528.

——— and Cantril, H. How nations see each other. Urbana: University of Illinois Press, 1953.

Burke, R. G. Local government and politics in Uganda. Syracuse: Syracuse University Press, 1964.

Burnstein, E. and McRae, A. V. "Some effects of shared threat and prejudice in racially mixed groups." Journal of Abnormal and Social Psychology, 1962, 62, 257-263.

Butt, A. Nilotes of the Anglo-Egyptian Sudan and Uganda. London: International African Institute, 1960.

Byrne, D. "Attitudes and attraction." In L. Berkowitz (ed.) Advances in experimental social psychology, Vol. 4. New York: Academic Press, 1969.

——— and Nelson, D. "Attraction as a linear function of proportion of positive reinforcements." Journal of Personality and Social Psychology, 1965, 1, 659-663.

Campbell, D. T. "Enhancement of contrast as a composite habit." Journal of Abnormal and Social Psychology, 1956, 53, 350-355.

———. "Common fate, similarity, and other indices of the status of aggregates of persons as social entities." Behavioral Science, 1958, 3, 14-25.

———. "Methodological suggestions from a comparative psychology of knowledge processes." Inquiry, 1959, 2, 152-182.

———. "Distinguishing differences of perception from failures of communication in cross-cultural studies." In F. Northrop and H. Livingston (eds.) Cross-cultural understanding: Epistemology in anthropology. New York: Harper & Row, 1964.

———. "Stereotypes and perception of group differences." American Psychologist, 1967, 22, 812-829.

——— and Kral, T. P. "Transposition away from a rewarded stimulus card to a non-rewarded one as a function of a shift in background." Journal of Comparative and Physiological Psychology, 1958, 51, 592-595.

Campbell, D. T. and LeVine, R. A. "Ethnocentrism and intergroup relations." In R. Abelson, E. Aronson, W. McGuire, T. Newcomb, M. Rosenberg and P. Tannebaum (eds.) Theories of cognitive consistency: A sourcebook. Chicago: Rand McNally, 1968.

———. "Field manual anthropology." In R. Naroll and R. Cohen (eds.) A handbook of method in cultural anthropology. Garden City, N.Y.: Natural History Press, 1970.

Carter, L. F. "The identification of 'racial' membership." Journal of Abnormal and Social Psychology, 1948, 43, 279-286.

Cartwright, D. and Harary, F. "Structural balance: a generalization of Heider's theory." Psychological Review, 1956, 63, 277-293.

Clarke, R. B. and Campbell, D. T. "A demonstration of bias in estimates of Negro ability." Journal of Abnormal and Social Psychology, 1955, 51, 585-588.

Cliffe, L. and Puritt, P. "Arusha: mixed urban and rural communities." In L. Cliffe (ed.) One party democracy. Nairobi: East African Publishing House, 1967.

Cohen, R. "An investigation of the diagnostic processing of contradictory information." European Journal of Social Psychology, 1971, 1, 475-492.

Cohen, R. and Middleton, J. From tribe to nation in Africa: Studies in incorporation processes. San Francisco: Chandler, 1970.

Colson, E. "African society at the time of the scramble." In L. Gann and P. Duignan (eds.) Colonialism in Africa 1870-1960. Vol. 1. The history and politics of colonialism 1870-1914. Cambridge, Eng.: Cambridge University Press, 1969.

Coser, L. A. The functions of social conflict. Glencoe, Ill.: Free Press, 1956.

Daniels, R. E. "By rites a man: a study of the societal and individual foundations of tribal identity among the Kipsigis of Kenya." Ph.D. dissertation, University of Chicago, 1970.

Davis, J. A. "Structural balance, mechanical solidarity, and interpersonal relations." American Journal of Sociology, 1963, 68, 444-462.

– – –. "Clustering and structural balance in graphs." Human Relations, 1967, 20, 181-188.

Deutsch, M. and Collins, M. Interracial housing: A psychological evaluation of a social experiment. Minneapolis: University of Minnesota Press, 1951.

Diab, L. N. "Some factors determining national stereotypes." International Mental Health Research Newsletter, 1963, 5, 15-16.

Dion, K. L. "Cohesiveness as a determinant of ingroup-outgroup bias." Journal of Personality and Social Psychology, 1973, 28, 163-171.

Dittes, J. E. "Attractiveness of a group as a function of self-esteem and acceptance by the group." Journal of Abnormal and Social Psychology, 1959, 59, 77-82.

Dollard, J., Doob, L. W., Miller, N. E., Mowrer, O. H. and Sears, R. R. Frustration and aggression. New Haven: Yale University Press, 1939.

Driberg, J. H. The Lango. London: T. Fisher Urwin, Ltd., 1923.

Druckman, D. "Ethnocentrism in the Inter-Nation Simulation." Journal of Conflict Resolution, 1968, 12, 45-68.

Dudycha, G. J. "The attitudes of college students toward war and the Germans before and during the Second World War." Journal of Social Psychology, 1942, 15, 317-324.

Dunn, R. E. and Goldman, M. "Competition and noncompetition in relation to satisfaction and feelings toward own-group and nongroup members." Journal of Social Psychology, 1966, 68, 299-311.

Dyson-Hudson, N. Karamojong politics. London: Oxford University Press, 1966.

Edari, R. "Ethnic relations and prospects for national integration in Kenya." Ph.D. dissertation, Northwestern University, 1971.

Edgerton, R. B. " 'Cultural' vs. 'ecological' factors in the expression of values, attitudes, and personality characteristics." American Anthropologist, 1965, 67, 442-447.

Ehrlich, H. J. The social psychology of prejudice. New York: John Wiley, 1973.

– – – and Rinehart, J. W. "A brief report on the methodology of stereotype research." Social Forces, 1965, 43, 564-575.

Eiser, J. R. "Enhancement of contrast in the absolute judgment of attitude statements." Journal of Personality and Social Psychology, 1971a, 17, 1-10.
———. "Categorization, cognitive consistency and the concept of dimensional salience." European Journal of Social Psychology, 1971b, 1, 435-453.
——— and Stroebe, W. *Categorization and social judgement.* London: Academic Press, 1972.
Elliot, D. N. and Wittenberg, B. H. "Accuracy of identification of Jewish and non-Jewish photographs." Journal of Abnormal and Social Psychology, 1955, 51, 339-341.
Enloe, C. H. *Ethnic conflict and political development.* Boston: Little Brown, 1973.

Fallers, L. "Equality, modernity, and democracy in the new states." In C. Geertz (ed.) *Old societies and new states.* Glencoe, Ill.: Free Press, 1963.
Fallers, M. C. *The Eastern Lacustrine Bantu.* London: International African Institute, 1960.
Fearn, H. *An African economy: A study of the economic development of the Nyanza Province of Kenya.* London: Oxford University Press, 1961.
Feldman, J. M. "Stimulus characteristics and subject prejudice as determinants of stereotype attribution." Journal of Personality and Social Psychology, 1972, 21, 333-340.
Fosbrooke, H. A. "An administrative survey of the Masai social system." Tanganyika Notes and Records, 1948, 26, 1-50.
Freud, S. *Group psychology and the analysis of the ego.* London: Hogarth, 1921. [Standard Edition, Vol. XVIII, 1955.]
———. *Civilization and its discontents.* London: Hogarth, 1930. [Standard Edition, Vol. XXI, 1961.]

Gardner, R. C., Wonnacott, E. J. and Taylor, D. M. "Ethnic stereotypes: a factor analytic investigation." Canadian Journal of Psychology, 1968, 22, 35-44.
Geertz, C. (ed.) *Old societies and new states.* Glencoe, Ill.: Free Press, 1963.
Girling, F. K. *The Acholi of Uganda.* London: Colonial Research Studies 30, 1960.
Good, C. M. *Dimensions of East African culture.* East Lansing, Michigan: African Studies Center, 1966.
Gould, P. R. "Tanzania 1920-1963: the spatial impress of the modernization process." World Politics, 1970, 22, 149-170.
Greenberg, J. H. *Languages of Africa.* The Hague: Mouton, 1963.
Guetzkow, H. *Multiple loyalties: Theoretical approach to a problem in international organization.* Princeton: Princeton University Press, 1955.
Guilford, J. P. *Psychometric methods.* New York: McGraw-Hill, 1954.
Gulliver, P. and Gulliver, P. H. *The Central Nilo-Hamites.* London: International African Institute, 1960.
Gulliver, P. H. "A history of the relations between the Arusha and the Masai." EAISR Conference Papers, June, 1957.
———. *Social control in African Society: A study of the Arusha.* London: Routledge & Kegan Paul, 1963.

Harman, H. H. *Modern factor analysis.* Chicago: University of Chicago Press, 1960.
Heider, F. "Attitudes and cognitive organization." Journal of Psychology, 1946, 21, 107-112.
———. *The psychology of interpersonal relations.* New York: John Wiley, 1958.

Helson, H. *Adaptation-level theory.* New York: Harper & Row, 1964.

Hickman, G. M. and Dickens, W. H. G. *The lands and peoples of East Africa.* London: Longmans, 1960.

Himmelfarb, S. "Studies in the perception of ethnic group numbers. I: Accuracy, response bias, and anti-Semitism." Journal of Personality and Social Psychology, 1966, 4, 347-355.

Homans, G. C. *Social behavior: Its elementary forms.* New York: Harcourt, Brace & World, 1961.

Hoyle, B. S. "The economic expansion of Jinja, Uganda." Geographical Review, 1963, 53, 377-388.

Huntingford, G. W. B. *The Nandi of Kenya.* London: Routledge & Kegan Paul, 1953a.

–––. *The Southern Nilo-Hamites.* London: International African Institute, 1953b.

Jacobs, A. H. "Masai age groups and some functional tasks." EAISR Conference Papers, 1958.

Jones, A. H. "Spatial patterns of modernization." M.A. thesis, Makerere University, 1971.

Jones, R. A. and Ashmore, R. D. "The structure of intergroup perception: categories and dimensions in views of ethnic groups and adjectives used in stereotype research." Journal of Personality and Social Psychology, 1973, 25, 428-438.

Katz, D. and Braly, K. W. "Racial stereotypes of 100 college students." Journal of Abnormal and Social Psychology, 1933, 28, 280-290.

–––, Gutek, B. A., Kahn, R. L. and Barton, E. *Bureaucratic encounters: A pilot study in the evaluation of government services.* Ann Arbor: Survey Research Center, Institute for Social Research, 1975.

Klineberg, O. and Zavalloni, M. *Nationalism and tribalism among African students.* The Hague: Mouton, 1969.

LaFontaine, J. S. *The Gisu of Uganda.* London: International African Institute, 1959.

Lambert, H. E. *The use of indigenous authorities in tribal administration: Studies of the Meru.* Capetown: Communications of the School of African Studies 16, 1947.

–––. *Kikuyu social and political institutions.* London: International African Institute, 1956.

Lambert, W. E. and Klineberg, O. *Children's views of foreign peoples.* New York: Appleton-Century-Crofts, 1967.

Lawrence, J. C. D. *The Iteso.* London: Oxford University Press, 1957.

LeVine, R. A. "Outsiders' judgments: an ethnographic approach to group differences in personality." Southwestern Journal of Anthropology, 1966, 22, 101-116.

–––. "Ethnocentrism and intergroup conflict in stateless societies." Presented at Conference on Rage, Aggression, and Violence, Center for Advanced Study in the Behavioral Sciences, Stanford, California, April, 1972.

––– and Campbell, D. T. *The Gusii of Southwest Kenya: Interviews for the Cross-Cultural Study of Ethnocentrism.* Evanston: Northwestern University, 1964. (Also available as HRAFlex Volumes #FL8-001, 002, New Haven, Conn.: Human Relations Area Files, 1972.)

–––. *Ethnocentrism: Theories of conflict, ethnic attitudes and group behavior.* New York: John Wiley, 1972.

LeVine, R. A. and LeVine, B. *Nyansongo: A Gusii Community in Kenya.* New York: John Wiley, 1966.

Lindblom, G. *The Akamba in East Africa.* Upsala: University of Sweden, 1920.
Lindzey, G. and Rogolsky, S. "Prejudice and identification of minority group member-ship." Journal of Abnormal and Social Psychology, 1950, 45, 37-53.

MacCrone, I. D. *Race attitudes in South Africa.* London: Oxford University Press, 1937. (Reprinted 1957, 1965, Witwatersrand University Press.)
Malcolm, D. W. *Sukumaland: An African people and their country.* London: Oxford University Press, 1953.
Manners, R. A. "The Kipsigis–change with alacrity." In P. Bohannon and G. Dalton (eds.) *Markets in Africa.* New York: Doubleday, 1965.
Mapp, R. E. "Cross-national dimensions of ethnocentrism." Canadian Journal of African Studies, 1972, 6, 73-96.
Marealle, T. L. M. "The Wachagga of Kilimanjaro." Tanganyika Notes and Records, 1952, 32, 57-64.
Mayer, T. *Gusii.* London: Colonial Research Studies 3, 1965.
Meenes, M. A. "A comparison of racial stereotypes of 1935 and 1942." Journal of Social Psychology, 1943, 17, 327-336.
Merton, R. K. *Social theory and social structure.* Glencoe, Ill.: Free Press, 1949, 1957.
––– and Rossi, A. "Contributions to the theory of reference group behavior." In R. Merton (ed.) *Social theory and social structure.* Glencoe, Ill.: Free Press, 1957.
Middleton, J. *The central tribes of the Northeastern Bantu.* London: International African Institute, 1953.
––– and Kershaw, G. *The Kikuyu and Kamba of Kenya.* London: International African Institute, 1965.
Miller, J. G. "Living systems: structure and process." Behavioral Science, 1965, 10, 337-379.
Mitchell, J. C. "The Kalela dance." Rhodes-Livingstone Institute Paper 27, Manchester University Press, 1956.
Morris, H. F. R. "The making of Ankole." Uganda Journal, 1958, 22, 1.
Murdock, G. P. *Social structure.* New York: Macmillan, 1949.
Murphy, R. F. "Intergroup hostility and social cohesion." American Anthropologist, 1957, 59, 1018-1035.
Myrdal, G. *An American dilemma.* New York: Harper, 1944.

Newcomb, T. M. "An approach to the study of communicative acts." Psychological Review, 1953, 60, 393-404.
–––. "The prediction of interpersonal attraction." American Psychologist, 1956, 11, 575-586.
–––. *The acquaintance process.* New York: Holt, Rinehart & Winston, 1961.
–––. "Stabilities underlying changes in interpersonal attraction." Journal of Abnormal and Social Psychology, 1963, 66, 376-386.
–––. "Interpersonal balance." In R. Abelson, E. Aronson, W. McGuire, T. Newcomb, M. Rosenberg and P. Tannenbaum (eds.) *Theories of cognitive consistency: A sourcebook.* Chicago: Rand McNally, 1968.
Norman, W. "Cluster analysis: a diametric rationale and procedure." University of Michigan, 1968. (unpublished)

O'Connor, A. M. *An economic geography of East Africa.* London: G. Bell, 1966.
Ogot, B. A. *History of the Southern Luo. Vol. 1.* Nairobi: East African Publishing House, 1967.

Oliver, S. C. "Individuality, freedom of choice, and cultural flexibility of the Kamba." American Anthropologist, 1965, 67, 421.

Osogo, J. *A history of the Baluyia*. London: Oxford University Press, 1966.

Osgood, C. E. "Cognitive dynamics in human affairs." Public Opinion Quarterly, 1960, 24, 341-365.

–––. "Studies on the generality of affective meaning systems." American Psychologist, 1962, 17, 10-28.

–––, Suci, G. and Tannenbaum, P. H. *The measurement of meaning*. Urbana: University of Illinois Press, 1957.

Osgood, C. E. and Tannenbaum, P. H. "The principle of congruity in the prediction of attitude change." Psychological Review, 1955, 62, 42-55.

Peabody, D. "Trait inferences: evaluative and descriptive aspects." Journal of Personality and Social Psychology Monograph Supplement, 1967, 7, No. 4, Whole No. 644.

Pepinsky, H. B. and Patton, M. J. *The psychological experiment: A practical accomplishment*. New York: Pergamon Press, 1971.

Peristiany, J. G. *The social institutions of the Kipsigis*. London: Routledge, 1939.

Postman, L. "The experimental analysis of motivational factors in perception." In J. Brown et al. (eds.) *Current theory and research in motivation*. Lincoln: University of Nebraska Press, 1953.

–––, Bruner, J. S. and McGinnies, E. "Personal values as selective factors in perception." Journal of Abnormal and Social Psychology, 1948, 43, 142-154.

Przeworski, A. and Teune, H. "Equivalence in cross-national research." Public Opinion Quarterly, 1967, 30, 551-568.

Rabbie, J. M. and Horwitz, M. "Arousal of ingroup-outgroup bias by a chance win or loss." Journal of Personality and Social Psychology, 1969, 13, 269-277.

Rabbie, J. M. and Wilkens, G. "Intergroup competition and its effect on intragroup and intergroup relations." European Journal of Social Psychology, 1971, 1, 215-234.

Reigrotski, E. and Anderson, N. "National stereotypes and foreign contacts." Public Opinion Quarterly, 1959, 23, 515-528.

Richards, A. I. *Economic development and tribal change*. Cambridge, Eng.: W. Heffer, 1954.

–––. *East African chiefs*. London: Faber & Faber, 1960.

–––. *The multicultural states of East Africa*. Montreal: McGill-Queen's University Press, 1969.

Richardson, L. F. *Statistics of deadly quarrels*. London: Stevens, 1960.

Rigby, P. J. A. "Aspects of residence and cooperation in a Gogo village." EAISR Conference Papers, 1962a.

–––. "Witchcraft, kinship, and authority in Gogo." EAISR Conference Papers, 1962b.

Rokeach, M. *The open and closed mind*. New York: Basic Books, 1960.

Root, A. "The Karamojong." East African Annual, 1965, 59-64.

Roscoe, J. *The Northern Bantu*. London: Cambridge University Press, 1915.

Rosenberg, M. J. and Abelson, R. P. "An analysis of cognitive balancing." In M. Rosenberg, C. Hovland, W. McGuire, R. Abelson and J. Brehm (eds.) *Attitude organization and change*. New Haven: Yale University Press, 1960.

Rosenblatt, P. C. "Origins and effects of group ethnocentrism and nationalism." Journal of Conflict Resolution, 1964, 8, 131-146.

Saberwal, S. *The Embu of Kenya: Interviews for the Cross-Cultural Study of Ethno-centrism.* Evanston: Northwestern University, 1964. (Also available as HRAFlex Volumes #FL5-001, 002, New Haven, Conn.: Human Relations Area Files, 1972.)

———. *The traditional political system of the Embu of Central Kenya.* Nairobi: East African Publishing House, 1970.

Sangree, W. H. "The Bantu Tiriki of Western Kenya." In J. Gibbs (ed.) *Peoples of Africa.* New York: Holt, Rinehart & Winston, 1965.

———. *Age, prayer, and politics in Tiriki, Kenya.* London: Oxford University Press, 1966.

Scodel, A. and Austrin, H. "The perception of Jewish photographs by non-Jews and Jews." Journal of Abnormal and Social Psychology, 1957, 54, 278-280.

Shann, G. N. "The early development of education among the Chagga." Tanganyika Notes and Records, 1956, 45, 21-32.

Sherif, M. and Sherif, C. W. *Groups in harmony and tension.* New York: Harper, 1953.

Sherif, M., Harvey, O. J., White, B. J., Hood, W. R. and Sherif, C. W. *Intergroup conflict and cooperation: The Robber's Cave experiment.* Norman: University of Oklahoma Press, 1961.

Sinha, A. K. P. and Upadhyaya, O. P. "Change and persistence in the stereotypes of university students towards different ethnic groups during Sino/Indian border disputes." Journal of Social Psychology, 1960, 52, 31-39.

Sobel, L. "Demographic determinants of social distance in East Africa." M.A. thesis, Northwestern University, 1970.

Sofer, C. and Sofer, R. "Recent population growth in Jinja." Uganda Journal, 1953, 17, 38-53.

Soja, E. W. *The geography of modernization in Kenya.* Syracuse: Syracuse University Press, 1968.

Spence, K. *Behavior theory and conditioning.* New Haven: Yale University Press, 1956.

Stahl, K. M. *History of the Chagga people of Kilimanjaro.* The Hague: Mouton, 1964.

Sumner, W. G. *Folkways.* New York: Ginn, 1906.

Sumner, W. G., Keller, A. G. and Davie, M. R. *The science of society.* New Haven: Yale University Press, 1927.

Suttles, G. D. *The social construction of communities.* Chicago: University of Chicago Press, 1972.

Taft, R. "Ethnic stereotypes, attitudes, and familiarity: Australia." Journal of Social Psychology, 1959, 49, 177-186.

Tajfel, H. and Wilkes, A. L. "Classification and quantitative judgement." British Journal of Psychology, 1963, 54, 101-114.

Tarantino, A. "Lango wars." Uganda Journal, 1949, 13, 109.

Taylor, B. K. *The Western Lacustrine Bantu.* London: International African Institute, 1962.

Thibaut, J. and Kelley, H. *The social psychology of groups.* New York: John Wiley, 1959.

Triandis, H. C. "Exploratory factor analyses of the behavioral component of social attitudes." Journal of Abnormal and Social Psychology, 1964, 68, 420-430.

———. *Attitude and attitude change.* New York: John Wiley, 1971.

———. *The analysis of subjective culture.* New York: John Wiley, 1972.

——— and Vassiliou, V. "Frequency of contact and stereotyping." Journal of Personality and Social Psychology, 1967, 7, 316-328.

Vinacke, W. E. "Stereotyping among national-racial groups in Hawaii: a study in ethnocentrism." Journal of Social Psychology, 1949, 30, 265-291.
———. "Explorations in the dynamics of stereotyping." Journal of Social Psychology, 1956, 43, 105-132.

Wagner, G. *The Bantu of North Kavirondo.* London: Oxford University Press, 1956.
Were, G. S. *A history of the Abaluyia of Western Kenya.* Nairobi: East African Publishing House, 1967.
Werner, O. and Campbell, D. T. "Translating, working through interpreters, and the problem of decentering." In R. Naroll and R. Cohen (eds.) *A handbook of method in cultural anthropology.* Garden City, N.Y.: Natural History Press, 1970.
Wesley, J. P. "Frequency of wars and geographical opportunity." Journal of Conflict Resolution, 1962, 6, 387-389.
Whiting, J. W. M. and Child, I. L. *Child training and personality: A cross-cultural study.* New Haven: Yale University Press, 1953.
Wilson, G. "Tribalism in Kenya." Nairobi, Marco Surveys, Report No. 8, 1961.
Wilson, W. and Miller, N. "Shifts in evaluations of participants following intergroup competition." Journal of Abnormal and Social Psychology, 1961, 63, 428-431.
Wilson, W., Chun, N. and Kayatani, M. "Projection, attraction and strategy choices in intergroup competition." Journal of Personality and Social Psychology, 1965, 2, 432-435.
Winans, E. V. *Shabala: The constitution of a traditional state.* Berkeley: University of California Press, 1962.
Wyatt, D. F. and Campbell, D. T. "On the liability of stereotype or hypothesis." Journal of Abnormal and Social Psychology, 1951, 46, 496-500.

Zajonc, R. B. "Attitudinal effects of mere exposure." Journal of Personality and Social Psychology, 1968, 9, 1-27.
Zawadski, B. "Limitations of the scapegoat theory of prejudice." Journal of Abnormal and Social Psychology, 1942, 43, 127-141.
Ziegler, M., King, M., King, J. and Ziegler, S. "Tribal stereotypes among Ethiopian students." Journal of Cross-Cultural Psychology, 1972, 3, 193-200.

ACKNOWLEDGMENTS

The research reported herein was supported primarily by a grant from the Carnegie Corporation of New York awarded to Northwestern University in 1963. Later analyses, completed after the Carnegie grant had expired, were funded through NSF Grant GSOC-7103704. Robert A. LeVine, co-principal investigator of the CCSE project, was an active participant in all phases of planning and completing the East African survey. His continuing advice and support in the preparation of this volume is gratefully acknowledged by the authors.

ABOUT THE AUTHORS

MARILYNN B. BREWER received her Ph.D. in social psychology from Northwestern University in 1968. She is currently Associate Professor of Psychology at the University of California at Santa Barbara. She has co-authored a book on research methodology, *Principles of Research in Social Psychology*, and is actively engaged in both experimental and field research in the areas of person perception and social judgment.

DONALD T. CAMPBELL is Professor of Psychology at Northwestern University. He has published extensively over the past twenty-five years in the fields of behavioral science, social psychology, experimental psychology and methodology, and clinical psychology, among others. Many of his works have become seminal to the disciplines. He is presently President of the American Psychological Association, and has previously been president of the Midwestern Psychological Association (1967) and of the Division of Personality and Social Psychology of the APA (1969). He was the recipient in 1970 of one of the Awards for Distinguished Scientific Contribution given by the APA.

APPENDIX A.

Background Information on Groups Surveyed

KENYA

1. Kikuyu

    Language-culture grouping: Bantu
    Topography: sufficient rainfall (40"+); high land elevation (5,000'+)
    Population:[a] 1,291,493 total; 343/sq. mi.
    Economy:[c] mixed farming; cash crops of coffee and cotton
    Advancement rating:[d] 3 (High advanced)
    Comments: Kikuyu secret societies were responsible for the famous Mau-Mau uprising. Kikuyu reserves are surrounded by land alienated to Europeans; many became "squatters" on European farms and worked for the owners in order to remain on land they considered their own. Nairobi, the largest city in East Africa, is contained in an Extra-provincial District adjacent to Kikuyu lands.
    Major ethnography sources: Lambert (1956); Middleton (1953); Middleton and Kershaw (1965).

2. Embu

    Language-culture grouping: Bantu
    Topography: moderate annual rainfall (40"-50"); population concentrated on east slopes of Mt. Kenya
    Population:[a] 292,276 total; 183/sq. mi.
    Economy: mixed farming; Kenya's second largest coffee exporter
    Advancement rating: 2 (Intermediate)
    Comments: Embuland is almost a continuation of Kikuyuland but with less favorable ecological situation (lower altitudes, less rain, poorer soil) and somewhat less contact with Europeans.
    Major ethnography sources: Middleton, (1953); Saberwal (1970)

3. Meru

    Language-culture grouping: Bantu
    Topography: annual rainfall increases from lowlands (under 20") to the mountain slopes (70"+)
    Population:[a] 468,223 total; 125/sq. mile
    Economy: mixed farming; Kenya's largest coffee exporter
    Advancement rating: 2 (Intermediate)
    Comments: Meru are ethnically similar to Kikuyu and Embu but are located

farther from the European Highlands; lacking in transportation and communication facilities and industrial development. Meru are distinguished from related Bantu by the relative importance of kinship groups.

Major ethnography sources: Lambert (1947); Middleton (1953)

4. Kamba

Language-culture grouping: Bantu

Topography: more than half the area has insufficient (less than 20″) annual rainfall; some areas, near the district capital cities of Machakos and Kitui, have sufficient rainfall (40″-50″).

Population:[a] 832,642 total; 48/sq. mi.

Economy: varies, according to rainfall zone, from mixed farming to subsistence agriculture to pastoralism and hunting and gathering.

Advancement rating: 2 (Intermediate)

Comments: The Kamba occupy two large districts with important ecological variations. The good farming areas are in the west, closer to the European Highlands, while for large stretches of the eastern portions, the few pastoralists that live there must supplement their diet with hunting and gathering. The Kamba stress the importance of the clan as a mutual aid society.

Major ethnography sources: Lindblom (1920); Middleton (1953); Middleton and Kershaw (1965); Oliver (1965)

5. Luhya

Language-culture grouping: Bantu

Topography: almost entirely excellent rainfall (60″+), good soil

Population:[a] 954,029 total; 353/sq. mi. (much denser—up to 1800/sq. mi. in South)

Economy: mixed farming and subsistence agriculture; some fishing

Advancement rating: 2 (Intermediate)

Comments: Abaluyia consists of at least 18 disparate sub-groups and many autonomous villages, characterized by considerable internecine hostilities. The southern sub-groups, particularly the Maragoli (where the survey was conducted), also have a history of warfare with the Luo, but some Luhya groups, such as the Bunyala, were on better terms with Luo than with other Luhya.

Major ethnography sources: Fearn (1961); Osogo (1966); Sangree (1965, 1966); Wagner (1956); Were (1967)

6. Gusii

Language-culture grouping: Bantu

Topography: entire district has 50″+ annual rainfall, parts up to 80″

Population:[a] 518,226 total; 690/sq. mi.

Economy: mixed farming

Advancement rating: 2 (Intermediate)

Comments: The Gusii are relatively prosperous but culturally static (e.g., the continued practice of trephining). Historically, the group has been characterized by frequent internecine warfare.

Major ethnography sources: LeVine and LeVine (1966); Mayer (1965)

7. Kipsigis

Language-culture group: Nilo-Hamitic (Southern Nilotic; "Kalenjin")
Topography: entire district between 50"-70" annual rainfall
Population:[a] 386,951 total; 183/sq. mi.
Economy: mixed farming; maize for cash, tea plantations, some shopkeeping
Advancement rating: 2 (Intermediate)
Comments: Kipsigis lands are bordered on three sides by land alienated to Europeans. One of the few places in East Africa with soil and rainfall suitable for growing tea, Kericho District has a number of large tea plantations owned by Europeans. Generally, Kipsigis farmers are too well off to be interested in emigrant labor, so most plantation laborers are Luo, Luhya, and Gusii. Many Kipsigis have become shopkeepers who sell consumer goods to plantation workers. Despite their agricultural prosperity, Kipsigis still place emphasis on cattle as a measure of wealth. Traditionally, Kipsigis are well-known for having no fear of night, which has been significant in their military history.

Major ethnography sources: Hickman and Dickens (1960); Manners (1965); Peristiany (1939)

8. Nandi

Language-culture grouping: Nilo-Hamitic (Southern Nilotic; "Kalenjin")
Topography: entire district between 50"-70" annual rainfall
Population:[a] 118,859 total; 167/sq. mi.
Economy: mixed farming, with emphasis on pastoralism
Advancement rating: 2 (Intermediate)
Comments: The Nandi were among the most troublesome groups during the period of formation of the Protectorate government. The object of five punitive expeditions, their herds were largely destroyed and they were confined to a reserve. Ethnically they are very similar to the Kipsigis but have not received the same training in agricultural techniques and development.

Major ethnography sources: Huntingford (1953a, 1953b)

9. Masai

Language-culture grouping: Nilo-Hamitic (Eastern Nilotic)
Topography: mostly under 20" annual rainfall, with some pockets of sufficient rainfall (30"-50")
Population:[a] 177,424 total; 12/sq. mi.
Economy: pure pastoralism
Advancement rating: 1 (Low advanced)
Comments: Devoted to maintaining their pastoral way of life centered around

cattle, the adaptations the Masai have made to modern conditions have generally served the purpose of maintaining the status quo. The most admired and feared ethnic group east of Lake Victoria in the mid-nineteenth century, they have suffered a marked reversal in status during the period of modernization.

Major ethnography sources: Banow (1965); Fosbrooke (1948); Jacobs (1958)

10. Luo

Language-culture grouping: Western Nilotic
Topography: mostly sufficient (40"+) annual rainfall
Population:[a] 1,133,553 total; 282/sq. mi.
Economy: mixed farming; some trade, fishing
Advancement rating: 2 (Intermediate)
Comments: Luo territory includes the part of Kisumu on the Kavirondo Gulf which, as an important center for the pre-colonial trade that flourished on Lake Victoria, was linked to Mombasa by the Kenya-Uganda Railway at the beginning of the century. Many Luo and Luhya were put to work on the construction of this railroad, which early set the pattern of wage labor and emigration for these groups. To neighboring groups, the most salient distinguishing feature of the Luo is that they do not practice circumcision and also that they "eat fish." The Luo have maintained an extended family system and play a leadership role in trade union movements and politics.

Major ethnography sources: Butt (1960); Fearn (1961); Ogot (1967); Wagner (1956)

UGANDA

1. Ganda

Language-culture grouping: Bantu
Topography: mostly sufficient (40"+) annual rainfall, more in the "elephant grass zone" littoral of Lake Victoria
Population:[b] 1,834,128 total; 128.6/sq. mi.
Economy: peasant cultivation; coffee and cotton as cash crops; some industry
Advancement rating: 3 (High advanced)
Comments: The Ganda city of Kampala and its environs form the nerve center of the nation, the focus of commerce, industry, government, religion, and education. The Ganda have been very receptive to education and have a tradition of encouraging talent in appointive posts. The British early recognized Ganda political sophistication; they enlarged Buganda at the expense of neighboring groups, gave Ganda chiefs more power and autonomy than other native rulers, and gave Ganda free-hold rights to land and put them in administration posts over other ethnic groups.

Major ethnography sources: Fallers (1960); Richards (1954, 1960)

2. Nyoro

    Language-culture grouping: Bantu
    Topography: mostly sufficient rainfall (40"-60" annually)
    Population:[b] 126,875 total; 26.9/sq. mi.
    Economy: subsistence agriculture with some small income from cash crops
    Advancement rating: 2 (Intermediate)
    Comments: Once the most powerful kingdom in Uganda, and the chief rival
            of Buganda, the Nyoro now form a demoralized group, feeling
            poor, cheated, and resentful of their loss of eminence. The British
            allocated considerable Nyoro territory to districts of other groups
            and put Ganda chiefs in Nyoro district administration.
    Major ethnography sources: Baker (1954, 1958); Beattie (1960, 1971); Burke
             (1964); Taylor (1962)

3. Toro

    Language-culture grouping: Bantu
    Topography: mostly 40" annual rainfall, rising to 65"+ in Ruwenzori
            Mountains
    Population:[b] 347,479 total; 73.2/sq. mi.
    Economy: peasant cultivation; coffee and cotton cash crops; copper mines
            and salt deposits
    Advancement rating: 2 (Intermediate)
    Comments: During the 19th century, Toro was merely a province of Bun-
            yoro. The district has many ecological advantages but rapid
            economic advancement has been held back by lack of transporta-
            tion and communication facilities.
    Major ethnography sources: O'Connor (1966); Taylor (1962)

4. Soga

    Language-culture grouping: Bantu
    Topography: all sufficient (40"+) annual rainfall, over 50" in "elephant grass
            zone"
    Population:[b] 660,507 total; 191.8/sq. mi.
    Economy: peasant cultivation; primarily cotton, some coffee, for market
    Advancement rating: 2 (Intermediate)
    Comments: In Soga territory, Jinja, located at the point where Lake Victoria
            empties into the Nile, is the site of Owen Falls Dam and a
            hydro-electric power station which attracts immigrants from the
            Northern Province. However, industrial development has not been
            up to expectations. The Soga are still more traditional and their
            population more ethnically and culturally uniform than Ganda.
    Major ethnography sources: Fallers (1960); Hoyle (1963); Richards (1960);
             Sofer and Sofer (1953)

5. Ankole

    Language-culture grouping: Bantu
    Topography: mostly sufficient (40"+) annual rainfall

Population:[b] 529,712 total; 89.4/sq. mi.

Economy: primarily subsistence agriculture; some pastoralists; some ground-
          nuts and coffee for cash crops

Advancement rating: 2 (Intermediate)

Comments: The relatively slow economic development of the Ankole has
          been blamed on late introduction of cash crops and lack of access
          to markets. Historically, the pastoral Bahima dominated over the
          agricultural Bahera subgroup. The Banyankole maintained friend-
          ship with stronger, hostile neighboring groups by frequent gifts of
          cattle.

Major ethnography sources: Morris (1958); Roscoe (1915); Taylor (1962)

6. Gisu

Language-culture grouping: Bantu

Topography: located on the slopes of Mt. Elgon with rich, deep volcanic loam
          soil, sufficient annual rainfall (40"-75")

Population:[b] 352,885 total; 215.4/sq. mi.

Economy: mixed farming; varied cash crops including maize, coffee, cotton;
          large cattle herds

Advancement rating: 2 (Intermediate)

Comments: The politically and economically powerful kin groups may be a
          force for conservatism among the Gisu who lag behind other
          ethnic groups with comparable resources in respect to urbaniza-
          tion and education.

Major ethnography sources: Allan (1965); LaFontaine (1959)

7. Teso

Language-culture grouping: Nilo-Hamitic (Eastern Nilotic)

Topography: almost all areas with 40"+ annual rainfall

Population:[b] 453,474 total; 105.3/sq. mi.

Economy: mixed farming; cotton grown for cash crop; leads nation in cattle
          exports

Advancement rating: 2 (Intermediate)

Comments: Teso are the most progressive non-Bantu group in the survey,
          considered by the British to have a model district in agriculture
          and animal care.

Major ethnography sources: Allan (1965); Burke (1964); Lawrence (1957)

8. Lango

Language-culture grouping: Western Nilotic

Topography: almost all 40"+ annual rainfall but with a long dry season

Population:[b] 352,943 total; 79.1/sq. mi.

Economy: annual crops; raise cattle and cotton for market

Advancement rating: 2 (Intermediate)

Comments: In the 200 years preceding British colonialism, the Lango were a
          very powerful and warlike group, warring both internally and

with their neighbors—especially the various sub-groups of the Acholi. Lango economy and status system was based on cattle, which are still of considerable importance.

Major ethnography sources: Butt (1960); Driberg (1923); Tarantino (1949)

9. Acholi

Language-culture grouping: Western Nilotic

Topography: poor soil; mostly 40''+ annual rainfall but large areas in the east and northwest under 40''

Population: [b] 285,530 total; 26.5/sq. mi.

Economy: subsistence agriculture; some cotton for cash

Advancement rating: 2 (Intermediate)

Comments: Once part of the Bunyoro-Kitara Kingdom, Acholi are culturally very close to Lango but with somewhat less emphasis on cattle as the symbol of wealth and status and more emphasis on maintenance of chiefly power.

Major ethnography sources: Girling (1960)

10. Karamojong

Language-culture grouping: Nilo-Hamitic (Eastern Nilotic)

Topography: almost entire district under 40'' annual rainfall

Population: [b] 171,945 total; 15.8/sq. mi.

Economy: pastoralism; semi-nomadism to dry areas during rainy season to permanent watering holes for dry season

Advancement rating: 1 (Low advanced)

Comments: The Karamojong live almost entirely unaffected by European contact, the only real change in their life-style being the elimination of constant warfare. The men and boys in cattle camps still subsist on milk, blood, and meat.

Major ethnography sources: Dyson-Hudson (1966); Root (1965)

TANZANIA

1. Chagga

Language-culture grouping: Bantu

Topography: located on the slopes of Mt. Kilimanjaro, zones of 40'' to 90'' annual rainfall

Population: [b] 359,094 total; 179.5/sq. mi.

Economy: mixed farming; variety of cash crops including coffee

Advancement rating: 3 (High advanced)

Comments: The Chagga appear to be the richest and most progressive group in Tanzania. Chagga themselves took over all commerce on Mt. Kilimanjaro, confining the Asian population to one town in the plains. They are noted for a high standard and rate of literacy.

Major ethnography sources: Allan (1965); Marealle (1952); Shann (1956);
Stahl (1964)

2. Pare

Language-culture grouping: Bantu
Topography: terraced villages and grassland; adequate (40″) annual rainfall
Population: [b] 108,436 total; 34.4/sq. mi.
Economy: mixed farming; some cash crops
Advancement rating: 2 (Intermediate)
Comments: The Pare are closer to some Nilotic groups than most Bantu, with
           some historical connection with the Luo. In recent times, the
           Pare have shown considerable economic advancement, maintain-
           ing close relations with Chagga and Sambaa Bantu.
Major ethnography sources: Butt (1960); Huntingford (1953b)

3. Sambaa

Language-culture grouping: Bantu
Topography: population concentrated in Usambara Mountains with annual
             rainfall zones from 30″ to 90″
Population: [b] 263,887 total; 74.3/sq. mi.
Economy: mixed farming
Advancement rating: 2 (Intermediate)
Comments: The Sambaa, though Bantu-speaking, are distinguished from their
           otherwise linguistically and culturally similar coastal neighbors by
           their concept of "rulership," involving a highly centralized power-
           ful state. Migrants tend to go to large towns, rather than adjacent
           farms and plantations, for wage labor and tend to be rather
           long-term urban dwellers.
Major ethnography sources: Winans (1962)

4. Arusha

Language-culture grouping: mixed Nilo-Hamitic and Bantu (Masai dialect)
Topography: located on the slopes of Mt. Meru; annual rainfall zones from
             30″ to 90″
Population: [b] 142,391 total; 123.8/sq. mi.
Economy: mixed farming with bananas, maize, coffee, and onions for market
Advancement rating: 2 (Intermediate)
Comments: With mixed ethnic origins, the Arusha have had a symbiotic
           relationship with the Masai, trading agricultural products for
           pastoral products from them. Traditionally, the Arusha admired
           and imitated Masai to a high degree, freely acknowledging their
           cultural and historical dependence on them, but many modern
           Arusha resent this dependence and are very ambivalent in their
           attitudes toward Masai. Arusha tend to be conservative, though
           agriculturally developed. Large areas of Arusha land have been
           alienated to Europeans.
Major ethnography sources: Cliffe and Puritt (1967); Gulliver (1957, 1963);
                            Gulliver and Gulliver (1960)

5. Meru

Language-culture grouping: mixed Bantu and Nilo-Hamitic
Topography: located on the slopes of Mt. Meru with annual rainfall zones
             from 30″ to 90″

Population: [b] (included in Arusha figures)
Economy: mixed farming and cash crops
Advancement rating: 2 (Intermediate)
Comments: During the late 19th century, Meru were continually raided and
           subjugated by the Arusha, accounting for their mixed ethnic
           origins. More recently, the Meru have been quicker to shed their
           ties to Masai culture and those in the Western region have shown
           rapid economic advancement. (Meru and Arusha are included in
           the same governmental district, hence the combined district
           population figures.)
Major ethnography sources: Gulliver and Gulliver (1960)

6. Sukuma

Language-culture grouping: Bantu
Topography: rainfall zones ranging from 20″ to 30″-40″
Population: [b] 977,062 total; density ranges, by district, from 32.7 to 153.3/
           sq. mi.
Economy: mixed farming and subsistence agriculture; some cotton for
           market
Advancement rating: 2 (Intermediate)
Comments: Sukuma occupy large tracts of land of marginal rainfall and
           fertility, portions of which are overpopulated. The government
           has sponsored a variety of development programs and redistribu-
           tion schemes in the Sukuma districts which have met with only
           moderate success.
Major ethnography sources: Allan (1965); Malcolm (1953)

7. Nyamwezi

Language-culture grouping: Bantu
Topography: annual rainfall from 20″ to 40″
Population: [b] 365,743 total; density ranges, by district, from 6.5 to
           39.2/sq. mi.
Economy: mixed farming and subsistence agriculture
Advancement rating: 2 (Intermediate)
Comments: As a tribe, the Nyamwezi overlaps with the Sukuma, Sukuma
           meaning "people of the north" and Nyamwezi "people of the
           south." Ethnically and linguistically they are not distinguishable.
Major ethnography sources: Abrahams (1967a, 1967b) (See also Sukuma
                            sources)

8. Gogo

Language-culture grouping: Bantu
Topography: entire district under 30″ annual rainfall
Population: [b] 236,152 total; 36.6/sq. mi.
Economy: pastoral; some subsistence agriculture
Advancement rating: 1 (Low advanced)
Comments: The Gogo society is extremely open, with frequent and easy
           assimilation of other ethnic groups. In addition, constant up-

heavals, due to droughts and famines in the area, have led to a
"blurring" of ethnic origins. Economic values still center on cattle.

Major ethnography sources: Rigby (1962a, 1962b)

9. Luo

Language-culture grouping: Western Nilotic
Topography: most of district has 40"+ rainfall
Population:[b] 145,029 total; 96.7/sq. mi.
Economy: mixed farming; fishing
Advancement rating: 2 (Intermediate)
Comments: The tribal lands of the Luo are artificially divided by the Kenya-
Tanzania international border, but there is no corresponding
social or economic division. The Luo of Tanzania are too few to
have much national influence, unlike the role of the Kenya Luo.

Major ethnography sources: (see Kenya Luo)

10. Masai

Language-culture grouping: Nilo-Hamitic (Eastern Nilotic)
Topography: almost entirely under 30" annual rainfall
Population:[b] 64,276 total; 2.8/sq. mi.
Economy: pure pastoralist
Advancement rating: 1 (Low advanced)
Comments: Like the Luo, Masai territory is divided between Kenya and
Tanzania. The Tanzania Masai tend to be somewhat poorer, less
educated, and less numerous than the Kenya Masai.

Major ethnography sources: (see Kenya Masai)

———————————————————

[a]Population figures based on 1962 Kenya District Census
[b]Population figures based on 1957 General African Census
[c]Under types of economy:

Mixed farming = stock-keeping and cultivation equally important
Subsistence agriculture = low-yield cultivation
Peasant cultivation = more prosperous cultivation; stock-keeping relatively minor

[d]See Chapter 4 for discussion of advancement ratings

APPENDIX B.

Demographic Characteristics of Respondents in Each Ethnic Group

Legend:
M.I. = Average Respondent Moderization Index (Scale:-2.00-+2.00)

Literacy
1 = Illiterate
2 = Reads only tribal language
3 = Speaks and reads English

Education
0 = None
1 = Some Elementary
2 = Completed Elementary
3 = Some Secondary
4 = Completed Secondary
5 = Some College/University

KENYA	Literacy	Marital Status	Males	Females	Age		Education	
Kikuyu	1: 9	Single:	13	9	12-15 yrs:	0	0:	22
	2: 12	Married						
(M.I.= .30)	3: 29	(Mono):	19	6	16-18:	12	1:	7
		Married						
		(Poly):	2	0	19-24:	18	2:	13
		Widowed:	0	1	25-34:	15	3:	6
					35-44:	4	4:	2
		Total	34	16	45 +:	1	5:	0
Embu	1: 19	Single:	7	4	12-15 yrs:	0	0:	20
	2: 2	Married						
		(Mono):	18	9	16-18:	3	1:	6
(M.I.= -.09)	3: 29	Married						
		(Poly):	7	0	19-24:	18	2:	16
		Widowed:	3	2	25-34:	14	3:	4
					35-44:	11	4:	4
		Total	35	15	45 +:	4	5:	0
Meru	1: 14	Single:	11	0	12-15 yrs:	0	0:	20
	2: 6	Married						
		(Mono):	23	7	16-18:	7	1:	0
(M.I.= .03)	3: 30	Married						
		(Poly):	0	9	19-24:	27	2:	20
		Widowed:	0	0	25-34:	15	3:	4
					35-44:	1	4:	6
		Total	34	16	45 +:	0	5:	0
Kamba	1: 20	Single:	15	8	12-15 yrs:	0	0:	20
	2: 2	Married						
		(Mono):	16	7	16-18:	0	1:	10
(M.I.= .06)	3: 28	Married						
		(Poly):	4	0	19-24:	21	2:	10
		Widowed:	0	0	25-34:	21	3:	8
					35-44:	6	4:	2
		Total	35	15	45 +:	2	5:	0

KENYA (continued)	Literacy	Marital Status	Males	Females	Age		Education	
Luhya	1: 19	Single:	10	5	12-15 yrs:	0	0:	20
	2: 22	Married						
		(Mono):	19	9	16-18:	10	1:	21
(M.I.= -.90)	3: 9	Married						
		(Poly)	4	2	19-24:	12	2:	0
		Widowed:	1	0	25-34:	16	3:	9
		Total	34	16	35-44:	9	4:	0
					45 +:	3	5:	0
Gusii	1: 22	Single:	7	3	12-15 yrs:	0	0:	23
	2: 7	Married						
		(Mono):	20	9	16-18:	2	1:	13
(M.I.= -.58)	3: 21	Married						
		(Poly):	8	2	19-24:	13	2:	5
		Widowed:	0	1	25-34:	22	3:	8
		Total	35	15	35-44:	11	4:	0
					45 +:	2	5:	1
Kipsigis	1: 20	Single:	10	9	12-15 yrs:	0	0:	20
	2: 5	Married						
		(Mono):	18	5	16-18:	5	1:	11
(M.I.= .05)	3: 25	Married						
		(Poly):	5	3	19-24:	13	2:	8
		Widowed:	0	0	25-34:	12	3:	8
		Total	33	17	35-44:	5	4:	2
					45 +:	15	5:	1
Nandi	1: 20	Single:	11	6	12-15 yrs:	0	0:	20
	2: 20	Married						
		(Mono):	16	8	16-18:	10	1:	20
(M.I.= -.85)	3: 10	Married						
		(Poly):	8	1	19-24:	19	2:	0
		Widowed:	0	0	25-34:	14	3:	10
		Total	35	15	35-44:	6	4:	0
					45 +:	1	5:	0

KENYA (continued)	Literacy		Marital Status	Males	Females	Age		Education	
Masai	1: 41	Single:		5	0	12-15 yrs:	0	0:	41
	2: 3	Married (Mono):		9	3	16-18:	0	1:	3
(M.I.* -1.85)	3: 6	Married (Poly):		24	9	19-24:	15	2:	6
		Widowed:		0	0	25-34:	25	3:	0
						35-44:	8	4:	0
		Total		38	12	45 +:	2	5:	0
Luo	1: 18	Single:		12	4	12-15 yrs:	0	0:	18
	2: 10	Married (Mono):		10	7	16-18:	2	1:	11
(M.I.= -.24)	3: 22	Married (Poly):		15	1	19-24:	16	2:	10
		Widowed:		1	0	25-34:	16	3:	8
						35-44:	10	4:	2
		Total		38	12	45 +:	6	5:	1
UGANDA									
Ganda	1: 4	Single:		19	6	12-15 yrs:	1	0:	2
	2: 9	Married (Mono):		21	3	16-18:	5	1:	13
(M.I.=1.75)	3: 37	Married (Poly):		1	0	19-24:	9	2:	3
		Widowed:		0	0	25-34:	21	3:	6
						35-44:	14	4:	21
		Total		41	9	45 +:	0	5:	5
Yoro	1: 11	Single:		13	6	12-15 yrs:	1	0:	11
	2: 9	Married (Mono):		23	3	16-18:	3	1:	11
(M.I.=.49)	3: 30	Married (Poly):		4	1	19-24:	18	2:	6
		Widowed:		0	0	25-34:	19	3:	5
						35-44:	4	4:	17
		Total		40	10	45 +:	5	5:	0

UGANDA (continued)	Literacy	Marital Status	Males	Females	Age		Education	
Toro	1: 19	Single:	8	8	12-15 yrs:	0	0:	20
	2: 19	Married						
		(Mono):	21	6	16-18:	1	1:	12
(M.I.= -.50)	3: 12	Married						
		(Poly):	5	0	19-24:	12	2:	8
		Widowed:	1	1	25-34:	7	3:	1
		Total	35	15	35-44:	15	4:	8
					45 +:	15	5:	1
Soga	1: 13	Single:	10	5	12-15 yrs:	0	0:	20
	2: 27	Married						
		(Mono):	19	9	16-18:	4	1:	13
(M.I.=.67)	3: 10	Married						
		(Poly):	7	0	19-24:	8	2:	7
		Widowed:	0	0	25-34:	22	3:	7
		Total	36	14	35-44:	12	4:	3
					45 +:	4	5:	0
Gisu	1: 24	Single:	8	5	12-15 yrs:	0	0:	20
	2: 8	Married						
		(Mono):	18	7	16-18:	0	1:	2
(M.I.=.17)	3: 18	Married						
		(Poly):	3	0	19-24:	13	2:	0
		Widowed:	6	3	25-34:	14	3:	18
		Total	35	15	35-44:	17	4:	7
					45 +:	6	5:	3
Ankole	1: 5	Single:	18	10	12-15 yrs:	0	0:	20
	2: 19	Married						
		(Mono):	13	4	16-18:	0	1:	4
(M.I.=.29)	3: 26	Married						
		(Poly):	4	1	19-24:	20	2:	16
		Widowed:	0	0	25-34:	15	3:	1
		Total	35	15	35-44:	9	4:	8
					45 +:	6	5:	1

UGANDA (continued)	Literacy	Matrial Status	Males	Females	Age		Education	
Teso	1: 21	Single:	9	3	12-15 yrs:	0	0:	20
	2: 3	Married						
		(Mono):	17	9	16-18:	0	1:	4
(M.I.= -.08)	3: 26	Married						
		(Poly):	10	0	19-24:	10	2:	16
		Widowed:	0	2	25-34:	24	3:	5
					35-44:	15	4:	3
		Total	36	14	45 +:	1	5:	2
Lango	1: 19	Single:	13	5	12-15 yrs:	0	0:	19
	2: 12	Married						
		(Mono):	20	9	16-18:	4	1:	16
(M.I.= -.53)	3: 19	Married						
		(Poly):	1	1	19-24:	21	2:	3
		Widowed:	1	0	25-34:	21	3:	5
					35-44:	4	4:	7
		Total	35	15	45 +:	0	5:	0
Acholi	1: 11	Single:	11	10	12-15 yrs:	0	0:	14
	2: 5	Married						
		(Mono):	19	4	16-18:	3	1:	1
(M.I.= .73)	2: 34	Married						
		(Poly):	4	1	19-24:	12	2:	9
		Widowed:	1	0	25-34:	25	3:	17
					35-44:	8	4:	6
		Total	35	15	45 +:	2	5:	3
Karamojong	1: 21	Single:	19	2	12-15 yrs:	0	0:	27
	2: 18	Married						
		(Mono):	10	12	16-18:	1	1:	14
(M.I.= -1.20)	3: 11	Married						
		(Poly):	6	1	19-24:	10	2:	5
		Widowed:	0	0	25-34:	29	3:	3
					35-44:	9	4:	1
		Total	35	15	45 +:	1	5:	0

TANZANIA	Literacy		Marital Status Males	Females	Age		Education	
Chagga	1: 11	Single:	12	14	12-15 yrs:	0	0:	9
	2: 26	Married						
		(Mono):	13	6	16-18:	9	1:	26
(M.I.= -.48)	3: 13	Married						
		(Poly):	2	0	19-24:	20	2:	5
		Widowed:	1	2	25-34:	15	3:	4
					35-44:	6	4:	6
		Total	28	22	45 +:	0	5:	0
Pare	1: 12	Single:	22	5	12-15 yrs:	1	0:	11
	2: 15	Married						
		(Mono):	14	1	16-18:	4	1:	17
(M.I.= .13)	3: 23	Married						
		(Poly):	8	0	19-24:	14	2:	15
		Widowed:	0	0	25-34:	18	3:	6
					35-44:	9	4:	1
		Total	44	6	45 +:	4	5:	0
Sambaa	1: 9	Single:	10	11	12-15 yrs:	0	0:	8
	2: 10	Married						
		(Mono):	17	9	16-18:	3	1:	11
(M.I.= .17)	3: 31	Married						
		(Poly):	3	0	19-24:	19	2:	24
		Widowed:	0	0	25-34:	21	3:	6
					35-44:	7	4:	0
		Total	30	20	45 +:	0	5:	1
Arusha	1: 1	Single:	14	11	12-15 yrs:	2	0:	1
	2: 13	Married						
		(Mono):	22	3	16-18:	5	1:	14
(M.I.=1.06)	3: 36	Married						
		(Poly):	0	0	19-24:	19	2:	18
		Widowed:	0	0	25-34:	22	3:	16
					35-44:	2	4:	1
		Total	36	14	45 +:	0	5:	0

TANZANIA (continued)	Literacy		Marital Status Males	Females	Age		Education	
Meru	1: 1	Single:	22	5	12-15 yrs:	0	0:	1
	2: 13	Married (Mono):	17	6	16-18:	3	1:	13
(M.I.= 1.05)	3: 36	Married (Poly):	0	0	19-24:	26	2:	19
		Widowed:	0	0	25-34:	20	3:	14
					35-44:	1	4:	3
		Total	39	11	45 +:	0	5:	0
Sukuma	1: 12	Single:	12	10	12-15 yrs:	0	0:	20
	2: 10	Married (Mono)	20	4	16-18:	4	1:	6
(M.I.=.31)	3: 28	Married (Poly):	3	0	19-24:	21	2:	9
		Widowed:	1	0	25-34:	13	3:	11
					35-44:	8	4:	4
		Total	36	14	45 +:	4	5:	0
Nyamwezi	1: 17	Single:	4	10	12-15 yrs:	0	0:	20
	2: 7	Married (Mono):	26	4	16-18:	2	1:	6
(M.I.=.10)	3: 26	Married (Poly):	1	0	19-24:	17	2:	7
		Widowed:	3	2	25-34:	14	3:	14
					35-44:	12	4:	3
		Total	34	16	45 +:	5	5:	0
Gogo	1: 18	Single:	22	10	12-15 yrs:	0	0:	19
	2: 5	Married (Mono):	9	2	16-18:	17	1:	11
(M.I.=.10)	3: 27	Married (Poly):	1	0	19-24:	17	2:	9
		Widowed:	2	4	25-34:	6	3:	8
					35-44:	3	4:	3
		Total	34	16	45 +:	7	5:	0

TANZANIA (continued)	Literacy		Marital Status Males	Females	Age		Education	
Luo	1: 22	Single:	11	5	12-15 yrs:	0	0:	22
	2: 6	Married (Mono):	9	8	16-18:	3	1:	11
(M.I.= -.52)	3: 22	Married (Poly)	11	3	19-24:	20	2:	7
		Widowed:	3	0	25-34:	16	3:	9
					35-44:	8	4:	1
		Total	34	16	45 +:	3	5:	0
Masai	1: 50	Single:	1	0	12-15 yrs:	0	0:	50
	2: 0	Married (Mono):	9	3	16-18:	1	1:	0
(M.I.= -2.00)	3: 0	Married (Poly):	25	8	19-24:	17	2:	0
		Widowed:	0	4	25-34:	15	3:	0
					35-44:	11	4:	0
		Total	35	15	45 +:	6	5:	0

APPENDIX C.

"Objective" Intergroup Relations

Kenya

Legend:
Physical distance: 4 = adjacent   Cultural similarity:
                     3 = 1 tribal territory between   + = high similarity
                     2 = 2 tribal territories between   0 = intermediate similarity
                     1 = more remote   - = high dissimilarity

		Kikuyu	Embu	Meru	Kamba	Luhya	Gusii	Kipsigis	Nandi	Masai	Luo
Kikuyu	Distant		4	3	3	1	1	2	1	4	1
	Sim.		+	+	0	0	0	-	-	-	-
Embu	Distant	4		4	4	1	1	1	1	3	1
	Sim.	+		+	0	0	0	-	-	-	-
Meru	Distant	3	4		4	1	1	1	1	2	1
	Sim.	+	+		0	0	0	-	-	-	-
Kamba	Distant	3	4	4		1	1	2	1	4	1
	Sim.	0	0	0		0	0	-	-	-	-
Luhya	Distant	1	1	1	1		3	2	4	2	4
	Sim.	0	0	0	0		+	-	-	-	-
Gusii	Distant	1	1	1	1	3		4	3	4	4
	Sim.	0	0	0	0	+		-	-	-	-
Kipsigis	Distant	2	1	1	2	2	4		4	4	3
	Sim.	-	-	-	-	-	-		+	0	-
Nandi	Distant	1	1	1	1	4	3	4		2	4
	Sim.	-	-	-	-	-	-	+		0	-
Masai	Distant	4	3	2	4	2	4	4	2		4
	Sim.	-	-	-	-	-	-	0	0		-
Luo	Distant	1	1	1	1	4	4	3	4	4	
	Sim.	-	-	-	-	-	-	-	-	-	

Correlation between objective and perceived similarity: r = .41

Uganda

Physical Distance: 4 = adjacent
                   3 = 1 tribal territory between
                   2 = 2 tribal territories between
                   1 = more remote

Cultural similarity:
+ = high similarity
0 = intermediate
- = high dissimilarity

		Ganda	Nyoro	Toro	Soga	Ankole	Gisu	Teso	Acholi	Lango	Karamojong
Ganda	Distant		4	4	4	3	2	2	2	3	1
	Sim.		0	0	+	0	0	-	-	-	-
Nyoro	Distant	4		4	3	3	1	2	3	3	1
	Sim.	0		+	0	+	0	-	-	-	-
Toro	Distant	4	4		2	4	1	1	2	2	1
	Sim.	0	+		0	+	0	-	-	-	-
Soga	Distant	4	3	2		2	3	3	1	2	2
	Sim.	+	0	0		0	0	-	-	-	-
Ankole	Distant	3	3	4	2		1	1	1	2	1
	Sim.	0	+	+	0		0	-	-	-	-
Gisu	Distant	2	1	1	3	1		4	1	2	3
	Sim.	0	0	0	0	0		-	-	-	-
Teso	Distant	2	2	1	3	1	4		3	4	4
	Sim.	-	-	-	-	-	-		-	-	+
Acholi	Distant	2	3	2	1	1	1	3		4	2
	Sim.	-	-	-	-	-	-	-		+	-
Lango	Distant	3	3	2	2	2	2	4	4		2
	Sim.	-	-	-	-	-	-	-	+		-
Karamojong	Distant	1	1	1	2	1	3	4	2	2	
	Sim.	-	-	-	-	-	-	+	-	-	

Correlation between objective and perceived similarity: r = .66

Tanzania

Physical Distance: 4 = adjacent   Cultural similarity:
               3 = 1 tribal territory between   4 = high similarity
               2 = 2 tribal territories between   0 = intermediate
               1 = more remote   - = high dissimilarity

		Chagga	Pare	Sambaa	Meru	Arusha	Sukuma	Nyamwezi	Luo	Masai	Gogo
Chagga	Distant		4	3	4	3	1	1	1	4	2
	Sim.		+	+	0	-	-	-	-	-	-
Pare	Distant	4		4	3	2	1	1	1	4	2
	Sim.	+		+	0	-	-	-	-	-	-
Sambaa	Distant	3	4		2	1	1	1	1	3	2
	Sim.	+	+		0	-	-	-	-	-	-
Meru	Distant	4	3	2		4	2	1	1	4	2
	Sim.	0	0	0		+	-	-	-	-	-
Arusha	Distant	3	2	1	4		2	1	1	4	1
	Sim.	-	-	-	+		-	-	-	+	0
Sukuma	Distant	1	1	1	2	2		4	3	4	2
	Sim.	-	-	-	-	-		+	-	-	-
Nyamwezi	Distant	1	1	1	1	1	4		3	2	4
	Sim.	-	-	-	-	-	+		-	-	-
Luo	Distant	1	1	1	1	1	3	3		2	1
	Sim.	-	-	-	-	-	-	-		-	-
Masai	Distant	4	4	3	4	4	4	2	2		4
	Sim.	-	-	-	-	+	-	-	-		0
Gogo	Distant	2	2	2	2	1	2	4	1	4	
	Sim.	-	-	-	-	0	-	-	-	0	

Correlation between objective and perceived similarity: r = .43

APPENDIX D.

Matrices of Intergroup Ratings

D.3.1.a. Intergroup Liking Scores - Kenya

Ratings given to

	A	B	C	D	E	F	G	H	I	J
A		+ 2.5	+ 5.8	-2.7	+ 4.2	+0.6	- 3.0	- 5.8	- 1.2	+ 1.6
B	+12.8		+10.1	+2.3	- 1.7	-1.9	- 1.8	-10.7	- 0.2	- 4.7
C	-20.2	+21.6		-5.2	- 3.1	+2.4	+ 0.4	- 5.7	+ 8.5	+ 1.9
D	+38.3	- 3.2	+ 0.5		- 4.8	+1.5	- 0.5	- 5.4	-16.4	-10.0
E	- 7.1	- 1.1	+ 1.2	+3.8		-0.1	- 1.6	- 3.2	+ 4.2	- 3.5
F	+24.3	- 2.1	- 0.9	+0.9	+ 4.4		- 8.7	- 1.9	-12.9	- 4.1
G	- 7.2	- 4.6	- 1.5	-2.9	- 2.2	-6.7		+30.4	- 7.6	+ 2.0
H	- 0.7	0.0	- 9.6	+2.6	- 2.5	-0.8	- 0.5		+ 8.1	+ 7.9
I	-24.6	- 6.9	- 3.4	+2.3	- 9.4	-3.3	+19.8	+10.1		+ 3.4
J	-24.5	- 2.2	- 1.7	-0.8	+17.5	+7.2	- 1.4	- 5.1	+ 5.7	

Ratings given by

Reciprocity: r = .03

D.3.1.b. Intergroup Liking Scores - Uganda

Ratings given to

	A	B	C	D	E	F	G	H	I	J
A		-11.8	+13.9	+9.4	-0.1	+5.3	- 2.3	+ 0.6	- 4.7	- 9.2
B	- 6.8		+ 3.3	+1.5	+0.9	+2.7	- 4.6	- 0.1	+ 1.3	+ 6.2
C	- 4.1	+22.1		-3.7	+3.7	-2.9	- 5.1	- 0.8	- 4.3	+ 3.9
D	+24.8	- 1.5	- 6.8		-2.2	-0.6	- 5.8	+ 0.2	- 8.2	+ 3.7
E	+ 7.6	- 5.1	+10.7	-0.1		+2.1	- 2.1	- 5.7	- 3.0	+ 4.2
F	+12.4	+ 4.3	+ 8.9	+0.5	-0.6		- 4.4	- 3.8	- 1.9	-16.6
G	+ 9.3	+ 2.1	- 3.8	-1.5	-0.8	-5.2		+ 2.0	- 2.5	+ 4.6
H	-19.1	- 0.9	- 4.9	-4.6	-1.2	+0.1	- 2.4		+25.9	+ 3.3
I	-14.1	- 0.8	- 1.9	+9.1	-1.3	-0.5	+ 4.8	+12.7		- 6.8
J	- 8.4	- 4.1	- 9.4	-3.4	+2.8	-2.4	+29.6	- 8.7	- 3.0	

(Ratings given by)

Reciprocity: r = .35

D.3.1.c. Intergroup Liking Scores - Tanzania

Ratings given to

	A	B	C	D	E	F	G	H	I	J
A		+ 6.3	- 1.9	+10.1	- 0.5	- 0.3	- 3.2	+ 0.7	- 7.8	+ 2.6
B	+ 2.8		+16.5	+ 0.9	- 2.2	+ 8.1	- 5.2	+ 3.3	-10.2	- 6.6
C	+ 7.4	+15.1		+ 0.2	- 3.6	- 3.2	- 4.9	- 4.5	- 1.7	0.0
D	+10.9	+ 4.6	- 5.6		-15.5	- 3.4	- 2.0	+ 1.5	+ 6.5	+ 1.7
E	+ 2.1	- 2.2	- 5.1	-10.2		+ 2.6	+ 6.6	+ 1.4	+10.5	- 5.2
F	- 9.5	- 4.8	+ 4.8	+ 0.8	- 1.5		+19.4	+ 0.6	- 6.7	+ 3.6
G	-10.0	- 1.9	+ 2.9	+ 1.9	- 0.8	+12.4		+ 3 2	- 3.8	- 0.5
H	+ 6.0	- 2.1	- 3.6	- 0.3	- 4.6	+ 2.5	- 9.8		+ 7.1	+ 1.0
I	- 4.3	- 4.0	- 2.4	- 5.4	+30.1	-11.2	- 2.4	-11.8		- 1.1
J	+ 0.2	- 4.4	- 0.5	+ 0.6	- 0.2	- 0.3	+ 5.1	+ 1.9	- 7.6	

(Ratings given by)

Reciprocity: r = .49

D.3.2.a. Intergroup Social Distance Ratings - Kenya

Ratings given to

Ratings given by

	A	B	C	D	E	F	G	H	I	J
A		+2.4	+1.7	+0.5	+0.8	-1.1	-1.9	-1.5	-0.9	+0.1
B	+3.1		+2.6	+2.7	-0.3	-1.3	-1.9	-1.9	-2.4	-0.6
C	+0.2	+2.1		+1.7	+0.1	-0.8	-1.2	-1.0	-0.9	-0.1
D	+1.4	+0.7	+0.7		0.0	-0.3	-0.3	-0.7	-1.3	-0.3
E	+0.5	-0.3	-0.5	-0.2		+0.5	+0.1	+0.7	-1.5	+0.8
F	+0.7	+0.4	+0.5	0.0	+0.8		-0.5	-0.5	-1.4	0.0
G	-0.1	-0.1	-0.1	-0.1	-0.1	-0.1		+0.9	-0.1	-0.2
H	-0.1	-1.0	-0.8	-0.5	+0.4	+0.2	+2.9		-0.3	-0.6
I	-0.2	-1.5	-1.5	+1.4	-1.8	-1.1	+3.1	+3.4		-1.9
J	-1.5	-1.2	-1.2	+1.6	+2.5	+0.4	+0.1	-0.8	+0.1	

Reciprocity: r = .52

D.3.2.b. Intergroup Social Distance Ratings - Uganda

Ratings given to

Ratings given by

	A	B	C	D	E	F	G	H	I	J
A		-0.6	+2.6	+2.2	+1.9	+1.7	-0.3	-2.1	-2.1	-3.2
B	-0.8		+1.7	+1.2	+1.8	0.0	-0.4	+0.1	+0.3	-3.9
C	-0.1	+2.5		+0.1	+2.7	-0.9	-0.8	-1.1	-0.7	-1.6
D	+2.9	+1.4	+1.4		+0.4	-0.2	-0.3	-1.8	-1.3	-2.4
E	+1.3	+1.5	+2.2	+0.7		-0.7	-0.9	-1.4	-1.1	-1.7
F	+2.2	+1.3	+2.3	+1.7	+1.2		-0.9	-1.9	-1.9	-4.0
G	+0.2	+0.1	+0.4	+0.2	-0.4	-0.6		-0.2	-0.1	+0.4
H	-0.5	-0.1	+0.1	0.0	-0.3	-0.6	+0.2		+1.6	-0.4
I	-0.4	+0.7	+0.3	+0.5	-1.0	-1.2	+0.9	+2.0		-1.9
J	-0.5	-0.9	-0.7	-1.0	-0.5	-0.9	+3.3	+0.8	+0.4	

Reciprocity: r = .72

D.3.2.c. Intergroup Social Distance Ratings - Tanzania

Ratings given to

Ratings given by	A	B	C	D	E	F	G	H	I	J
A		+2.5	+0.5	+2.0	+0.8	+0.2	-0.4	-1.1	-2.4	-2.0
B	+1.3		+3.0	-1.7	-0.2	+0.3	+0.2	-2.2	-0.5	-0.1
C	+2.7	+2.9		+1.6	-1.3	+1.6	+1.9	-2.7	-3.9	-2.9
D	+0.8	+0.7	-0.5		+0.2	+0.5	+0.2	-0.9	-0.2	-0.7
E	+0.4	+0.6	-0.2	+0.5		+0:3	+0.3	-1.0	+0.1	-0.9
F	-0.4	-0.1	+0.2	-0.9	-0.9		+3.3	+0.1	-1.4	+0.2
G	-0.2	+0.6	+1.0	-1.1	-1.6	+3.2		+0.1	-1.9	-0.2
H	+2.0	-0.4	-0.9	-1.5	-0.6	+1.7	+0.1		+0.3	-0.6
I	+1.7	-0.9	-0.9	-0.9	+4.7	-0.9	-0.9	-0.9		-0.9
J	+1.0	+1.0	+0.4	-0.7	-0.2	-0.3	+1.0	-1.0	-1.2	

Reciprocity: r = .40

D.3.3.a. Intergroup Familiarity - Kenya

Ratings given to

Ratings given by	A	B	C	D	E	F	G	H	I	J
A		1.7	1.3	1.7	1.2	0.6	0.5	0.6	1.0	1.4
B	2.9		2.1	2.3	1.4	0.5	0.8	0.8	0.6	1.4
C	2.8	2.4		1.9	0.9	0.7	0.4	0.6	0.9	1.1
D	2.9	0.8	0.8		0.6	0.2	0.1	0.2	1.3	2.1
E	0.9	0.4	0.2	0.4		0.3	0.2	0.6	0.1	1.1
F	1.3	0.7	0.6	1.1	2.0		1.2	0.7	0.6	2.6
G	1.4	0.4	0.5	0.7	1.2	1.5		3.2	1.0	2.0
H	1.0	1.0	1.1	1.0	1.5	1.7	1.8		1.4	1.2
I	0.1	0.0	0.0	0.7	0.2	0.2	0.4	0.7		0.2
J	1.3	0.3	0.3	0.6	1.8	1.1	0.5	0.5	0.3	

Reciprocity: r = .27

D.3.3.b. Intergroup Familiarity - Uganda

Ratings given to

Ratings given by

	A	B	C	D	E	F	G	H	I	J
A		1.8	2.1	2.7	1.6	1.8	0.9	0.9	0.9	0.3
B	2.7		2.8	1.6	2.1	0.5	0.5	0.5	0.8	0.2
C	1.6	2.8		0.4	2.0	0.1	0.3	0.3	0.2	0.1
D	2.9	0.3	0.3		0.5	0.6	0.5	0.3	0.2	0.1
E	2.2	1.1	1.5	0.4		0.1	0.5	0.0	0.0	0.1
F	2.9	2.6	2.6	2.3	2.0		1.9	1.8	1.6	1.8
G	3.6	0.7	0.8	1.9	0.4	1.3		0.4	0.4	1.0
H	2.0	1.2	0.9	1.0	1.1	1.0	1.2		3.3	0.9
I	1.6	1.2	0.9	1.1	1.2	1.0	1.7	2.6		1.0
J	0.9	0.4	0.2	0.4	0.4	0.7	2.7	2.1	1.8	

Reciprocity: r = .45

D.3.3.c. Intergroup Familiarity - Tanzania

Ratings given to

Ratings given by

	A	B	C	D	E	F	G	H	I	J
A		1.6	1.0	1.5	1.1	0.3	0.6	0.4	0.7	0.3
B	1.9		2.3	1.4	1.5	1.2	2.1	1.3	1.7	1.6
C	1.4	3.9		0.7	0.2	0.6	0.8	0.3	0.1	0.4
D	1.9	1.2	0.8		2.1	0.6	0.5	0.2	1.0	0.3
E	1.7	1.3	1.0	2.3		0.8	0.8	0.6	2.7	0.7
F	0.8	0.4	0.6	0.2	0.2		3.1	1.1	0.2	0.9
G	0.8	0.9	1.1	0.2	0.2	3.7		0.7	0.2	1.3
H	0.6	0.2	0.2	0.0	0.2	1.0	0.3		0.1	0.0
I	0.8	0.0	0.0	0.0	1.8	0.0	0.0	0.0		0.0
J	0.7	0.3	0.3	0.2	0.2	1.2	1.3	0.2	0.5	

Reciprocity: r = .74

D.6.1.a. Evaluative Rating Bias Scores - Kenya

Ratings given to

Ratings given by	A	B	C	D	E	F	G	H	I	J
A	+ 71.9	+ 6.4	+ 10.1	- 32.2	+ 9.3	- 23.0	- 33.3	+ 2.1	- 16.2	+ 4.9
B	+ 41.2	+54.7	- 14.6	- 22.9	+ 1.6	- 3.7	- 21.0	-11.6	- 10.9	-12.8
C	- 12.4	+47.1	+103.8	- 19.5	-18.0	- 11.3	- 26.6	-30.2	- 49.5	+16.6
D	-133.2	-14.7	- 14.0	+241.7	-12.8	- 1.1	- 10.4	+16.0	- 31.3	-40.2
E	+ 12.4	-18.1	- 14.4	- 33.7	+59.8	+ 7.5	- 37.8	- 5.4	+ 34.3	- 4.6
F	+ 50.7	+ 0.2	- 0.1	- 25.4	- 8.9	+117.8	- 46.5	+16.9	- 82.4	-22.3
G	+ 9.9	-18.6	- 17.9	- 36.2	- 6.7	- 41.0	+231.7	+22.1	-112.2	-31.1
H	+17.5	-22.0	- 18.3	- 35.6	-16.1	- 4.4	- 11.7	+41.7	+ 53.4	- 4.5
I	- 24.9	-20.4	- 21.7	- 19.0	-27.5	- 37.8	- 23.1	-53.7	+196.0	+32.1
J	- 33.1	-14.6	- 12.9	- 17.2	+19.3	- 3.0	- 21.3	+ 2.1	+ 18.8	+61.9

D.6.1.b. Evaluative Rating Bias Scores - Uganda

Ratings given to

Ratings given by	A	B	C	D	E	F	G	H	I	J
A	+206.5	- 36.6	- 1.0	-119.0	- 4.4	- 9.0	- 6.0	- 13.7	-11.8	- 5.1
B	-103.8	+156.1	- 11.3	+ 10.7	- 13.7	+ 0.7	- 10.3	- 14.0	+11.9	- 26.4
C	-116.4	- 30.5	+128.1	- 3.9	+ 20.7	- 10.9	- 13.9	- 20.6	+ 8.3	+ 39.0
D	+ 10.4	- 22.7	- 19.1	+148.9	- 30.5	- 19.1	- 40.1	- 46.8	-10.9	+ 29.8
E	- 28.0	- 13.1	- 2.5	- 2.5	+101.1	- 12.5	- 19.5	- 44.2	-19.3	+ 40.4
F	+ 93.2	- 6.9	- 10.3	- 28.3	- 8.7	+128.7	- 40.3	- 9.0	- 8.1	-110.4
G	+ 17.1	- 5.0	- 24.4	- 15.4	- 20.8	- 26.4	+101.6	- 24.1	-10.2	+ 7.5
H	+ 7.3	- 16.8	- 21.2	- 4.8	- 10.6	- 13.2	- 13.2	+144.1	-33.0	- 48.3
I	- 58.0	- 3.1	- 6.5	+ 12.5	- 22.9	- 26.5	+ 3.5	+ 46.8	+71.7	- 17.6
J	- 28.4	- 21.5	- 31.9	- 7.9	- 10.3	- 11.9	+ 38.1	- 18.6	+ 1.3	+ 91.0

D.6.1.c. Evaluative Rating Bias Scores - Tanzania

Ratings given to

Ratings given by

	A	B	C	D	E	F	G	H	I	J
A	+61.5	+34.9	+ 8.1	+ 1.1	- 1.7	- 19.9	- 38.6	+ 3.8	- 50.8	+ 2.0
B	+ 8.5	+90.9	- 0.9	+ 5.1	+ 7.3	+ 44.1	- 11.6	- 9.2	-115.8	- 18.0
C	-26.4	-13.0	+160.2	-10.8	- 6.6	- 31.8	- 50.5	- 20.1	+ 16.3	- 16.9
D	-29.4	- 1.0	- 25.8	+67.2	-49.6	+ 3.2	- 4.5	- 24.1	+ 72.3	- 7.9
E	- 8.2	+ 4.2	- 19.6	+15.4	+ 8.6	+ 7.4	+ 25.7	- 16.9	- 8.5	- 7.7
F	-28.3	-27.9	- 14.7	-15.7	- 0.5	+119.3	+ 41.6	- 33.0	- 27.6	- 12.8
G	-20.3	-15.9	- 9.7	- 6.7	+ 1.5	+ 9.3	+138.6	- 19.0	- 42.6	- 34.8
H	+38.4	-31.2	- 35.0	-16.0	- 2.8	- 37.0	- 45.7	+103.7	+ 26.1	- 0.1
I	+ 2.7	-29.9	- 37.7	-38.7	+40.5	- 72.7	- 65.4	+ 12.0	+211.4	- 21.8
J	+ 1.9	-10.7	- 24.5	- 0.5	+ 3.7	- 21.5	+ 10.8	+ 3.2	- 80.4	+118.4

D.6.2.a. Achievement Rating Bias Scores - Kenya

Ratings given to

Ratings given by

	A	B	C	D	E	F	G	H	I	J
A	+ 40.8	- 5.6	- 0.8	- 4.8	+ 8.3	-19.2	-15.1	- 2.9	- 1.1	+ 0.1
B	- 21.8	+33.8	+14.6	+18.6	+ 4.7	-16.8	-18.7	-11.5	- 7.7	+ 4.5
C	+ 4.6	-11.8	+59.0	-33.0	-19.9	-15.4	-10.3	-11.1	+ 39.7	- 2.1
D	+ 89.3	- 2.1	-13.3	+21.7	+ 5.8	- 2.7	+ 0.4	+14.6	-105.6	- 8.4
E	- 88.8	- 0.2	- 6.4	- 6.4	+26.7	+12.2	- 8.7	+13.5	+ 50.3	+ 7.5
F	+ 67.8	- 1.6	- 8.8	-17.8	+ 4.3	+34.8	- 7.1	+10.1	- 42.1	-39.9
G	+ 56.2	- 4.2	-11.4	+ 3.6	+ 2.7	- 3.8	+89.3	+19.5	-137.7	-14.5
H	-101.6	+10.0	- 9.2	+ 2.8	+ 2.9	- 8.6	- 2.5	+20.7	+ 83.5	+ 1.7
I	- 1.6	-14.0	-11.2	+29.8	-37.1	- 9.6	-26.5	-29.3	+ 97.5	+ 1.7
J	- 45.2	- 4.6	-12.8	-14.8	+ 1.3	+28.8	- 1.1	-23.9	+ 22.9	+49.1

D.6.2.b. Achievement Rating Bias Scores - Uganda

Ratings given to

	A	B	C	D	E	F	G	H	I	J
A	+110.7	-43.9	-11.4	+22.2	+ 4.4	- 11.5	- 6.0	+ 0.7	- 8.9	-56.6
B	- 16.4	+54.0	-20.5	- 9.9	-17.7	- 9.6	-14.1	+ 8.6	+ 1.0	+24.3
C	+ 42.8	+11.2	+ 8.7	-14.7	-28.5	- 17.4	- 3.9	+ 3.8	- 1.8	- 0.5
D	- 16.7	+ 6.7	+14.2	+36.8	-24.0	- 16.9	+ 7.6	- 9.7	- 6.3	+ 8.0
E	+ 2.8	+ 2.2	-47.3	- 8.7	+52.5	- 11.4	- 3.9	- 5.2	+ 2.2	+16.5
F	- 6.6	-30.2	+ 6.3	- 5.1	-13.9	+119.2	-10.3	-11.6	-11.2	-36.9
G	- 35.4	+20.0	+19.5	- 0.9	+ 2.3	- 9.6	- 6.1	- 7.4	- 2.0	+19.3
H	- 8.5	-37.1	+ 5.4	- 5.0	+ 3.2	- 7.7	- 2.2	+48.5	+ 1.9	+ 1.2
I	- 27.2	+ 8.2	+11.7	- 1.7	+ 4.5	- 14.4	- 0.9	+ 3.8	+37.2	-21.5
J	- 45.8	+ 8.6	+13.1	-13.3	+16.9	- 21.0	+39.5	-31.8	-12.4	+45.9

Ratings given by

D.6.2.c. Achievement Rating Bias Scores - Tanzania

Ratings given to

	A	B	C	D	E	F	G	H	I	J
A	+27.0	- 6.3	-13.4	+ 1.3	- 0.6	-15.9	+ 4.5	- 6.2	+ 8.9	+ 0.4
B	+ 1.4	+ 3.1	0.0	+ 5.7	+ 6.8	+23.5	- 7.1	- 6.8	-10.7	-16.2
C	- 1.6	-11.9	+55.0	- 4.3	+ 1.8	- 4.5	- 2.1	-14.8	+18.3	-36.2
D	+75.3	- 4.0	- 7.1	+30.6	-23.3	-19.6	- 0.2	- 2.9	-35.8	-13.3
E	+63.6	+ 6.3	- 4.8	- 4.1	+ 3.0	- 4.3	+ 7.1	- 4.6	-38.5	-24.0
F	-51.7	- 7.0	- 6.1	- 8.4	+ 3.7	+92.4	- 0.2	- 9.9	-14.8	+ 1.7
G	-35.4	- 5.7	- 7.8	- 3.1	+ 5.0	+41.7	+37.1	- 0.6	- 9.5	-22.0
H	-41.4	+ 1.3	-12.8	+ 3.9	+20.0	-39.3	-12.9	+53.4	+ 1.5	+26.0
I	-19.0	+19.7	+ 2.6	-21.7	-22.6	-71.9	-23.5	- 0.2	+91.9	+44.4
J	-18.5	+ 4.2	- 5.9	- 0.2	+ 5.9	- 2.4	- 3.0	- 7.7	-11.6	+38.9

Ratings given by

D.6.3.a. Potency Rating Bias Scores - Kenya

Ratings given to

Ratings given by

	A	B	C	D	E	F	G	H	I	J
A	- 3.4	- 3.9	-3.6	+ 0.8	+ 1.9	+ 4.2	+3.5	-3.3	+ 4.1	+ 0.1
B	+13.1	-10.4	+7.9	+11.3	-20.6	+ 4.7	+2.0	+0.2	-12.4	+ 4.6
C	+ 7.4	-15.1	-3.8	-12.4	- 2.3	- 3.0	-0.7	+0.5	+22.9	+ 6.9
D	+ 8.3	+ 4.8	+1.1	- 9.5	+ 2.6	+ 4.9	+3.2	+0.4	-12.2	- 3.2
E	- 8.1	+ 5.4	-0.3	+ 6.1	- 3.2	+ 0.5	-1.2	+6.0	-13.6	+ 2.4
F	+ 2.3	+ 2.8	-7.9	+ 0.5	- 4.4	-11.1	-1.8	-4.6	+ 4.8	+19.8
G	- 2.5	+ 7.0	+1.3	+ 7.7	+ 2.8	+ 7.1	-7.6	+2.6	+25.0	-43.0
H	- 6.7	- 1.2	+9.1	+13.5	+ 4.6	+ 4.9	-0.8	+2.4	-11.2	-14.2
I	+ 1.9	+ 8.4	-0.3	-16.9	+14.2	+ 1.5	+4.8	+3.0	-23.6	+ 7.4
J	-11.9	+ 2.6	-3.1	- 0.7	- 1.6	-13.3	-1.0	-6.8	+16.6	+19.6

D.6.3.b. Potency Rating Bias Scores - Uganda

Ratings given to

Ratings given by

	A	B	C	D	E	F	G	H	I	J
A	+ 9.1	- 1.4	- 6.2	- 4.0	+ 3.9	- 4.0	- 0.9	- 3.8	+ 5.2	- 5.8
B	+23.0	+ 3.5	-11.3	- 8.1	+ 3.8	- 4.1	+ 3.0	- 7.9	-17.9	+16.1
C	+18.5	+19.0	-34.8	+ 6.4	- 6.7	+ 2.4	+ 4.5	- 4.4	- 2.4	- 2.4
D	- 1.4	+ 5.1	+ 8.3	-36.5	+ 5.4	+ 4.5	+10.6	+ 2.7	+ 8.7	- 7.3
E	+ 8.5	- 2.0	+11.2	+ 3.4	-16.7	- 1.6	+ 3.5	- 3.4	- 0.4	- 2.4
F	-15.4	-14.9	+ 5.3	+ 9.5	- 8.6	+23.5	+ 4.6	- 7.3	- 3.3	+ 6.7
G	-11.0	- 0.5	+10.7	+ 8.9	+ 7.8	+ 1.9	-16.0	- 3.9	+ 1.1	+ 1.1
H	-18.5	- 9.0	+ 3.2	+ 3.4	+ 5.3	-22.6	+ 6.5	+26.6	+ 9.6	- 4.4
I	+ 3.3	- 1.2	+ 3.0	+ 4.2	+ 4.1	- 0.8	- 2.7	- 1.6	- 0.6	- 7.6
J	-16.0	+ 1.5	+10.7	+ 4.9	+ 1.8	+ 0.9	-13.0	+ 3.1	+ 0.1	+ 6.1

D.6.3.c. Potency Rating Bias Scores - Tanzania

Ratings given to

	A	B	C	D	E	F	G	H	I	J
A	- 2.3	+ 7.0	- 1.6	- 1.0	+2.8	+ 1.8	+ 7.5	- 1.1	-15.6	+ 2.5
B	- 8.4	-38.1	+ 5.3	+ 5.9	+3.7	+ 3.7	+ 2.4	+ 6.8	+ 9.3	+ 9.4
C	+21.4	-40.3	-11.9	+ 4.7	+0.5	+ 2.5	+10.2	- 4.4	+ 8.1	+ 9.2
D	+14.2	+ 1.5	- 2.1	-17.5	+3.3	+ 1.3	+ 2.0	- 5.6	+13.9	-11.0
E	+ 9.2	+ 1.5	- 1.1	- 8.5	+1.3	+ 2.3	- 5.0	- 4.6	+14.9	-10.0
F	+10.4	+16.7	+ 2.1	+ 5.7	+0.5	-20.5	-17.8	- 0.4	- 4.9	+ 8.2
G	+ 4.7	+16.0	- 2.6	+ 5.0	+0.8	+ 1.8	-17.5	- 2.1	-14.6	+ 8.5
H	-30.7	+ 5.6	- 2.0	- 0.4	-5.6	+ 5.4	+ 3.1	+18.5	+ 6.0	+ 0.1
I	-14.8	+14.5	+ 7.9	+ 1.5	-9.7	+ 2.3	+ 8.0	- 2.6	-15.1	+ 8.0
J	- 3.7	+15.6	+ 6.0	+ 4.6	+2.4	- 0.6	+ 7.1	- 4.5	- 2.0	-24.9

Ratings given by

APPENDIX E.

Intragroup Attraction Correlations

E.1. Intragroup Correlations Between Attraction Ratings and Physical Distance

Ethnic Group	Correlation	Ethnic Group	Correlation
Kikuyu	.45	Gisu	-.36
Embu	.81	Teso	-.08
Meru (K)	.91	Acholi	.72
Kamba	.28	Lango	.82
Luhya	.54	Karamojong	.76
Gusii	-.23	Chagga	.53
Kipsigis	.57	Pare	.44
Nandi	.74	Sambaa	.54
Masai (K)	.07	Meru (T)	.79
Luo (K)	.49	Arusha	.89
Ganda	.67	Sukuma	.43
Nyoro	.77	Nyamwezi	.60
Toro	.89	Luo (T)	.40
Soga	.76	Masai (T)	.31
Ankole	.89	Gogo	.30

Average Intragroup Correlation = .60

E.2.   Intragroup Correlations Between Attraction Ratings and Perceived Similarity

Ethnic Group	Correlation	Ethnic Group	Correlation
Kikuyu	.77	Gisu	.81
Embu	.76	Teso	.04
Meru (K)	.88	Acholi	.90
Kamba	.84	Lango	.66
Luhya	.16	Karamojong	.86
Gusii	.38	Chagga	.90
Kipsigis	.94	Pare	.75
Nandi	.31	Sambaa	.65
Masai (K)	.83	Meru (T)	.55
Luo (K)	.86	Arusha	.60
Ganda	.68	Sukuma	.93
Nyoro	.65	Nyamwezi	.87
Toro	.38	Luo (T)	.67
Soga	.71	Masai (T)	.96
Ankole	.58	Gogo	.13

Average Intragroup Correlation = .74

E.3. Intragroup Correlations Between Attraction Ratings and Outgroup Advancement
      Factor Scores for Kenya and Uganda

Ethnic Group	Correlation
Kikuyu	-.02
Embu	.36
Meru (K)	-.02
Kamba	.60
Luhya	.36
Gusii	.56
Kipsigis	-.20
Nandi	.27
Masai (K)	-.03
Luo (K)	-.11
Ganda	.76
Nyoro	.44
Toro	.10
Soga	.59
Ankole	.53
Gisu	.82
Teso	.38
Acholi	-.33
Lango	.07
Karamojong	-.42

Average Intragroup Correlation = .28

E.4. Intragroup Correlations Between Attraction Ratings and Achievement Ratings
(Average Achievement Rating Received by Each Group)

Ethnic Group	Correlation	Ethnic Group	Correlation
Kikuyu	.30	Gisu	.51
Embu	.70	Teso	.61
Meru (K)	.25	Acholi	.08
Kamba	.85	Lango	.31
Luhya	.52	Karamojong	.15
Gusii	.72	Chagga	.41
Kipsigis	-.07	Pare	.32
Nandi	-.25	Sambaa	.52
Masai (K)	-.38	Meru (T)	.42
Luo (K)	-.26	Arusha	-.06
Ganda	.29	Sukuma	.10
Nyoro	.26	Nyamwezi	.40
Toro	-.06	Luo (T)	.56
Soga	.73	Masai (T)	.06
Ankole	.37	Gogo	.57

Average Intragroup Correlation = .34

E.5.   Intragroup Correlations Between Attraction Ratings and Outgroup
        Population Size

Ethnic Group	Correlation	Ethnic Group	Correlation
Kikuyu	.36	Gisu	.54
Embu	.63	Teso	.86
Meru (K)	.16	Acholi	-.16
Kamba	.73	Lango	-.13
Luhya	.60	Karamojong	-.11
Gusii	.91	Chagga	-.17
Kipsigis	-.25	Pare	.25
Nandi	-.16	Sambaa	.14
Masai (K)	-.49	Meru (T)	-.05
Luo (K)	.29	Arusha	-.16
Ganda	.63	Sukuma	.66
Nyoro	.27	Nyamwezi	.90
Toro	.04	Luo (T)	.68
Soga	.91	Masai (T)	-.26
Ankole	.55	Gogo	.51

Average Intragroup Correlation = .37

E.6.   Intragroup Correlations Between Attraction Ratings and Intergroup
        Evaluative Ratings

Ethnic Group	Correlation	Ethnic Group	Correlation
Kikuyu	.68	Gisu	.81
Embu	.64	Teso	.65
Meru (K)	.61	Acholi	-.28
Kamba	-.72	Lango	.79
Luhya	.33	Karamojong	.58
Gusii	.59	Chagga	.65
Kipsigis	.19	Pare	.41
Nandi	.52	Sambaa	.79
Masai (K)	-.29	Meru (T)	.01
Luo (K)	.70	Arusha	-.26
Ganda	.10	Sukuma	.77
Nyoro	.65	Nyamwezi	.64
Toro	.25	Luo (T)	.46
Soga	.93	Masai (T)	.82
Ankole	.92	Gogo	.71

Average Intragroup Correlation = .53

E.7.   Intragroup Correlations Between Attraction Ratings and Intergroup
       Achievement Ratings

Ethnic Group	Correlation	Ethnic Group	Correlation
Kikuyu	.46	Gisu	.58
Embu	.85	Teso	.58
Meru (K)	.17	Acholi	.11
Kamba	.79	Lango	.44
Luhya	.58	Karamojong	.56
Gusii	.63	Chagga	.31
Kipsigis	.07	Pare	.30
Nandi	-.42	Sambaa	.40
Masai (K)	-.33	Meru (T)	.53
Luo (K)	-.10	Arusha	-.01
Ganda	.49	Sukuma	.34
Nyoro	-.06	Nyamwezi	.68
Toro	-.02	Luo (T)	.18
Soga	.74	Masai (T)	-.18
Ankole	.14	Gogo	.57

Average Intragroup Correlation = .33

APPENDIX F.

Trait Attributions by Different Types of Outgroups

High Frequency Trait Attributions for each Ethnic Group
by Different Types of Outgroups

Rated Group	Self Attributions	All Types of Outgroups	Near Outgroups	Remote Outgroups	Similar Outgroups	Dissimilar Outgroups
Group #1	Peaceful (self) Peaceful (others) Hardworking men Hardworking women Backbite Intelligent Handsome men Friendly Pushy Progressive Wealthy Thrifty Not generous Religious	Quarrelsome (others) Dishonest (others) Hardworking men Hardworking women Backbite Intelligent Beautiful women Pushy Progressive Wealthy Thrifty Not generous	Dishonest (selves) Clean Cruel Sexually strict Conservative Proud	Hot-tempered Sexually loose Light-skinned	Quarrelsome (selves) Peaceful (others) Clean Independent Brave Cruel Hot-tempered Conservative Proud Witchcraft	Light-skinned
Group #2	Peaceful (Selves) Peaceful (others) Honest (others) Obedient Hardworking men Gentle Friendly Intelligent Clean Handsome men Light-skinned Sexually strict Pushy Progressive Conservative Wealthy Thrifty Religious Proud	Independent Obedient Lazy men Lazy women Backbite Intelligent Clean Not generous Sexually loose Pushy Progressive Conservative Wealthy Thrifty Religious Proud	Dishonest (selves) Quarrelsome (others)	Gentle Light-skinned	Dishonest (selves) Peaceful (others) Handsome men	Peaceful (selves) Quarrelsome (others) Gentle Friendly Effeminate Light-skinned Powerful magic

F-2

Rated Group	Self Attributions	All Types of Outgroups	Near Outgroups	Remote Outgroups	Similar Outgroups	Dissimilar Outgroups
Group #3	Peaceful (selves) Peaceful (others) Honest (others) Hardworking women Intelligent Handsome men Beautiful women Light-skinned Clean Pushy Progressive Wealthy Not thrifty Religious Proud	Dishonest (selves) Dishonest (others) Beautiful women Light-skinned Clean Pushy Progressive Not generous Backbite Proud	Intelligent Sexually strict Wealthy Thrifty		Obedient Intelligent Effeminate Wealthy Thrifty	
Group #4	Peaceful (selves) Honest (others) Obedient Hardworking women Brave Strong Hot-tempered Uncivilized Sexually loose Handsome men Beautiful women Light-skinned Friendly Wealthy Not thrifty Not proud	Quarrelsome (selves) Quarrelsome (others) Independent Lazy men Lazy women Brave Cruel Uncivilized Hot-tempered Backbite Dirty	Uninterested adv. Conservative Unintelligent Poor	Powerful magic Sexually loose Sexually strict Effeminate	Dishonest (selves) Dishonest (others) Powerful magic Uninterested adv. Conservative Not generous Poor Proud	Sexually loose Sexually strict Effeminate Unintelligent

	Peaceful (selves) Peaceful (others) Honest (others)	Quarrelsome (selves)	Quarrelsome (selves)	Quarrelsome (selves)
Group #5	Obedient			
	Independent	Independent		
	Hardworking women			
	Lazy men			
	Brave	Brave		
	Strong	Strong		
	Friendly			
	Dirty Dark-skinned	Dirty	Unattractive men	Unattractive men
	Unintelligent	Unintelligent		
	Cruel	Cruel		
	Hot-tempered	Hot-tempered		
	Sexually strict			
	Uncivilized	Uncivilized		
	Uninterested adv.	Uninterested adv.		
	Conservative			
	Wealthy	Poor		
	Not thrifty		Not proud	
	Not proud			

	Peaceful (selves) Peaceful (others) Honest (others)	Quarrelsome (selves) Quarrelsome (others)	Quarrelsome (selves)	Dishonest (others)
Group #6	Obedient	Independent		Backbite
	Friendly	Cruel		
	Brave	Brave		
	Strong	Strong		
	Handsome men	Lazy men		Handsome men
	Beautiful women	Lazy women		Beautiful women
	Light-skinned	Dirty		Sexually loose
	Sexually loose			
	Hot-tempered	Hot-tempered	Wealthy	Wealthy
	Wealthy	Uncivilized		Not generous
	Not thrifty	Uninterested adv.		Proud
	Not proud	Conservative		

F-4

Rated Group	Self Attributions	All Types of Outgroups	Near Outgroups	Remote Outgroups	Similar Outgroups	Dissimilar Outgroups
Group #7	Peaceful (selves)					
	Peaceful (others)					
	Honest (others)					
	Obedient					
	Hardworking men					Weak
	Hardworking women				Lazy men	
	Gentle			Gentle		
	Friendly					
	Strong	Unintelligent	Effeminate	Weak	Effeminate	
	Dirty	Dirty				
	Sexually strict	Uninterested adv.				
	Uninterested adv.	Uncivilized				
	Conservative	Poor				
	Poor					
	Not thrifty					
	Witchcraft					
	Powerful magic					
	Religious					
	Not proud					
Group #8	Peaceful (selves)					
	Peaceful (others)					
	Obedient					
	Hardworking men		Lazy men	Hardworking men		
	Brave	Gentle				
	Strong		Weak	Strong		
	Hot-tempered					
	Clean	Clean				
	Intelligent					
	Progressive					
	Handsome men	Unattractive men	Backbite	Not generous		
	Dark-skinned	Dark-skinned				
	Poor					
	Not thrifty	Not thrifty				
	Sexually strict					
	Witchcraft	Witchcraft				
	Religious					
	Proud	Proud				

Rated Group	Self Attributions	All Types of Outgroups	Near Outgroups	Remote Outgroups	Similar Outgroups	Dissimilar Outgroups
Group #9	Peaceful (selves) Honest (others) Hardworking women Gentle Clean Handsome men Beautiful women Friendly Pushy Progressive Thrifty Not proud	Light-skinned	Peaceful (selves) Peaceful (others) Honest (others) Handsome men Weak Friendly		Peaceful (selves) Peaceful (others) Honest (others) Friendly Not proud	
Group #10	Peaceful (selves) Peaceful (others) Honest (others) Hardworking men Hardworking women Clean Handsome men Beautiful women Friendly Wealthy Not thrifty Religious		Not proud Wealthy	Dishonest (selves) Dishonest (others) Conservative	Peaceful (others) Not proud Hardworking men Hardworking women Brave Wealthy Hot-tempered Friendly Unintelligent	Quarrelsome (others) Dishonest (others)

[205]

F-6

Rated Group	Self Attributions	All Types of Outgroups	Near Outgroups	Remote Outgroups	Similar Outgroups	Dissimilar Outgroups
Group #11	Peaceful (selves)					
	Peaceful (others)					
	Honest (others)					
	Obedient					Obedient
	Hardworking women	Lazy men				
	Friendly	Weak			Hot-tempered	
	Backbite					
	Intelligent					
	Clean					Effeminate
	Handsome men		Effeminate			
	Sexually strict					
	Pushy					
	Progressive					
	Conservative					
	Poor		Poor	Not proud	Poor	
	Thrifty				Not proud	
	Powerful magic	Witchcraft				
	Religious					
Group #12	Peaceful (selves)				Peaceful (selves)	
	Peaceful (others)				Peaceful (others)	
	Honest (others)					
	Dishonest (selves)					
	Obedient					
	Hardworking women		Lazy women		Lazy women	
	Lazy men		Lazy men		Lazy men	
	Gentle				Gentle	
	Friendly					
	Backbite					
	Intelligent					
	Clean				Clean	
	Weak		Weak		Weak	
	Handsome men	Handsome men	Effeminate		Effeminate	
	Beautiful women	Beautiful women				
	Light-skinned	Light-skinned				
	Sexually strict		Sexually loose		Sexually loose	
	Conservative					
	Wealthy					
	Poor					
	Not thrifty				Witchcraft	
	Religious					
	Not proud					

F-7

Rated Group	Self Attributions	All types of Outgroups	Near Outgroups	Remote Outgroups	Similar Outgroups	Dissimilar Outgroups
Group #13	Peaceful (selves)		Dishonest (selves)		Dishonest (selves)	
	Peaceful (others)		Dishonest (others)		Dishonest (others)	
	Honest (others)					
	Obedient					
	Hardworking women		Lazy women		Lazy women	
	Gentle		Gentle		Gentle	
	Friendly					
	Backbite		Backbite		Backbite	
	Intelligent					
	Clean					
	Handsome men					
	Beautiful women					
	Pushy					
	Progressive					
	Poor				Not generous	
	Not thrifty				Powerful magic	
	Religious		Witchcraft		Witchcraft	
	Not proud					
Group #14	Peaceful (selves)				Peaceful (selves)	
	Peaceful (others)				Peaceful (others)	
	Gentle		Gentle		Gentle	
	Friendly		Friendly		Friendly	
	Weak	Lazy men		Weak	Obedient	Weak
	Handsome men	Lazy women			Handsome men	
	Beautiful women	Light-skinned	Beautiful women		Beautiful women	
	Backbite	Sexually loose	Witchcraft		Effeminate	
	Poor		Thrifty		Backbite	
	Thrifty		Not proud		Thrifty	
	Not proud				Not proud	

F-8

Rated Group	Self Attributions	All Types of Outgroups	Near Outgroups	Remote Outgroups	Similar Outgroups	Dissimilar Outgroups
Group #15	Peaceful (selves)				Peaceful (others)	
	Peaceful (others)					
	Honest (others)					
	Obedient				Obedient	
	Hardworking men					
	Hardworking women				Lazy women	
	Weak				Weak	
	Intelligent					
	Clean					
	Handsome men					
	Beautiful women					
	Light-skinned	Light-skinned				
	Sexually strict					
	Friendly					
	Progressive					
	Conservative					
	Powerful magic	Witchcraft				
	Religious	Powerful magic			Religious	
	Proud					
Group #16	Peaceful (selves)				Peaceful (selves)	
	Peaceful (others)					
	Obedient					
	Hardworking women					
	Friendly		Gentle		Gentle	
	Sexually strict				Backbite	
	Not thrifty					
	Not proud					

F-9

Rated Group	Self Attributions	All Types of Outgroups	Near Outgroups	Remote Outgroups	Similar Outgroups	Dissimilar Outgroups
Group #17	Peaceful (selves)				Quarrelsome (selves)	
	Peaceful (others)				Quarrelsome (others)	
	Honest (others)				Dishonest (selves)	
	Obedient		Obedient		Obedient	
	Hardworking men					
	Brave					
	Gentle	Gentle				
	Clean	Weak				
	Strong					
	Intelligent			Unintelligent		
	Handsome men		Light-skinned		Light-skinned	
	Beautiful women				Beautiful women	
	Witchcraft	Witchcraft				
	Powerful magic	Powerful magic				
	Sexually strict		Sexually loose		Sexually strict	
	Hot-tempered				Sexually loose	
	Conservative			Conservative		
	Poor	Poor				
	Not thrifty				Not thrifty	
	Not generous					
	Religious		Religious			Religious
	Not proud					Pushy
	Unadvanced					
Group #18	Peaceful (selves)		Peaceful (others)	Backbite		Backbite
	Peaceful (others)		Peaceful (selves)	Witchcraft		Witchcraft
	Honest (others)			Powerful magic		Powerful magic
	Obedient	Religious		Lazy women	Lazy women	
	Clean		Friendly	Not proud	Not proud	
	Friendly			Gentle	Gentle	
				Not thrifty	Not thrifty	
				Poor		Poor

F-10

Rated Group	Self Attributions	All Types of Outgroups	Near Outgroup	Remote Outgroups	Similar Outgroups	Dissimilar Outgroups
Group #19	Peaceful (others)					
	Quarrelsome (selves)		Quarrelsome (selves)	Dishonest (selves)		Quarrelsome (selves)
	Honest (others)		Backbite			Backbite
	Obedient					Obedient
	Hardworking men					
	Hardworking women		Dirty	Conservative	Conservative	Dirty
	Strong	Weak	Hot-tempered			Hot-tempered
	Handsome men					
	Friendly		Not proud			Not proud
	Sexually strict		Sexually strict			Sexually strict
	Religious					
	Poor					
	Not thrifty					
Group #20	Peaceful (selves)		Quarrelsome (others)			Quarrelsome (others)
	Peaceful (others)		Dishonest (others)			Dishonest (others)
	Honest (others)					
	Obedient					
	Hardworking men					
	Strong					
	Brave					
	Handsome men				Handsome men	
	Beautiful women					
	Clean		Dirty		Dirty	
	Friendly				Cruel	
	Sexually strict					
	Pushy, progressive		Uncivilized		Uncivilized	
	Conservative					
	Light-skinned					
	Wealthy					
	Thrifty				Not thrifty	
	Religious					
	Not proud					

F-11

Rated Group	Self Attributions	All Types of Outgroups	Near Outgroups	Remote Outgroups	Similar Outgroups	Dissimilar Outgroups
Group #21	Peaceful (selves) Peaceful (others)	Lazy men Dirty Uncivilized	Unintelligent Unattractive men Dark-skinned	Dishonest (selves) Dishonest (others) Cruel Hot-tempered	Independent Cruel Hot-tempered	Dishonest (selves) Unintelligent
Group #22	Peaceful (selves) Peaceful (others) Honest (others) Obedient Hardworking men Hardworking women Friendly Handsome men Beautiful women Light-skinned Sexually strict Thrifty Religious Not proud	Weak Lazy men Lazy women Effeminate Dirty	Handsome men Light-skinned		Handsome men	
Group #23	Peaceful (selves) Peaceful (others) Honest (others) Hardworking men Hardworking women Brave Friendly Strong Clean Handsome men Beautiful women Light-skinned Wealthy Progressive	Sexually loose		Not proud		Not proud

F-12

Rated Group	Self Attributions	All Types of Outgroups	Near Outgroups	Remote Outgroups	Similar Outgroups	Dissimilar Outgroups
Group #24	Peaceful (selves) Peaceful (others) Honest (others) Obedient Hardworking men Friendly Sexually strict Uninterested Adv. Conservative Poor Religious Not proud	Hot-tempered	Hardworking men Not thrifty Witchcraft		Peaceful (others) Honest (others) Obedient Hardworking men Gentle, friendly Sexually loose Intelligent Progressive Strong, clean Witchcraft Powerful magic	Cruel Hot-tempered Unattractive men
Group #25	Peaceful (others) Quarrelsome (selves) Honest (others) Dishonest (selves) Hardworking men Hardworking women Brave Strong Intelligent Friendly Clean Handsome men Dark-skinned Sexually strict Poor Thrifty	Hardworking men Strong Dark-skinned	Peaceful (others) Honest (others)	Quarrelsome (selves) Cruel Hot-tempered Unattractive men	Peaceful (others) Honest (others) Friendly Handsome men Conservative Not thrifty	

F-13

Rated Group	Self Attributions	All Types of Outgroups	Near Outgroups	Remote Outgroups	Similar Outgroups	Dissimilar Outgroups
Group #26	Peaceful (selves) Peaceful (others) Honest (others) Hardworking men Strong Friendly Hot-tempered Dark-skinned Sexually strict Powerful magic Pushy Not thrifty	Strong Dark-skinned Unattractive men	Hot-tempered Progressive Not thrifty		Quarrelsome (others) Dishonest (others) Independent Hot-tempered Proud Progressive Not thrifty	
Group #27	Quarrelsome (selves) Hardworking women Sexually strict Hot-tempered Not thrifty		Quarrelsome (selves) Uninterested adv. Hot-tempered Not thrifty		Uninterested adv. Sexually loose Hot-tempered Not thrifty Unintelligent	
Group #28	Peaceful (selves) Peaceful (others) Honest (others) Obedient Hardworking men Intelligent Brave Strong Clean Handsome men Dark-skinned Sexually strict Progressive Not thrifty Powerful magic Religious Proud	Unattractive men Dark-skinned	Strong Dirty Hot-tempered Proud			

F-14

Rated Group	Self Attributions	All Types of Outgroups	Near Outgroups	Remote Outgroups	Similar Outgroups	Dissimilar Outgroups
Group #29	Peaceful (selves)	Peaceful (selves)				
	Peaceful (others)	Peaceful (others)				
	Honest (others)				Honest (others)	
	Obedient		Obedient			
	Hardworking men	Hardworking men				
	Hardworking women		Hardworking women		Hardworking women	
	Gentle					
	Friendly					
	Brave				Brave	
	Strong	Strong				
	Intelligent					
	Clean					
	Handsome men					
	Beautiful women					
	Sexually strict				Sexually strict	
	Pushy					
	Progressive				Progressive	
	Conservative					
	Wealthy	Wealthy				
	Thrifty				Thrifty	
	Witchcraft		Not thrifty		Witchcraft	
	Powerful magic		Witchcraft		Powerful magic	
	Religious		Powerful magic			
	Not proud				Not proud	
Group #30	Peaceful (selves)	Peaceful (selves)				
	Peaceful (others)	Peaceful (others)				
	Honest (others)	Honest (others)				
	Obedient					
	Hardworking men				Hardworking men	
	Hardworking women			Lazy women	Hardworking women	
	Gentle		Gentle		Gentle	
	Friendly	Friendly				
	Intelligent					
	Clean		Clean		Clean	
	Handsome men					
	Beautiful women					
	Dark-skinned					
	Sexually loose					
	Pushy					
	Conservative				Conservative	
	Poor		Poor		Poor	
	Powerful magic					
	Religious					
	Not proud		Not proud		Not thrifty	

INDEX